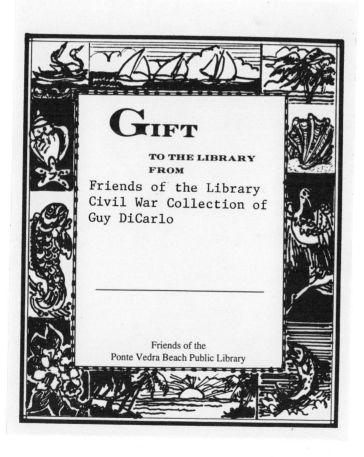

My Life in the Irish Brigade

The Civil War Memoirs of
Private William McCarter, 116th Pennsylvania Infantry

Edited by
Kevin E. O'Brien

My Life in the Irish Brigade: The Civil War Memoirs of
Private William McCarter, 116th Pennsylvania Infantry

edited by Kevin E. O'Brien

Savas Publishing Company
1475 S. Bascom Avenue, Suite 204,
Campbell, California 95008 (800) 848-6585

Copyright © 1996 Kevin E. O'Brien
Copyright © 1996 of maps Savas Publishing Company

Includes bibliographic references and index

Printing Number
10 9 8 7 6 5 4 3 2 1 (First Hardcover Edition)

ISBN 1-882810-07-4

This book is printed on 50-lb. Glatfelter acid-free paper

The paper in this book meets or exceeds the guidelines for permanence and durability of the Committee on Production Guidelines for Book Longevity of the Council on Library Resources

To my mother, Regina Flynn Neill,

who taught me how to read and
gave me a love of learning

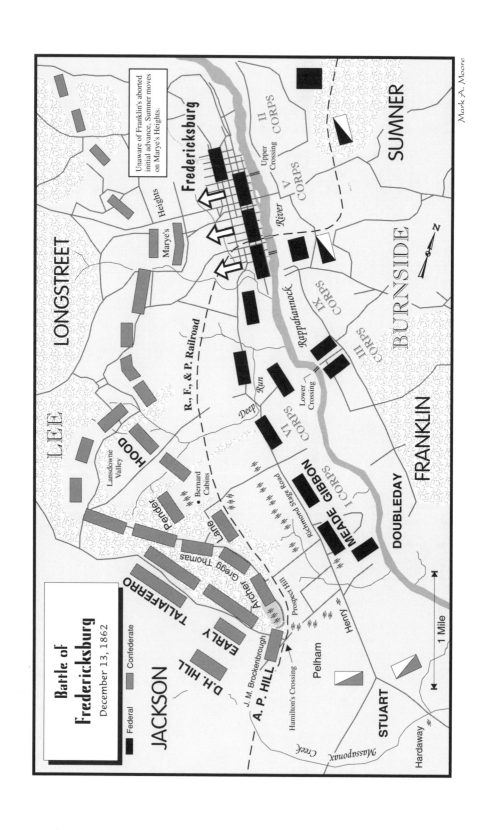

Battle of
Fredericksburg
December 13, 1862

■ Federal   ■ Confederate

Unaware of Franklin's aborted
initial advance, Sumner moves
on Marye's Heights.

Fredericksburg

Marye's
Heights

II CORPS

Upper
Crossing

River

V CORPS

Rappahannock

IX CORPS

III CORPS

Lower
Crossing

Deep
Run

VI CORPS

I CORPS

MEADE

GIBBON

Richmond Stage Road

Bernard
Cabins

Lansdowne
Valley

HOOD

Pender

Lane

Gregg Thomas

Archer

Prospect Hill

R., F., & P. Railroad

LEE

LONGSTREET

JACKSON

D. H. HILL

EARLY

TALIAFERRO

A. P. HILL

J. M. Brockenbrough

Hamilton's Crossing

Pelham

Henry

STUART

Hardaway

Massaponax
Creek

BURNSIDE

FRANKLIN

DOUBLEDAY

SUMNER

N

1 Mile

Mark A. Moore

Table of Contents

continued. . .

Cartography & Illustrations

Brig. Gen. Thomas F. Meagher
The first commander of the legendary Irish Brigade
Image courtesy of Leib Image Archives, York, PA

Foreword

The Irish Brigade has fostered a myriad of books and articles over the years. Considering some of the elite units of the Civil War, the historian William F. Fox mused, "The Irish Brigade was, probably, the best known of any brigade organization, it having made an unusual reputation for dash and gallantry."[1] The sterling qualities of the Irish Brigade were exhibited on many battlefields, and both its members and observers felt compelled to write at length of its experiences.

Prior to the Civil War, the Irish struggled to subsist in the United States. They repeatedly felt the wrath of an isolationist, Know-Nothing society that generally despised the Irish. Often the specter of the Irish-Catholics paving the way for a Papal coup d'etat sparked violent and deadly Nativist riots throughout America. The Very Reverend William Corby, C.S.C., once wrote, "still we have the mortification of hearing, through the press, from the pulpit, and even in legislative halls, the hue and cry: 'Catholics will destroy our free institutions!'"[2] In quieter times, American society simply ignored the Irish. This benign neglect allowed them some economic leeway and even a foundation for political opportunity, but the Irish still failed to breach the final wall of prejudice—social acceptance. Oddly enough, the Civil War provided the means to assail this last barrier.

When the Civil War broke out many Irishmen viewed the conflict ambivalently as they attempted to scratch out a hand-to-mouth existence. Irish community leaders, however, keenly felt the importance of volunteering their services to the United States. They hoped to uphold and defend the valuable liberties that Americans took for granted and in the process prove themselves worthy of their adopted country. Irish political exile and alluring elocutionist, Thomas Francis Meagher, donned a Federal uniform and formed what would eventually become the legendary Irish Brigade, composed of modern Celts from New York, Massachusetts, and Pennsylvania. At least forty other units formed during the war boasted rosters with overwhelmingly Irish surnames, but Meagher's legions easily became the most famous. Meagher deliberately focused attention on his brigade's Irish heritage so that the United States would appreciate its sacrifices as the work of a composite group of Irish-Americans. Unlike the other Irish units during the war, the Irish Brigade promoted interest and good will through its actions and its words. Members of Meagher's Irish Brigade constantly crusaded to keep its name and exploits before the public, and in doing so "increased their renown."[3] Many of the officers published tracts during the war ranging from newspaper articles to religious sermons on the faithfulness and integrity of the Irish.

After the war, former officers and chaplains published book-length memoirs of life in the Irish Brigade. The most influential works came from a triumvirate of the brigade's veterans: a staff officer, a field officer, and a chaplain. Captain David P. Conyngham, one-time aide to General Meagher, wrote a lengthy tome on the brigade in 1867. His writing, which transcended his short-lived service with the unit, provided valuable insight into the quality of the men composing the Irish Brigade. Conyngham's flowing prose made him an excellent candidate to write the unit's history, although no one seemed concerned that Conyngham was a novelist rather than an historian. The commander of the 116th Pennsylvania Infantry, Lt. Col. St. Clair Augustin Mulholland, further elaborated on Conyngham's theme of the Irish being "fearless in danger and peerless in battle."[4] Mulholland penned lavish articles and books professing that "The soldiers who gathered around our flag in this great war were not only heroes but patriots and saints as well."[5] The third brigade scribe, Father William Corby, published his memoirs of chaplain life in the Irish Brigade in 1893. The Catholic priest and then-President of the University of Notre Dame dwelt like the others on the merits of the Irish. Lashing out at Nativist intolerance, Corby appealed, "Let the press temper its language and be inspired by the noble, manly spirit of our forefathers. . . .Why should they [the Irish] be debarred rights purchased by the purest blood of their noblest sons?"[6] The Irish Brigade's sacrifice on battlefields like Fredericksburg did much to dispel anti-Irish, anti-immigrant fears. They had proven their loyalty both on the field and through the written word, thereby winning grudging approval through their blood and their ink. A recent historian observed that Meagher's soldiers "had, in a way, fought and won two wars."[7]

A renaissance of modern history has given us additional studies on the Irish Brigade, including Joseph M. Hernon, Jr., *Celts, Catholics and Copperheads: Ireland Views the American Civil War*, (Columbus, 1968); Steven J. Wright, *The Irish Brigade*, (Springfield, 1992); and, Joseph G. Bilby's *Remember Fontenoy!*, (Hightstown, 1995), a history of the 69th New York. Each offers a scholarly approach to the units of the brigade. Essays exploring different aspects and personalities of the brigade were recently made available in *A History of the Irish Brigade*, (Fredericksburg, 1995), which includes a brief look at William McCarter by Kevin E. O'Brien, the editor of the work in which this Foreword appears. Fordham University published the wartime correspondence of a color bearer in the 28th Massachusetts, *Irish Green & Union Blue: The Civil Letters of Peter Welsh*, (New York, 1986), which provides the first look into the common soldier of the Irish Brigade. A unique marriage of three common soldiers' diaries and letters in *The Civil War Notebook of Daniel Chisholm*, (New York, 1989), chronicles daily life in the 116th Pennsylvania during the last year of the war.

So why do we need yet another Irish Brigade study? William McCarter's memoir, *My Life in the Irish Brigade*, offers an insight missing from all of the other published sources. Outside of Peter Welsh of the 28th Massachusetts and the conglomerated Daniel Chisholm of the 116th Pennsylvania, every available published primary source is the work, exclusively, of officers and educated men of influence. The common soldiers, Welsh and Chisholm et. al., write very tersely in the immediacy of the moment and never elaborate on their thoughts or actions. Their records are deficient of the human element of emotion. *My Life in the Irish Brigade* rectifies this missing piece of the Irish Brigade literary puzzle. William McCarter was peculiarly suited to chronicle his experiences in the Irish Brigade. His education allowed him to give voice to the common soldier, and his astute eye for detail permits the modern reader to see the generals and battles as the men in the ranks perceived them.

McCarter served in some minor skirmishing and only one major battle, but the battle would affect the rest of his life and ultimately, become his life. His multiple wounds from the Battle of Fredericksburg left him crippled, yet those wounds also seared his war experiences indelibly into his memory. McCarter combines the romance of the nascent soldier with the cruel reality of battle. His candor is both illuminating and entertaining. He unwittingly gives credence to all the dignified attributes that so many of the Irish Brigade writers had stressed about the latent nobility of America's adopted children.

When I first read McCarter's unpublished manuscript ten years ago, I wondered why it had not yet been published. I am pleased that Kevin E. O'Brien has resurrected this fine memoir, whose publication will make it widely available to the general reading public. His own extensive catalogue of published articles on the Irish Brigade grace both sides of the Atlantic, and his exhaustive knowledge of the brigade's history eminently qualifies him to edit and footnote McCarter's war memories.

William McCarter's classic and provocative memoir, published here for the first time by Savas Publishing Company, will instantly appeal to every serious student of the Civil War.

Frank A. O'Reilly
Guinea, Virginia
June 1996

Editor's Preface

The air was alive with Confederate ordnance. Solid shot belched from Confederate cannon and shrapnel pattered when it hit the earth. Minie balls hissed as Southern riflemen unleashed volley after volley. Every cannon, every rifle, every gun that could be brought to bear by General Robert E. Lee's Army of Northern Virginia poured death and destruction at the Union troops assaulting Marye's Heights at Fredericksburg on December 13, 1862.

Private William McCarter of the 116th Pennsylvania, together with the rest of General Thomas F. Meagher's Irish Brigade, cringed under the cover of a lip of rising ground at the base of Marye's Heights. Confederate artillery had inflicted severe casualties on the brigade when it advanced through the city of Fredericksburg to its jumping off point for the attack against the heights. McCarter himself had been wounded in the left ankle from this barrage when an exploding shell killed one man and struck eight more.

The scene ahead was not encouraging. Major General William H. French's division had been shot to pieces when it attempted to seize a strategic sunken road occupied by the Confederates on the slope of Marye's Heights. "Fearful havoc had been made among the troops of the first assaulting division," wrote McCarter. "The dead and large numbers of the wounded lay thick in front of the heights."

Some men prayed, others hastily made last-minute checks of their muskets and equipment, and still others waited in silence. In a few minutes the word "Attention!" brought every man in the Irish Brigade to his feet. Next came the order, "Fix bayonets!" Private McCarter remembered that as the men attached bayonets to the sockets on their muskets, "the clink, clink, clink of the cold steel sounding along the line made one's blood run cold."

A bold, distinct Gaelic voice—loud enough to be heard above the noise of battle—yelled out: "Irish Brigade, advance!" The afternoon sun glittered on the frozen ground and the long lines of bayonets as the Irishmen rushed up the hill with wild huzzahs. The 28th Massachusetts had been chosen to be the center of the brigade because it carried the green flag of Ireland. The banner, decorated with a golden harp, a sunburst, and a wreath of shamrocks, bore the Gaelic motto, "Faugh a Ballagh," translated as "Clear The Way."

The soldiers of the Irish Brigade had not gone far when they were struck by a deluge of whining artillery shells, which burst in front, above, in the rear, and in the ranks of the attacking Federals. Holes opened in their lines, but the Irishmen closed them and pressed grimly forward. The Federal wounded littering the ground cheered and waved on the Irish. Officers and men fell rapidly, but others ran up to take their places.

After a steady but bloody advance, the Irish Brigade finally got within effective rifle-range of the defending Confederates. Partially hidden in a sunken road and protected by a stone wall across their front, the soldiers of Brig. Gen. Thomas R. R. Cobb's Georgia brigade prepared to loose a devastating volley into the faces of their enemy. Ironically and tragically, many of these Georgians were Irish immigrants. A few recognized the green flag of the 28th Massachusetts and the green sprigs of boxwood which every man in the Irish Brigade wore in his cap. They spread the word. "Oh, God, what a pity! Here comes Meagher's fellows!" was the groan in the Southern ranks.

Despite their ties of nationality, Cobb's veterans stood and opened fire with their rifles, shredding the ranks of the Irish Brigade. Showers of bullets mowed down men like grass before the scythe of the reaper. Dead and wounded Irishmen piled up in all directions. Bent over in the hail of lead, the survivors of the Irish Brigade dashed towards the front as if they were ducking hail in a storm.

The charge was stalled by a wooden rail fence about 60 yards from the Southern line. The intense fire from Cobb's Georgians splintered the fence, spattered mud in all directions, and decimated those men moving up behind it. But still, the Irish came on.

A strange and macabre sound was heard above the exploding artillery shells and pathetic screams of the wounded. The Confederates were cheering and applauding, overcome by the bravery of their Irish foe. Maj. Gen. George Pickett of Gettysburg fame wrote after the battle to his fiancée: "Your soldier's heart almost stood still as he watched those sons of Erin fearlessly rush to their death. The brilliant assault on Marye's Heights of their Irish Brigade was beyond description. Why, my darling, we forgot they were fighting us, and cheer after cheer at their fearlessness went up along our lines."[1]

What was left of the Irish Brigade stumbled to a halt about 30 yards from the stone wall and delivered a heavy fusillade into Cobb's men. With the luck of the Irish, Pvt. William McCarter reached this point without receiving a single scratch other than his earlier ankle wound. But such good fortune could not last forever, and a spent bullet struck him in the left shoulder as he fired his musket at the enemy. While this missile did not seriously harm him, another bullet cut the leather peak from his cap, leaving it dangling by a thread next to his ear. McCarter casually described this particular brush with death as a "close shaving."

It was evident that the Irish Brigade's assault had failed, just as had French's before it. "Yet our shattered and bleeding ranks held their ground," McCarter later penned, "determined to fight to the last. Irish blood was up." While Irish blood may have been up, nearly all its officers were down, and no one knew who was in command. One man behind McCarter was hit as he prepared to fire. The unlucky fellow never moved or spoke after he fell. As McCarter lifted his ramrod to send another cartridge home, a ball struck him in the arm near the shoulder. In shock from the blow, McCarter watched blood fill his shoe as dizziness and partial loss of sight further staggered his senses. The Irishman fell unconscious to the cold ground. When he finally regained consciousness a short while later and attempted to get up, another bullet skimmed his left wrist, leaving another painful wound. Yet another ball ripped through his cartridge box, scattering its contents, while the gravely wounded soldier listened to still more rounds whizzing by his head. He laid flat on the ground and placed his blanket roll in front of his head as protection.

A moment or two later, McCarter heard someone call out, "Fall back, men! Fall back!" Human flesh could endure no more. The remaining officers in the Irish Brigade were ordering a retreat. When the word was given to retire, Lt. Christian Foltz of the 116th Pennsylvania stooped over McCarter and said, "Bill, I wish I could get you out of here, but I can't. I see that Confederate who laid you there and I'll have a shot at him before I leave you."

Foltz picked up McCarter's loaded musket and aimed at someone behind the stone wall. He was dead before he could pull the trigger, shot through the forehead. McCarter's only companions now were the wounded, dying and dead. There were terrible sounds all around him. The shrieks and groans of the wounded, meaningless words and noises, curses and prayers. He listened to the hot whirl of streaking shrapnel and the deadly zip of rifleballs.

Trapped on the slope of Marye's Heights, McCarter assumed the lowest profile possible. Bullets ripped and tore the clothes on his back as he witnessed wave after wave of Union reinforcements advance towards the stone wall, only to be blown back by enemy fire so intense that McCarter described it as "the breath of hell's door."

Darkness and gloom settled upon the battlefield. Somehow, McCarter found the strength to alternately crawl and walk down the slope of Marye's Heights. A friend, Sergeant Stretchabok, together with another soldier from the 116th Pennsylvania, literally stumbled over McCarter after he had collapsed near the base of the hill. Stretchabok and his partner carried the wounded soldier to an ambulance.

He was lucky to be alive. Out of the 1,200 men in the Irish Brigade engaged at Fredericksburg, 545 were killed, wounded or missing—a 45% casualty rate.[2] Three of five regimental commanders in the Irish Brigade—Maj. Joseph O'Neill of the 63rd New York, Col. Nugent of the 69th New York, and Col. Dennis Heenan of the 116th Pennsylvania—fell wounded. The correspondent of Great Britain's *London Times*, who viewed the Irish Brigade's assault from behind Southern lines, wrote afterwards:

> Never at Fontenoy, Albuera, or at Waterloo was more undaunted courage displayed by the sons of Erin. The bodies which lie in dense masses within 40 yards of Colonel Walton's guns are the best evidence what manner of men they were who pressed on to death with the dauntlessness of a race which has gained glory on a thousand battlefields, and never more richly deserved it than at the foot of Marye's Heights on the 13th day of December, 1862.[3]

Unfortunately, little documentation exists on William McCarter's early life. His army enlistment papers reveal that he was born in Derry, Ireland, during 1840 or 1841. When he volunteered for Union army service, McCarter was a Philadelphia resident and earned his living as a currier—a tanner of animal hides. He was married to Annie McCarter and had several children by the outbreak of the Civil War.

Although a family man, McCarter enlisted on August 23, 1862. When asked after the war why he joined the Federal army, McCarter answered: "because of my love for my whole adopted country, not the North, nor the South, but the Union, one and inseparable, its form of government, its institutions, its Stars and Stripes, its noble, generous, brave and intelligent people ever ready to welcome, and to extend the hand of friendship to the downtrodden and oppressed of every clime and people." He entered service as a private in Company A, 116th Pennsylvania Infantry, a regiment raised by Col. Dennis Heenan, a well-known and respected commander of local militia.

William McCarter was five feet, ten inches tall and had blue eyes and brown hair. Throughout his life he was afflicted by a bad stammer, which made it difficult for listeners to understand him. Perhaps to compensate for this affliction, he developed extraordinary skills as a writer. His penmanship was exemplary. Comrades in the 116th Pennsylvania asked him to write letters home for them when they learned of McCarter's flourish with the pen. His skill eventually came to the attention of Col. Heenan and Brig. Gen. Thomas F. Meagher, commanding general of the Irish Brigade. McCarter became General Meagher's adjutant thanks to his ability to write crisp, well-drafted military communications.

The 116th Pennsylvania headed for the nation's capital with many other newly-raised regiments from the North and mustered in the Army of the Potomac during early September 1862. Spared the horrors of Antietam on the seventeenth of that month, McCarter and his comrades dug trenches, drilled, and learned the art of soldiering in base camps near Washington, D.C. On October 6, 1862, the regiment was ordered to proceed to Harper's Ferry, where it joined the already famous Irish Brigade, commanded by Thomas F. Meagher, an exiled Irish revolutionary and prominent New York lawyer.

The Irish Brigade, officially the Second Brigade, First Division, Second Corps of the Army of the Potomac, was already the stuff of legend. Known by its distinctive emerald-green battleflags, the brigade had made a name for itself during Maj. Gen. George B. McClellan's Peninsula Campaign of 1862, where it had served capably as a rearguard, protecting retreating Federal forces at Gaines' Mill, Savage Station, and White Oak Swamp. The three original regiments of the Irish Brigade—the 63rd, 69th, and 88th New York—lost nearly 500 men as McClellan slogged toward the rear through across Virginia's muddy roads and through her miasmic swamps. "I wish that I had twenty thousand more men like yours," said McClellan to Meagher after the Union Army reached safety at Harrison's Landing.

A few months later at Antietam, Meagher's Irishmen assailed a powerful position, driving against Confederates drawn up in a sunken road. Cheering and waving swords and hats, the soldiers of the Irish Brigade dashed themselves against the Southern line—a position soon to be known as the Bloody Lane—only to be met by hundreds of rifles flashing like a quarter-mile long bolt of lightning. Before it was relieved by other Federal troops, Meagher's Irish Brigade had lost 540 killed, wounded, and missing in about fifteen minutes of furious combat.

Despite their veteran status, the New York Irishmen greeted the rookies of the 116th Pennsylvania warmly, grateful for reinforcements. Lieutenant Colonel St. Clair Mulholland, second-in-command of the 116th, remembered that Meagher himself passed around a canteen of whiskey when the Pennsylvanians arrived.

Although the December 13, 1862 assault on Mayre's Heights was the climax of his relatively short military career, McCarter saw action well before the Fredericksburg Campaign. His first exposure to enemy lead was with the Irish Brigade during its capture of Charlestown, West Virginia on October 16, 1862. The young Irishman was also in the skirmish line two weeks later during the brief but brutal clash at Snicker's Gap in Virginia in early November. Thus, when McCarter and his fellow Pennsylvanians marched south with the New York Irish regiments during the opening days of the Fredericksburg campaign in late October 1862, McCarter had already "seen the elephant." Further strengthened by the 28th Massachusetts, a predominantly Irish unit from Boston, Meagher commanded five regiments in the reconstituted Irish Brigade when it made its famous assault against the impregnable Southern stronghold on Mayre's Heights.[4]

Courage, pluck, a simple faith in God's mercy and sheer luck enabled Pvt. William McCarter to survive the horrors of Fredericksburg. After spending five months in hospitals, he was discharged from the Union Army on May 12, 1863, because of his severe shoulder wound. McCarter had a tearful reunion with his wife Annie in Philadelphia and returned to civilian life. His Fredericksburg wounds were so severe that he collected a Federal pension for the rest of his life.

Additional tragedies awaited the crippled soldier, including the loss of his beloved Annie, who died on May 8, 1869. Eventually McCarter took a second wife, Eleanor Jane, and it was at her request, in addition to pressure from his family and friends, that he wrote *My Life in the Irish Brigade*, a detailed manuscript of his service with the 116th Pennsylvania Infantry. Somehow, his handwritten reminiscences on the Civil War, penned between 1875 and 1879, were donated to the Historical Society of Pennsylvania in Philadelphia.

McCarter's narrative on the Battle of Fredericksburg offers an intimate perspective on the experience of a combat infantryman in one of the most famous charges in American history. But his memoir is much, much more. McCarter had incredible powers of observation and a near photographic memory. These attributes, coupled with a facile pen, makes his memoir one of the most lively and informative ever published. He captures the daily life of soldiers in the Army of the Potomac in outstanding detail—including the drudgery of camp life and picket duty, the constant search for decent food and drinkable water, and battles with hostile Virginia weather.

McCarter's affiliation with Meagher's brigade, however, saturates his account with additional importance. *My Life in the Irish Brigade* fills holes in the historical record of the famous unit, and includes vivid, stimulating accounts of the obscure and all-but-forgotten actions at Charlestown and Snicker's Gap. Few writers compare with McCarter in describing the sensations of soldiers as they experienced the terror of war. His unique gifts as a writer breath life into the multitude of character's associated with McCarter's Civil War. His profiles of several prominent Union generals—George McClellan, Edwin Sumner, Winfield Hancock, Thomas Meagher, and others—are as penetrating as they are fresh, as insightful as they are incisive. After his severe wounding at Fredericksburg, McCarter spent a significant amount of time experiencing the trevails of Civil War medicine. His account of his recuperation in Union Army hospitals is both informative and frightening in the same instance. Confederate soldiers, Yankee troopers, Irish infantry, slave women, and Virginia civilians live again thanks to McCarter's skill with the pen.

William McCarter loved the Irish Brigade and its legendary commander, Thomas F. Meagher. Although he served in General Meagher's tent and broke bread with the man, his memoir details Meagher's faults as well as his virtues. Private McCarter honestly (and perhaps surprisingly) vividly describes the Irish general during one of the worst of his drunken escapades. No other Irish Brigade veterans would admit to the depth of Meagher's alcoholism. But McCarter did his best to help the general in a moment of need and went on to develop a close and intimate friendship with Meagher.

McCarter never formally published his memoirs. Recognizing the importance of his account, the *Philadelphia Weekly Times* on September 8, 1883, published excerpts from McCarter's reminiscences as part of the popular "Annals of the War" series. "Fredericksburg's Battle" offered the highlights of McCarter's moments on Marye's Heights.

Haunted by his memories, McCarter moved to Fredericksburg, Virginia in 1885, twenty-three years after the battle. He resided in the battle-scarred and historic city for nearly a year before moving to Washington, D.C., in 1886, where he found employment as a clerk for the U.S. Pension Office. Fated to be a widower, McCarter's second wife, Eleanor, died on September 27, 1890. He married Theodora Bartlett, aged 27, on July 17, 1894. He was 53 at the time of their wedding.

The old soldier continued to be tortured by the wounds received at Fredericksburg. In 1891, he successfully petitioned the U.S. Government for a pension increase because he could not sleep because of shoulder pain. Despite his severe wounds and their lingering complications, it was not enemy lead but a weak heart that took McCarter, who died on February 10, 1911. He was 71 years old.[5]

William McCarter was the only enlisted man in the Irish Brigade to leave a memoir of his service. His reminiscence chronicles the remarkable exploits of Irish immigrants who willingly threw themselves into battle to protect the flag that sheltered them when persecuted and exiled from their own native land. McCarter would undoubtedly have agreed with the sentiments of Cpl. Samuel Clear, a fellow soldier in the 116th Pennsylvania, who wrote the best epitaph for the most famous Irish unit in the Union Army: "The old Irish Brigade is a thing of the past," penned Clear. "There never was a better one pulled their triggers on the Johnnies."[6]

Kevin E. O'Brien
Scottsdale, Arizona
July 21, 1996

Acknowledgements

The roots of this book can be traced back some two years ago this November, on a cold and snowy night in Yosemite, California, at the 9th Annual West Coast Civil War Round Table Conference. There, before a crackling hot fire, my (future) publisher, Theodore P. Savas, and I sat discussing McCarter's delightful memoir. It did not take long before he realized the historical importance of McCarter's work, and Ted urged me to edit the memoirs for publication. I am indebted to him for his encouragement and assistance in preparing this manuscript for general consumption.

There are many other individuals who deserve mention, including: Mark A. Moore, for his outstanding maps; Lee Merideth for the excellent index; Virginia historian Frank A. O'Reilly, whose Foreword graces this book; and Ms. Amy Fleming, Coordinator for Rights and Reproduction, Historical Society of Pennsylvania, who arranged for permission to reprint the McCarter memoirs.

And of course, special thanks go to my wife Nancy, for her inspiration and support while I labored on McCarter's prose.

Private William McCarter
Postwar image, courtesy of the Historical Society of Pennsylvania

"You used your fingers to eat with, for knife and fork were not available here. A cup, if you had one, was dipped into so-called coffee. Black, greasy looking fluid. . . plentiful in buckets."

Chapter 1

My First Days as a Soldier in the Union Army

On August 23d, 1862, I enlisted in the 116th Regiment, Pennsylvania Volunteers, for three years, or the war.[1] The regiment then was encamped in Jones' Woods, near Hestonville, Philadelphia, receiving daily increase to its ranks.[2]

On September 1st at about ten a.m., marching orders from Washington were received unexpectedly for the regiment to report at that city at the earliest possible moment. Everything then was hurry and excitement, and by three p.m. the same afternoon, all baggage, equipment and tents were packed. The regiment went on its march out of Jones' Woods to the Baltimore Railroad Depot at Broad and Pine Streets, Philadelphia. On our arrival there, our Colonel [Dennis Hennan] was informed by the railroad authorities that transportation for his regiment could not possibly be furnished before eleven p.m. or midnight that night. Every available car and train was then engaged in the transportation of other regiments which arrived at the depot early in the morning and day. Consequently, the regiment was compelled to remain there until transportation was had.

At three a.m. next morning, conveyances arrived in the shape of dirty cattle-cars—rather uncomfortable vehicles for equipped soldiers to take a long ride in. However, off we got at that time. In that way bound for the seat of war, we were in the very best of good humor and spirits, some of the genuine Old Virginia Mountain Dew having fallen on the most of us during our detention in the depot.

As our train switched round a curve going out of the depot, the band on board, accompanied by the voices of the regiment, struck up the airs of "Jonny is Gone for a Soldier," "The Star Spangled Banner" and "John Brown's Body Lies Moldering in the Grave, As We Go Marching On." After the songs, three rousing cheers were given for Philadelphia and the girls we left behind us. Each man for himself then sought the most comfortable corner he could find for a nap. The train went rattling along on its way to Baltimore, where we arrived at two p.m. after a ride of eleven hours. I shall never forget the journey, the slowest and most uncomfortable one I ever experienced.

In Baltimore, Maryland
September 2nd, 1862

The city was full of soldiers on their way, like ourselves, to the Capital. Our regiment remained here until next day, awaiting transportation forward. During the afternoon and night, we were quartered in a large, unoccupied tobacco warehouse. Having had nothing to eat since leaving Philadelphia at three a.m. in the morning, we were naturally very hungry and would have been glad of the very coarsest victuals, having no rations whatever in our haversacks. What, in the shape of food, would a lot of hunger-bitten soldiers refuse? Our appetites, however, were gratified in a very unexpected and bountiful manner. At about six p.m. in the evening, a corporal of a Maine regiment, then stationed in or near Baltimore, brought the following written message on a small card, and presented it to our colonel: "Form your men in line, and march them to the Hall, three doors below, for supper provided for them by the patriotic Union citizens of Baltimore."[*]

A few members of the regiment on some occasions were slow and reluctant in carrying out the colonel's orders and commands. But at this time, when "grub" was named, and the command "fall in" was given,

---

[*] This was as near as I can recollect, the words of the invitation. I had a copy of the original, but lost it.

what a contrast. In less than five minutes, the line was formed and on its march to partake of the good things provided by the loyal people of Baltimore.[3] We entered the Hall named above, a very long and wide one. A long wooden table ran from one end of it to the other. It was covered with plain white muslin table cloths, something unusual for soldiers to see on a march. The table was actually loaded with large dishes full of corned beef sliced, sliced ham and tongue and cold roast-beef, besides a good supply of butter, and any quantity of hot coffee and bread. To all these luxuries, we did ample justice. After which, the command "Fall-in" was again given and obeyed. But not so freely and willingly as an hour before. The regiment marched back again to its quarters for the night, the tobacco warehouse. In the morning we partook of a breakfast similar to the supper the previous evening at the same place. At nine a.m., we boarded a train of regular passenger cars with one day's government rations in our haversacks, bound for Washington, where we arrived at 12:45 p.m. There we embarked, formed in line on the street near the Capitol and awaited further orders.*

In Washington, DC
September 3rd, 1862

Shortly after arriving here, the regiment was marched to the Soldier's Retreat for refreshments.[4] This was a large, temporary wooden

---

* Note: In all my army life experience, I must say, that the treatment our regiment received during its very short stay in Baltimore, as far as hospitality is concerned, far exceeded that of any other city in which we as a regiment ever were in. Little boys going around here and there among the troops, handing them small bags filled with tobacco and matches. Negroes going through the ranks supplying the men with good, fresh, clear drinking water, and little girls presenting thousands of small pin and needle cases, better known in the army as "housewives." But the bountiful supply of eatables provided in the Hall, and handed around there by a corps of beautiful ladies in attendance, assisted by several colored persons, was the most attractive and acceptable feature of the kindness and hospitality of the citizens of Baltimore. All who were the recipients cannot forget it as long as they live. On the morning of the 3rd, after partaking of a splendid breakfast, the regiment was drawn up in line on the pavement fronting the Hall. The band, accompanied by several good voices in the regiment, gave the ladies a parting salute by playing the tune and singing the beautiful patriotic lines commencing with "My Country 'tis of thee." The scene was a touching one—ladies leaning out of all the windows in that large five story building, waving white handkerchiefs. Soldiers cheered them on the street below. As our regiment filed off for the train, three rousing cheers, with caps waving, were given by our boys in blue—for the good and pretty ladies of the Monumental City, ladies pretty in looks as well as in deeds. Many of our men (myself included) looked back at the fair ones still waving their white handkerchiefs with tears in their eyes. We beckoned to them, although then at a distance. It was an affectionate adieu and farewell to Baltimore.

building erected near the railway station, where all soldiers passing through the city were entertained with coffee, bread and meat. It was a filthy, dirty place, containing long uncovered wooden tables. Tin cans full of something called coffee, without milk and scarcely any sugar, were brought in and set on these tables. Chunks of coarse, brown bread were thrown down on the bare boards. Fat, boiled salt beef (better known in the army as salthorse) in black, dirty looking metal and wooden pans deposited here and there along the tables, constituted the eatables. The custom then was "every man for himself."

You used your fingers to eat with, for knife and fork were not available here. A cup, if you had one, was dipped into so-called coffee. Black, greasy looking fluid, called coffee, was plentiful in buckets. Every allowance, however, should be made for this rough fare and treatment. When you take into consideration the fact that from eight to ten thousand men were said to be fed in that way there every day for months during the early part of the war, it was understandable. After partaking of the food at the Soldier's Retreat, the regiment marched to another larger wooden structure attached to the Retreat, there to be quartered for the night. In this place, long benches were stretched out in every direction for men to lay upon. No beds, or anything of the kind, were provided.

As the regiment was late in getting there, we had to do the best we would with what little room was left after other soldiers filled up the place. We made our beds on the floor for the night. Morning came and with it, orders to prepare to march. Breakfast was got at the Retreat, the fare being an exact duplicate of what was received the previous afternoon. Each man was provided with two days' rations. Early the same morning, a report was current that a heavy body of the enemy were threatening Point of Rocks, Maryland, and that a fight was daily expected there. Nor was the report false, for at about ten a.m., the news reached Washington that fighting had been going on since daybreak in the morning. At ten-thirty a.m., marching orders were received. But to where was not made known to any of the rank and file.

At eleven a.m., the regiment was on its march up Pennsylvania Avenue, heading in the direction of the Potomac. Every man could plainly see and feel that their destination was the scene of strife at Point of Rocks. We all expected the regiment would receive its first baptism of fire and blood there. At twelve p.m., we had reached the outskirts of the city and bade it farewell.

On the March from Washington, DC
September 4th, 1862

Our march was a rather pleasant one. The weather was dry, not oppressively hot, and the roads were in splendid marching order. On the second day, we were informed by the adjutant that our destination was Point of Rocks, exactly what we supposed. Late on the evening of the same when it nearly dark, we had reached Rockville, Maryland.[5]

Our expectations, however, in regards to participating in an engagement were not realized. It was already over. But we were informed that a skirmish really had occurred the day before, between a body of the enemy passing towards Harper's Ferry, Virginia, and some Union troops in which two or three of the latter were killed and a number wounded. Our regiment bivouacked that night in a small clump of woods in the vicinity. Next morning we commenced a backward movement towards Washington. A light, drizzling rain commenced falling early in the morning and continued all day. It did not delay the march of the regiment, although water completely soaked the clothing of the men and rusted all their firearms, bayonets, and brasses. At dark, a halt was made, good fresh rations supplied, tents pitched in an open field near the road, and fires kindled. After partaking of hot coffee, army biscuit (hardtack) and fine salt pork (my favorite dish anywhere), each man sought the shelter of his tent for the night.* Next morning, tents were taken down, rolled up, placed on board our army wagons, and the regiment again proceeded on its march. On the afternoon of the 7th, we arrived at a point within ten miles of Washington, surrounded by a beautiful country, although it was hilly and thickly wooded. Here we encamped, expecting to remain several days, and gave the place the name of "Camp Morris."

---

* Our style of cooking was as follows—As part of each ration, each man received two tablespoon fulls of ground coffee, and two of brown sugar which he deposited generally in two little bags, or his handkerchief if he had one. Then when he wanted hot coffee to drink, he would take a portion of the ground coffee and sugar from the little bags, put them in his tin cup, add water and boil on the fire. In cooking pork, a slice or lump it was run on the point of a sharp stick or long twig cut from a tree and held over the fire till done. In cold weather, the men considered pork a luxury when frozen hard and eaten raw on a march, cutting it with a knife like cheese. In getting the hardtack (biscuit) into shape for eating, the butt ends of our muskets had frequently to be used as a battering ram to bring the unruly article under subjection to our teeth.

Camp Morris, Ten miles from Washington
September 7th, 1862

On the morning of the 8th, those of us who were yet asleep in our tents were awakened at five a.m. by our usual morning call. The drum beat the call to fall in line for roll call. After roll call, each man cooked his own breakfast and enjoyed his morning smoke. At ten a.m., orders were given for inspection of arms and dress parade at eleven. After we did this, our colonel read instructions received from headquarters, designating the duties to be performed by the regiment during its stay at Camp Morris. In addition to drilling one hour each morning and evening, we were to do the following: dig rifle pits, throw up earthworks, construct a fort (afterwards named Fort McClellan) and fell trees for miles around in conjunction with other regiments in the vicinity. The point was to obstruct the march of the enemy should he make his advance northward and to protect the Capital.[6]

The regiment wasn divided into two sections, Section A and Section B. On the following morning, the whole regiment, except for a few men detailed for guard duty, commenced its labors. Regimental drill was conducted from eight to nine a.m. Section A worked on the fortifications from ten a.m. to twelve while Section B felled trees in the woods during the same hours. We all ate dinner between twelve p.m. and one p.m. At two, both sections resumed their labors again, continuing until four p.m.. From five to six p.m., we had regimental and battalion drill, sometimes dress parade. After this, supper was cooked and eaten. Then we had the evening smoke, enjoying storytelling interspersed with songs. We talked sense and considerable nonsense up to nine p.m. when tattoo was sounded, notifying every man to retire to his quarters for the night except those on guard. The following morning (and so on during our stay at Camp Morris), Section A took the place of Section B in the woods and Section B the place of Section A on the fortifications, dividing the two branches of the work equally among the regiment.*

The weather here was very hot and sultry during the day, and chilly, cold and damp at night from the heavy dew that fell. Sometimes the heavy dew completely wet through the covering and blankets of the

---

* I may note here that drunkenness up to this time was not seen in the regiment since leaving Philadelphia. This was true even through the regiment numbered between 700 and 750 men all told.

men laying in their tents. Several of them, not accustomed yet to the soldier's life and rough usage, were attacked with camp (typhoid) fever. They were removed to a Washington hospital. Two of them soon afterwards were reported to have died. Some three or four of the force at work on the fortifications were prostrated by sunstroke.*

On the morning of the 20th, marching orders were again received for the regiment to report at Washington the following day. Accordingly, on the morning of the 21st, everything was packed. By ten a.m. the regiment was in motion, advancing on the Capital where it arrived the same evening. We soldiers partook of refreshments at the Soldier's Retreat. Since every corner and spot in the place where before we passed a night was filled up by a fresh arrival of New England troops that day, we were compelled to make our beds for the night on mother earth, on the side of a green mound near the Capitol Building. There we had the starry heavens for our canopy. Small fires were kindled at which we warmed ourselves. Being very tired after our day's march of ten miles in pretty warm weather, loaded down with our equipment, very many of us found rest in sleep. It was hard to enjoy slumber on the cold, damp ground, exposed to the weather and the heavy falling dew of a clear, but chilly night.**

In the morning, sore throats and stiff joints were prevalent complaints among the men. At six a.m., roll was called, after which breakfast was served us at the Retreat (same fare as before). Gum blankets and overcoats were then issued. About noon, we commenced the march again, going out Pennsylvania Avenue and through Georgetown to the

---

* My own health at this time, thank God, never was better. This was true despite the fact that I always did my full share of regimental duties, besides writing scores of letters for my brothers in arms, to their dear ones then far away. My appetite was voracious. I never was in better spirits. I was always busy if not at my army duties. When I entered the army, my weight was 140 lbs. Now it was 154 and continued to increase to three days before the Battle of Fredericksburg, Virginia, on Dec. 13th, 1862. I made the scale touch the ground with 158 lbs. on it near Falmouth, Virginia (my highest weight).

** On leaving Camp Morris, the face of the country for many miles around presented an appearance only to be seen in time of war. Immense forests of almost every kind of American timber lay prostrate, cut down by the axe of the soldier. Lying in every direction and shape, they blocked up completely those roads over which the Rebel Army was expected to make an advance north. An Englishman, one of our number once in the British Army, and rather an eccentric genius, remarked in looking over the country at this time and place, "Well, that is one heterogeneous mass of compound confusion." And so it was. Horrid, black and bloody war transforms a paradise into a wilderness, and men into bloodhounds and fiends.

celebrated "Long Bridge" spanning the Potomac. After we crossed the span, our feet trod for the first time on the "Sacred Soil of Bloody Virginia."

On the Virginia Side of the Potomac Below Washington
September 22nd, 1862

The regiment remained here until next morning, sheltering during the night under sheds and in freight cars of a railway company whose depot was at this place. Nothing worthy of note occurred here. In the morning, the march was resumed, but only after an address from our major. He called the attention of the men to the fact that they were then in the "Enemy's Country." The major told us we would never know when or where or how the Rebs might suddenly appear or attack. He urged all to double diligence and activity in prosecuting faithfully their duties as soldiers of the United States Army. After a rather pleasant march and a bivouac for another night beside an old flourmill lately burned by the Rebels, the regiment arrived, by a rather circuitous route, at Fairfax Courthouse, Virginia, on September 24th. We pitched Sibley tents near the town and called the place "Camp Bardwell" in honor of our respected major.

Camp Bardwell, Fairfax Courthouse
Fairfax County, Virginia
September 24th, 1862

Fairfax Courthouse was a small town of one principal, long, uneven street, composed chiefly of small houses, grog, grocery, dry-goods and baker's shops. It was occupied by part of the Rebel Army twelve days previous to our arrival there. Upon evacuating it and after pillaging and robbing it, the Rebs set it on fire, destroying all the most valuable portion of the little town. Only a few small shops, three or four of them groggeries, and an old school house survived. The remaining buildings contained a number of wounded and dying Rebel soldiers, as well as their rusty, dirty muskets, roughly branded "C.S.A." The filth in the Southern uniforms would have nourished the sacred soil of old Virginia without the addition of the bones of its dying sons. *

---

*A very noticeable feature about this little town was the total and entire absence of all young and middle-aged men, the only inhabitants then being old men, women and

Our regiment, at this time not being brigaded, was here temporarily attached to General Siegel's Division[7] whose headquarters were about two miles distant from this camp. During our stay here, he paid us several visits for inspection, putting every regiment in this vicinity under strict military discipline. In looks, he much resembled the generality of his own countrymen, Germans. Siegel was short, stout and healthy. He usually inspected the troops on horseback. From his manners, talk and actions, Siegel left the impression on the minds of all the men that he was a good, skillful officer, capable of handling a large body of troops to the greatest advantage. Our duties here were very light, compared with those performed at Camp Morris, consisting chiefly in drilling, camp-guard and picket duty.

On the night of Sept. 28th, a rather amusing incident occurred between Colonel Heenan of our regiment and me. It happened to be my turn on guard at eleven p.m. at Post No. 2 facing the town. The night was very still and quiet, not a sound being heard but the tramp of my fellow sentinels over their different lonely beats. Heavy clouds threatening rain hung thick and dark overhead. Although the moon was full, that orb failed to completely pierce the blackness. Yet it gave sufficient light to show the approach of a man at a short distance.

Our camp was supposed to be one large square of four sides. It was divided into eight divisions or, to use the military term, posts. To prevent surprise by an enemy or intrusion by any person within our camp lines not duly authorized, four sentinels, fully armed, were placed one on each side of the square. They marched from one end to the other for two hours before being relieved and so on for twelve hours in daytime. At night, which was between the hours of 6 p.m. and 6 a.m., the guard

children, black and white. And upon inquiry as to how this was, we were informed that all the young men of the place and others capable of performing military duty had either gone into the Rebel Army or were forced into it. Those old men, women and children who remained often dealt with us. We purchased little knickknacks such as Virginia pumpkin pie, writing materials, tobacco, and matches. Occasionally, we even got from them a little grog. But the Southerners invariably treated us with the very essence of hatred and contempt, in words, motions and deeds. It showed conclusively, at least to us, the unhappy state of feeling between the people of the North and the South, even at this point. Often indeed did many of us feel like retaliating, and in a very severe way too, against such gross and repeated insults as we received here. But the rules and regulations from headquarters of the Commander-in-Chief (then Gen. Geo. B. McClellan) forbade such a course, under penalty of severe punishment. I suppose that a feeling of fear, caused by the close proximity of so many Union troops (about 15,000) in and around the town just at that time, only prevented acts of violence and bloodshed by these good people of Fairfax Courthouse upon our men, often branded with the name of "damned Yankees."

was doubled, manning all the posts. Between the town and Post No. 2, my position this night was a large cornfield full of dry, standing corn stalks, the ears of corn having been all taken off by the Rebels when recently in possession of the town. Anybody moving among these dry stalks would cause a cracking, rattling noise which would not fail to reach the ear of the sentinel at this point.

When the night guards went on duty, or soon afterwards, the "countersign" for that night was secretly communicated to them by a commanding officer. He received it from the headquarters of the district's general. This countersign was simply one word, the name of a man, city, town, or animal. Given secretly to the guard, the countersign was an important signal. No man could pass in or out of the lines after a certain hour in the evening unless he first named that word (the countersign) to the sentinel on duty. It prevented all entry and egress from the lines or camp without knowledge of the code word. The countersign this night was the word "Dresden," a city in Europe.

About eleven p.m. while walking over my beat, I heard a noise in the cornfield. It sounded like a person was moving among the dry stalks. At this time I had just reached the limit of my bounds and the beginning of my neighbor's. He also reached that point at the time I did. We both listened—louder and more distinct the noise became. We then concluded that it was some party approaching about the center of my own post. My neighbor dared not leave his beat to render me assistance. I at once hastened to the threatened point. I stood perfectly still at shoulder arms, musket loaded and primed and bayonet fixed. Nearer came the sound. At last, I faintly discovered by the weak, dim light of the moon, the form of a tall man approaching me. I let him advance within about ten yards of the point of my bayonet. Then by military rules and instructions, I commanded him to "Halt."

"Who comes there?" I asked.

He obeyed at once, and replied, "A friend."

"Advance, friend, and give the countersign," I replied.

"Can't give it, don't know it. I am Colonel Heenan of your regiment," he said, advancing to within three feet of my bayonet.

"Don't know you*, can't pass, stand your ground until the captain of the guard arrives," I replied at the top of my voice. "Captain of the guard, Post No. 2," I shouted.

This was at once telegraphed from one guard to the next and so on

---

*The guard is instructed to know nobody until he gives the countersign.

until it reached the guardhouse, where the captain was with the other guards not then on duty. In ten minutes, he was at my post with eight of his men. In the meantime, Col. Heenan slowly backed away upon my giving the first alarm. By the time the captain and his men reached me, he was clean out of sight in the cornfield again. The captain inquired what was the matter. I told him exactly how I had acted. "You did right," he said, "but you ought to have held him until my arrival. You would have been justified in pulling your trigger on him when he moved away."

They then left for their quarters, the captain giving me extra orders how to act in case the attempt was repeated. But it was not. Nothing whatever was said by anyone next day about the matter. By some means, the colonel got into camp that night but not through my avenue of admission, Post No. 2. I often met him afterwards and talked with him, but the subject of the "cornfield" was never broached by either party. But the results were not to die and be buried, as will be seen. This was the first time the faithful performance of my duty as a soldier was tested.

During our stay here, a painful and fatal accident occurred. A young soldier named Carson, a Philadelphian and a member of our regiment, lost his life.[8] He was carelessly lounging with others on the grass in front of his quarters when a loaded musket standing in one of the tents fell down, causing it to go off. The whole charge, a ball and three buckshot, lodged in his face and throat, causing death a few hours afterwards. His mother residing in Philadelphia was notified by telegraph of the accident and death of her son. She arrived in camp the next day to take the body home. He was an intelligent, active young man, a good soldier, cheerful company, very talkative, yet never profane or vulgar and beloved by all his comrades. His sudden and sad death cast a gloom over the entire regiment for some time afterwards. This was the first death from accident in our ranks.

A number of Philadelphia regiments were encamped near us here. Among them were the Scott Legion, 119th Pennsylvania, Collis' Zouaves, 118th Pennsylvania (Corn Exchange), and 119th Pennsylvania.

On September 29th, our colonel received orders to have his regiment in readiness to move at short notice. Each man was ordered to pack all his clothing in his knapsack. These knapsacks, together with the Sibley tents then in use by our men, were to be forwarded to

Washington. We only carried a change of shirt, drawers and socks. The regiment again commenced to march on Monday, October 6th.

None could imagine why such strange and unusual orders were given or what was in the wind. Sometime afterward, I ascertained that the movement was designed to meet an anticipated attack by Stonewall Jackson and his 35,000 men, then retreating before McClellan to Richmond. The Confederate Army had just been defeated at the Battle of Antietam, September 17th. The Rebs had suffered considerable loss. But although the attempt was well planned and carried out by some of the best generals in the Army of the Potomac, it proved an utter failure. The sly, insidious old Stonewall, thanks to his acknowledged matchless maneuvering, succeeded in evading his pursuers and in reaching Richmond, his Capital, in safety without further loss among his troops.[9]

As I stated before, our duties here were very light. Plenty of good rations to eat and plenty of time to eat and enjoy them. Plenty of fun and amusement and plenty of rest and ease. These good times prepared us for the hard and trying labors of the long march, the dangerous picket line and the bloody battlefield. Save the sad death by accident, our stay at Camp Bardwell will long be remembered with pleasure by many of the surviving members of the 116th Regiment, Pennsylvania Volunteers.

On the morning of October 6th, the regiment took up the line of march, again for Washington, bidding goodbye to the little town of Fairfax Courthouse, Virginia. After bivouacking for a night on the route and a three hour march in the morning, we entered the Capital for the third time since leaving Philadelphia.

In Washington, DC
October 7th, 1862

On this occasion, we fared better than on our last visit to the city. Having had to remain overnight before proceeding on our march for some reason not made known to any of our rank and file, we succeeded in finding pretty comfortable quarters for the night. We got a decent share of salthorse, bread and coffee in the old, familiar Soldier's Retreat. The afternoon of the day being clear and pleasant, a very intimate and attached comrade and I requested our colonel for leave of absence. We wanted a few hours to see the sights in Washington. Colonel Heenan very willingly complied. He also furnished us with passes to prevent our arrest by the Provost Guard, then constantly patrolling the streets, day and night, and arresting all straggling soldiers or those who could give no proper cause or authority for being away from their regiments.

It was fortunate that we had these passes. In passing along Pennsylvania Avenue, we were stopped five times by guards. But upon sharing our passes, we were immediately permitted to proceed. We visited the Treasury Buildings, Post Office, Smithsonian Institute, the Capitol, and then passed around the White House.

There, standing near one of the entrances and leaning against a small tree with a little cane in his hand, stood a man whom I at once recognized as Abraham Lincoln. I once before had a good view of him when he passed through Philadelphia after his election as President of the United States. He was plainly dressed in black or dark clothes and wore a high black hat. Lincoln, apparently deep in thought, cut at the grass with his cane. We stopped a moment through curiosity to have a good, quiet look at the great man, hoping, however, that he would not notice or speak to us. But it was not to be so. For almost as soon as we stopped, he raised his head. Seeing two soldiers, only privates, he raised his hat to us and said in a polite and friendly manner, "Good evening boys. What regiment?"

My comrade replied, "The 116th Pennsylvania, sir."

He then said, "God bless you."

We only answered, "Thank you, sir." Giving him as polite a military salute as we were capable of doing, we passed on our way. The two of us were much pleased, gratified and encouraged at such an unexpected interview with such a truly great and good man.

To fully satisfy my companion that this man who we had seen and talked with really was the President, we asked a sentinel at another entrance to the White House farther along. He said, "Yes, he comes out here nearly every evening that he is at home. About this hour for study and a quiet walk."[10]

We returned to our regiment again at about six p.m., much pleased and benefited by our walk through Washington. We had another decent night's rest here. In the morning, after roll call, the regiment was notified to be prepared to march at nine a.m. with three days rations. At the same time we were also notified that our destination was Harper's Ferry, Virginia. Accordingly, at the appointed hour, all was ready and again we bid adieu to the Capital.

On the March from Washington, DC
To Harper's Ferry, Jefferson County, Virginia
October 8th, 1862

We left Washington in the morning by a train of freightcars, on the Baltimore and Ohio Railroad, bound for Harper's Ferry, Virginia. The locomotive ran at about the rate of five miles per hour. This slow rate of speed was caused by three trains ahead of ours. They were carrying immense quantities of ammunition, dismounted heavy and light artillery and horses. Close behind us came two other trains carrying infantry with the same destination as ourselves. The weather was beautiful, clear and pleasantly warm. It was a sight to see so many railway cars rattling along, crowded on the platforms and on the top with cheering soldiers and their bright shining muskets and blue uniforms. Truly, it was grand and imposing to behold. The country over which we passed between Washington and Harper's Ferry was very uneven and generally heavily wooded, with here and there, neat and thrifty looking villages, composed of small houses clean and comfortable in appearance. Occasionally, a large factory or mill was seen, indicating that this section of country was, to a considerable extent, a manufacturing one. Judging from the demonstrations made by the people as we passed along, they were undoubtedly loyal to the Union. The men greeted us loudly with cheers, and the women waved white handkerchiefs out of windows and on the tops of houses.

At about seven p.m., we arrived at a village, the name of which I forget. A raiding party of Rebels had captured a few men of Colonel Rush's Philadelphia Lancers there.[11] At ten p.m., we arrived at a little town called Sandy Hook near Harper's Ferry. We bivouacked for the night on open ground near a mill-race, built fires, cooked our rations, and passed the night. With morning, we resumed our march on foot, and arrived opposite Harper's Ferry at nine a.m. The regiment crossed the Potomac River at that place on a pontoon bridge. While crossing, my cap was blown off by the wind into the water and lost. We marched through the town to Bolivar Heights on its outskirts. Orders were given to pitch our small field tents (called shelter tents) forwarded from Washington and to encamp for the present. On all our march from the Capital, until we arrived at Harper's Ferry, we found no ravages or spoils whatever made by the enemy.

Bolivar Heights, Harper's Ferry
Jefferson County, Virginia
October 9th, 1862

The town of Harper's Ferry is built at the foot of the narrow tongue of land that thrusts itself out like a cutwater, separating the Potomac and the Shenandoah Rivers. It is known as Bolivar Heights. Just across the Potomac are the Maryland Heights, Washington County, Maryland. Over the Shenandoah beyond Loudon Heights lies Virginia proper.

Before the war, Harper's Ferry had a population of about 2,000. But now, like Fairfax Courthouse, Virginia, it was inhabited only by old men, black and white, women and children and a garrison then of Union troops. The Confederate Army evacuated it on the 19th of September after burning all the stores and government buildings. The Rebs left the once beautiful and comfortable town a heap of black ruins, save for a few small, mean brick and log huts. The saddest and the most humiliating sight to us here, and perhaps the heaviest loss to the United States government in this section of the country, was the celebrated Harper's Ferry Arsenal and Armory. It was now one mass of ruins, with only a small portion of the stone work standing. Our own forces had applied the fire fiend to keep it out of Confederate hands. This once magnificent and immense government structure, which manufactured firearms and artillery of every caliber and gave constant employment to twelve or fifteen hundred men, was destroyed. It was located by the side of the town along the river's brink.

Here, drunkenness was very prevalent. We were informed that when the Rebel Army was in possession, it was even more so. To use the language of an old citizen there, "whiskey ran like water." Our regiment was here brigaded, becoming a portion of the famous Irish Brigade under the command of General Thomas Francis Meagher. The brigade was a part of Hancock's Division, Sumner's Corps (2nd Army Corps), Army of the Potomac, General George B. McClellan, Commander-in-Chief.[12]

Sketch of General Meagher

In personal appearance, General Meagher was about 35 years old, five feet-eight or ten inches high, of rather stout build, and had a clear high-colored complexion. He wore a heavy, dark brown moustache, closely trimmed. Except in battle, where he generally wore only the uniform of a private soldier, he nearly always appeared in the full dress of his rank. Meagher presented an exceedingly neat and clean soldierly appearance, marked and admired by all. He was a gentleman of no ordinary ability. In thorough military skill and in courage and bravery on the battlefield, he was second to none in the Army of the Potomac.

In polished, gentlemanly manners and bearing (when himself), he was head and shoulders above any other man occupying a similar position in the army that I ever knew or heard of. His conversation was dignified. In point of education, his equal was hard to find. He spoke fluently not only English, but also Greek, Hebrew, French, German, Welsh, and the native Irish language. The latter sounded like a mixture of all the others jumbled up together and was very seldom heard in the present day. Only a few of the natives of some of the wildest and most uncultivated parts of Ireland spoke it and even there that old, ancient language was fast going to decay.

In kindness and thoughtfulness for his men, he was the shining light and bright star of the whole Union Army. Meagher made unceasing efforts to have his soldiers all well provided for and made comfortable. He often brought some poor, sick or perhaps dying soldier into his own private tent in cold weather. Wrapping him up there in blankets, Meagher administered with his own hands such medicine as was prescribed by the brigade head doctor. In the surgeon's absence, the general prescribed for and administered himself such remedies as he thought were needed. As a physician, Meagher had considerable judgment.

He was one of the very few military leaders who never required or would ask any of his command to go where he would not go himself. Meagher was first to lead the way. He was a soldier who not only prided in doing his own duty but encouraged and helped all under him to do theirs. Glory, honor and praise to his memory as a soldier, firm and true to his government and his country.

But, alas, poor fellow, he had one besetting sin. It was the besetting sin of so many Irish then and now—intemperance. Meagher found an untimely grave in the broad waters of the Missouri, having either stumbled or fallen overboard drunk from a steamboat on that river. He was serving then his term of office as Governor of Montana. Meagher had been appointed Acting Governor after the close of the war.[13] Thus ended the eventful career of one of the truest and best soldiers that ever drew a sword in defense of the Union of his adopted country. His death and the reported cause of it was sad and melancholy. Yet his many acts of kindness, bravery and heroism will long be remembered and cherished with pleasure and pride by many an American and by thousands of his own native countrymen of the Emerald Isle.*

---

* The foregoing sketch of General Meagher is from my own personal knowledge of him for nearly two months prior to the Battle of Fredericksburg, Virginia, December 13, 1862, commencing at Harper's Ferry.

Lt. Col. St. Clair A. Mulholland
Commander, 116th Pennsylvania Infantry Regiment
Postwar image, courtesy of the U.S. Army Military History Institute

*"I must note that there was a special, uncomfortable time
experienced by every soldier on the eve of going into action.
Then his heart was, as it were, in his mouth. Brave,
Good and loyal men were not excepted."*

Chapter 2

The Capture of
Charlestown, West Virginia

Early on the morning of the 13th, our colonel sent me a message to be ready to accompany him to the headquarters of General Meagher, about 200 yards distant, at ten a.m. The general wanted to see me. I tried to think. Who could have told General Meagher about me or what could he want with me? I was a perfect stranger to him, one who perhaps he had never saw before except in the ranks and then in the distance. Had I been guilty of any crime or misdemeanor worthy of reproof or punishment?

The incident of the cornfield flashed upon my mind. Had I done wrong in refusing Col. Heenan admittance into the camp at the dead hour of nearly midnight without the countersign? Had I insulted him by telling him that I did not know him then in my position as a guard at my post? But even in this, I did not see how any charge could be brought against me for, in acting as I did, I was simply doing my duty. I was carrying out the instructions of my superior officer. In vain did any of my thoughts or ideas satisfy my mind as to the real nature of General Meagher's business with me.

I, however, rigged myself up in my dress uniform, brightened up all my buttons and brasses, and presented a pretty fair soldierly appearance. I was fit for inspection. I proceeded in accordance with orders to the tent of Colonel Heenan, whom I found all alone reading a Philadelphia newspaper. I saluted him and said, "Good morning, Colonel."

"Good morning, my man," he said, "what do you wish?"

"I have come here," I said, "by your orders received early this morning."

"Oh, yes," he replied. "Sit down a moment and look over this paper from home."

I sat down while he changed his camp dress for his full dress uniform. My feelings at this time I could not describe. Fear, courage, hope, dread, suspense and I know not what else took sole possession of me. I wondered what was coming.

After the colonel dressed, we got out of the tent. The colonel said, "We will now go over and see the general."

Meagher's tent or headquarters was not more than 100 yards distant. It was on the camp line of the 69th New York Infantry, one of the regiments of our Irish Brigade. On the way, the only remarks made by the colonel concerned the weather and healthy location of the various camps scattered all over Bolivar Heights and Loudon Heights. There were some 25,000 troops stationed there. He never in the remotest manner made the slightest allusion to the nature and object of our mission to General Meagher.

We reached our destination, stopping at the fly door of the general's tent. There stood one of his orderlies; Colonel Heenan inquired if the general was in. The orderly replied, "Yes." "Can I see him?" returned the colonel.

"I will ask," said the orderly turning around and going into the tent.

In a moment he returned and invited the colonel and myself to enter. We then did. Now comes the tug of war, I thought.

General Meagher was in fatigue dress, partly stretched out on a wooden bench covered with brown army blankets. His feet were propped up against an empty cracker (hardtack) box. Around him on the partly rough boarded floor of his tent were scattered newspapers. On a small, plain wooden table there were a few books, maps and a fieldglass. In another part of his tent stood a large empty box, covered with an India-rubber blanket. It held three canteens. Nearby was a bright tin bucket full of clear spring water with a tin cup attached by a string. Along one of the sides of the tent were placed three or four campstools and a writing desk, on which an inkstand and paper had been placed. These articles constituted the entire furniture of General Meagher's tent on Bolivar Heights, Harper's Ferry, Virginia.

On entering the tent, the usual military salute passed between the two commanders and me. The colonel then turned round to me standing close behind him and addressed Meagher, saying, "General, here is your man."

"Ah," said the general, "be seated."

I fetched one of the campstools for Colonel Heenan who sat down on it near to General Meagher. I then took a seat myself on another one nearby, facing them. Silence reigned for about half a minute, until it was broken by the general. With that pleasing smile on his countenance which he always wore when addressing personally any of his soldiers, he asked, "Well, you are from the Old Sod, ain't you?"

My reply was simply, "Yes, sir."

Meagher then put his hand into his coat breastpocket and pulled out a lot of papers. After looking them all over but seeming not to have found what he wanted, he called his orderly standing outside of the tent. The soldier immediately entered. The general asked him if he knew what had become of the piece of poetry titled "The Land of My Birth" with the name McCarter written on the back.

"Yes, sir," said the orderly, "you bid me put it into your portfolio."

Going over to the writing desk and opening a book thereon, the orderly took from one of its pockets the paper in question and handed it to General Meagher. He, in his habitual polite and gentlemanly manner, thanked the attendant. The man then retired. The general looked at the paper a moment. Then glancing at me, he held it out, asking "Is that your handwriting?" "Yes sir," I replied. I also stated, "Yes, sir, that is my handwriting."*

---

* How this paper got into the hands of General Meagher, I never learned. I remember, however, writing it at home in Philadelphia in the year 1860. Upon leaving the city with my regiment on the 1st of September for the seat of war, I accidentally put it with several other private papers into my memorandum book. When in camp near Washington, I pulled it out one day. When I was reading it over again, one of our lieutenants (Montgomery, afterwards killed at Fredericksburg) sitting on the grass nearby, happened to see the heading. He asked me to let him read it. I did so, after which he took such a fancy to it and the style of the penmanship that he offered me a $10 greenback on the spot for it. I at once refused, saying, "No sir, but if you accept it as a gift, it is yours." He very thankfully did so. Ever after, he was unremitting in his attention and kindness to me. Quite likely this was the channel through which General Meagher got possession of the paper, although I never knew for certain that it was.

Colonel Heenan interrupted our conversation by saying, "General, this is a man that I think we can trust. As my regiment requires a good man to distribute, collect and attend to its mail, I am thinking of giving him the position. My own staff recommend the appointment."

Then and not until then did I discover and, so agreeably too, the nature of our visit to General Meagher. But this was not all.

"Well, really, Colonel," said the general, "that is all very good. But he writes so well. I think with all respect to you and your regiment, I am in much need of a clerk for the brigade. He could make himself more useful and be of more service in that capacity than in the position you propose." Turning to me, he asked, "What say you yourself, McCarter?"

"Fix it between yourselves, gentlemen," said I, "I am satisfied."

"Thank you," responded the general.

"Now, Mac," said General Meagher, "Colonel Heenan and I will arrange it. And, in the meantime, you can go to your quarters and the colonel will instruct you this afternoon what to do. Before you go, just help yourself from either of those canteens on that box," pointing to it.

I did so and left, saluting both officers and returned to camp.* On reaching my regimental quarters, I found them deserted by all except by the guard. In my absence the regiment had gone away about half a mile to drill and returned soon after my own return from the tent of General Meagher.

About five p.m., Colonel Heenan came to my tent where I was comfortably seated (or rather squatted), partaking of some fine salt pork, coffee and hardtack which I had just cooked. Without any ceremony,

---

* It is a remarkable fact that my impediment in speaking never interfered with me in the full discharge of my military duties at anytime or under any circumstance, not even on guard or picket duty, the most trying of all to me in that respect. No one except a few of my most intimate companions ever noticed it. Why this was, I cannot tell. Probably the very healthy condition of my whole system, no doubt brought about by constant work and exercise in the pure open air, was the cause. Certain it was that my nervous system, especially which I have always found to govern my powers of articulation, was then stronger than it ever had been before or since. To this I attribute the fluency of speech which I then enjoyed and which was on many occasions so necessary in the performance of duty. A distinguished Philadelphia physician, who well knew my constitution, once said to me "Your speaking is the best index to your health in the world."

The conversation related here between myself, Colonel Heenan and General Meagher is not exactly verbatim. It is as near so as my memory and a few notes taken down soon after it occurred can make it.

the colonel edged in, and, sitting down beside me, said, "Well, the general says he must have you for his clerk when the brigade goes into winter quarters, which we expect will be soon. In the meantime and from now, you are appointed to take full charge of the mail of your regiment, making my own tent your headquarters for receiving and distributing. Write out on a slip of paper your authority which I will sign."[1]

I did so, after which the colonel attached his signature. I deposited the document in my memorandum book and still retain it to this day. Its signer's body has long been moldering in the grave. Only on one occasion was I called upon to produce the paper to satisfy the division head mail agent of the authority given me by my colonel. The general mail office of our division, General Hancock's, being in the town of Harper's Ferry about one and a half miles distant, my duty was to go there daily for the regiment's mail. This was no pleasant or easy matter. The roads then in that place, like all other Virginia highways that I ever saw, were rough, hilly, winding and narrow. They were well calculated to test the patience and endurance of man or beast to the utmost in getting over them.

The road over which my route lay to the town was then in a worse condition than it had ever been before. This had been caused by recent rain storms, so common in Virginia, together with being cut up into ruts and gullies by the passage of hundreds of batteries of artillery, Rebel and Union, as well as large bodies of cavalry and infantry of both armies. Nothing but mud, knee-deep, was to be found anywhere in or around Harper's Ferry for many miles. It was "Virginia mud," red, sticky, thick and staining, hard to remove when dry. However, a cavalry horse was set apart for my use. But not being much of a horseman and my route to the town being a constant jam from morning to night of moving bodies of troops arriving from other parts, I preferred Shank's mare to the animal appointed to carry me.

This, however, was not of long continuance. On the night of the 15th, orders were received for the Irish Brigade to march next morning to Charlestown, a small town about six or seven miles distant. We were to move on the Winchester Road, our purpose to drive a large force of the enemy, said to number 3,000 men, out of the town. These men had taken possession of the town only one day previous to our arrival on Bolivar Heights.

On the March from Bolivar Heights, Harper's Ferry, Virginia, to Charlestown, Virginia, and a Skirmish there "My First Engagement," October 16th, 1862

At daybreak on the morning of the 16th, every man asleep in his tent was awakened by the long roll of the kettle drums of our own regiment and the shrill notes of the bugle of the 4th New York Battery of Artillery adjoining us. Half an hour later, the cry "Fall in for roll call," sounded throughout the camp. In ten minutes, each company had formed in line. Each man answered to his name. Notified to be in readiness to march with the other regiments of the brigade at seven a.m. sharp, each soldier carried two days cooked rations, prepared the night before, and 40 rounds of ammunition. The Irish Brigade was to move in light marching order ready for action at a moment's warning.[2]

All camp equipment was to remain on the ground just as it stood. This indicated a return of the regiments to Bolivar Heights in two or three days at most and also that a brush with the Rebels at Charlestown on our approach was fully expected and calculated upon. At seven a.m., the bugle again sounded, calling all the regiments into line. Half an hour later, the whole Irish Brigade was in motion, advancing by the Winchester Road on Charlestown, fully prepared for a fight.

The brigade marched by regiments, four men abreast, and in the following order: 1) 69th New York, Gen. Meagher's own regiment, and brigade band as pioneers; 2) 4th New York Artillery (6 Guns); 3) 116th Pennsylvania; 4) 28th Massachusetts; 5) 63d New York; 6) 88th New York; 7) Ambulances, protected by a heavy guard.

The weather was bracing, bright and clear. The troops were in fine condition and good spirits.[3] The country over which we passed was picturesque and beautiful, more even and level than any other part of Virginia that I had seen up to this time. At about eleven a.m., we arrived at a point within three-quarters of a mile of Charlestown, on rising ground overlooking that little town lying before us in the valley below. "A halt" and "a rest at ease" were ordered. At the same time, our artillery was commanded to unlimber the guns and prepare for action. No trace or appearance whatever of the enemy could be seen. But from the conduct of our commanding officers, especially General Meagher who was always on the alert, all felt satisfied of the close proximity of the Rebs. They actually were closer than even the most knowing and watchful among our rank and file ever had the remotest idea of.

To our right, at about a quarter of a mile, lay a wide tract of land thickly covered with heavy and light timber. On our left, at about the same distance, laid another one of the same description. It was a well known fact that the thick, dark woods with which Virginia abounds were frequently resorted to by the Rebel army. The Johnnies used them as hiding places or covering from which to make sudden dashes and attacks upon Federal forces advancing or retreating on open and unprotected ground. Rebel masked batteries were often concealed in these forests and used with deadly effect against our moving and unsuspecting columns. Therefore, great caution and care had to be continually observed by our men when approaching or nearing such forests.

Accordingly, after a rest of ten minutes, skirmishers to the number of 100 men from the 69th New York were ordered out and deployed to the right and left. They advanced quietly and cautiously in the direction of the woods to reconnoiter them, while 100 picked men of the 28th Massachusetts went on a similar errand towards Charlestown, half a mile in our front. The latter had not far to go to find what they sought. On nearing the edge of the town, they were met by a squad of Rebel cavalry who fired upon them, as well as by a shower of bullets from Rebel muskets leveled at them out of windows and from the roofs of houses. Two of the men were killed and nine wounded. The others at once retreated to the main body, bringing their wounded comrades with them. The parties who had gone out to reconnoiter the woods had returned earlier, reporting no enemy to be found in those places.

Being now fully satisfied that the enemy in considerable force was in the town, a brief consultation of about ten minutes was held among the staff officers of all the regiments, presided over by General Meagher. It resulted in the decision to bombard the town. The artillery was then ordered to a more commanding position on the extreme right of our line and await orders to open fire.[4] Under the cover of these guns, the whole Irish Brigade was ordered to advance rapidly, enter the town, and drive the enemy out if possible to do so. Only my regiment, the 116th, was to remain behind to support the artillery.

All being now in readiness, the artillery in position and well supplied with shot and shell awaiting the signal to "Fire," my own regiment drew up in line of battle, a single line, some fifty yards in the battery's rear. We were on lower ground and ready to advance to the artillery's defense if the enemy attacked from any quarter. The other regiments, four in all, positioned on our left and anxiously waited for the order, "Forward, march."

Five, ten, fifteen, twenty, twenty-five, thirty minutes had now elapsed. Yet the gunners stood idle at their guns while the infantry framed all kinds of reasons for the delay. Five minutes later, the shout, "Look out there," from an artillery officer, greeted the hearing organs of the patiently waiting infantry. Two seconds later, a shell, with its fuse (or tail) still on fire, came "h-i-s-s-i-n-g" over our heads. It caused some slight shaking sensations among the troops, my own regiment especially, who were nearly all green and untried men never under fire until now. Our lieutenant-colonel [St. Clair A. Mulholland] at the top of his voice shouted, "Steady, men, steady." This was sufficient, no more "dodging" afterwards. The shell hit several hundred feet beyond, injuring no one, not even bursting. It came from a Rebel battery in a clump of woods on the other side of Charlestown hitherto unseen by us.

The ball was now opened by the enemy. "Boom, boom, boom," was the reply from three guns of our artillery. The cannons shook the earth and sent howling and screeching missiles through the air into the very center of the town. The artillerymen had fired three spherical case shot. This artillery round was a kind of shell, varying in size and powers of destruction. It contained from 50-100 musket balls, all connected or run together, in the center of which was a heavy charge of powder. The fuse, like that of a regular shell, was ignited when the shot left the gun. It caused the missile to burst in a designated area after the range of the place had been obtained. The length or form of the fuse was so regulated that the explosion of the shot took place exactly where and when it was intended to do, hurling the musket balls in every direction, each one of them being as deadly as if discharged from a rifle.

After the discharge of the three shot, all was still and quiet for a moment. The gunners keenly followed with their eyes, as best they could through the smoke, their messengers of death until they were lost to view in the streets of the ill-fated town, where they were expected to explode. No reply whatever came from the Rebel battery on the opposite hill beyond Charlestown. Nor was there any advance made by his infantry to capture or attack our artillery. A moment longer, then "Boom, boom, boom," from three more of our guns. This noise was followed by the same anxious gaze of the gunners looking for the results of their fire. They did not long remain in suspense. About ten minutes later, during which time our cannonade had ceased, a dense volume of smoke, then flame, burst high up in the air. It was located about at the center of the town, threatening destruction all around. This seemed to arouse the enemy. Their battery, hitherto almost silent, opened a rapid and steady fire on ours, making the affair for awhile an artillery duel.

The Rebels, now seeming to have got the exact range of our battery, commenced throwing solid shot, undoubtedly with the object of dismounting our guns. Our gunners worked with double energy. Up to this time, none of our artillerymen had been killed or hurt. But very soon afterwards, it was my own painful experience, as well as that of the great majority of my regiment, to witness the almost instant death of one of our brave artillerymen. When in the act of sponging out one of the guns, a solid shot from the Rebel battery hit him fair and square, tearing completely away both legs close up to his body. He was carried to the rear of my own regiment, a little behind the battery on lower ground, where he died in a very few minutes without uttering a word. He was rolled up in his "Winding Sheet," his blanket, and left on the field to be buried in his soldier's grave after the action was over, a martyr to the cause of liberty and humanity.

A few seconds afterwards, another missile of the same description and from the same source, took the entire head off of one of his comrades manning another of the guns, as clean as if cut off with a knife or axe. His body was not moved from where it fell during our stay on that part of the field of strife. Ten minutes after this occurrence, two more artillerymen had been severely wounded, one losing a hand and the other run over by the wheel of a gun carriage changing position. There were four casualties in this battery alone, two of them being sadly and fearfully fatal.*

At this time, when the ground around us began to assume the realities of a battlefield, a most amusing incident, occurred. It was also a disgraceful act of cowardice. I am sorry to say that it happened in my own regiment. I cannot pass over the incident without noticing that it was one thing to "play soldier" at home in Philadelphia where Rebel

---

* Please bear in mind the position of the infantry regiments of our brigade during this artillery fight. They were to advance and enter the town upon receipt of a particular signal which was to be given to that effect at a certain time. My regiment was in line of battle—a straight, single row of men posted about 50 yards in the rear of the artillery as its support. The four remaining regiments were in double line of battle (two rows of men, one of them close behind the other). All the regiments to a great extent were shielded and protected from the Rebel fire on our battery by the high hill on which it was posted. Our lines of battle were stationed at the base. Several of our men, however, were slightly hurt by fragments of Rebel shells bursting overhead and falling on them. But none was hit hard enough to prevent the full discharge of his military duty. [Note continued on p. 28]

bullets were not whizzing past the ears, and another to "be a soldier in reality" on the field of deadly conflict.

A certain lieutenant in my own company, Company A, was noted for his great pride and self-conceit. I will omit his name in respect for his distinguished family residing near Philadelphia. He was better known in the army by the nickname of "Squirt." Afraid of having his boots soiled by mud, Virginia mud especially, he would not hesitate to request and even command some of his men to clean them off. He would not stain his soft, white ladylike hands with a common soldier's tincup. A piece of fine, fat pork with its necessary companions, beans, would scare him into a fit. While in Philadelphia, this lieutenant was foremost in all military displays. In point of bravery, personal appearance and army knowledge, he was, in his own estimation and conceit, at least equal to or even superior to General George B. McClellan. So much for "playing soldier." Now there was the smell of powder far away from home.

But before relating the incident, I must note that there was a special, uncomfortable time experienced by every soldier on the eve of going into action. Then his heart was, as it were, in his mouth. Brave, good, loyal and true men were not even excepted. That time was the interval between the formation of the line of battle and the spoken command, "Charge, forward, march." These moments, few or many, were full of dread, fear and suspense. They were well calculated to test a

Signals Note: In the Army of the Potomac, there was a body of men called the "Signal Corps" which was of invaluable service to the Army. This Corps was controlled generally by the Commander-in-Chief. It was composed of officers and men selected from each brigade. Its work was constructing and working the army telegraph lines and watching the enemy's movements and reporting them immediately to headquarters. Two systems of signalling were used, namely the "telegraph" (running along the ground, fences, etc.) and the "flag." I had not the opportunity of seeing the former in operation, but the latter was fully displayed at our skirmish at Charlestown. "Flag signalling" (or telegraphing) was nearly always used in any action and was one of the most exposed and most dangerous branches of the service to the men engaged in it. For this purpose, three small flags were used, a white one with a red center, a red one with a white center, and a black one with a white center. Signals were transmitted with these flags from one place to another by the flag man "waving" his flag in certain directions from his station. Signal stations were generally on high hills, steeples of churches (as at Charlestown), roofs of houses, bends in roads, and on eminences from which the enemy's movements were visible to the flag men. Brave and cool men only were employed in this arm of the service. The duties required were of the most important, dangerous and trying kind, the flag men invariably being targets for the enemy's shot.

soldier's mettle. Invariably, the coward showed the white feather. A regiment or brigade stood in line of battle, ready at the word "go" to plunge into a fight. But the men dared not until so ordered. Shells flew thick over and past them, yet they could not advance or fall back. Oh, what misery! What a terrible situation, compelled to stand and take whatever punishment the foe may inflict without being permitted to protect yourself or even to retaliate or avenge.

Yet such was often the case in time of war. My comrades and I were placed in just such a position near Charlestown, Virginia. But when the command, "Forward, march," was then given, how different our feelings. For although marching to meet the enemy face to face in deadly conflict, we all felt a freedom, a courage. In my own case, it was a time of go-ahead, reckless courage. I was perfectly destitute of fear and utterly regardless for the time being of any or every consequence, life or death, heaven or hell.

But to proceed with the incident. My lieutenant was at his post of duty on the extreme right of Company A, then the head of the regiment. My own position was very near him. I was the fourth man from the head of the line, allowing me to have a full view of the lieutenant's conduct and actions while under Rebel fire. I was already somewhat suspicious of his bravery. After all his boasts, I wondered how he would act in an engagement.

The first shell thrown by the enemy, which passed far beyond us, high in the air, caused no pleasant sensations to the men of my regiment. This was not strange for raw troops. But the effect upon our gallant little lieutenant was far stronger and more marked. It gave unmistakable indications that at least one "white feather" resided in our immediate neighborhood. Immediately on seeing this missile coming, our lieutenant made one clean spring back, falling on his back on the ground as if shot. But a moment afterwards he regained his place again, although with a face contorted by fright. Oh, how pale he was, his limbs trembling as if palsied! Later, other shells began to come more frequently and closer to our men. The enemy seemed to have gotten the range of our artillery. One of them burst over the heads of the men in the regiment, wounding several with fragments. The poor, frail, weak, yet boastful nature of our dashing officer could stand it no longer. With trembling legs, almost declining to support a shaking body, and with an ashy, pale countenance, he spoke out in a voice that sounded like a frightened child, "I don't like them fiery-tailed things so near me. I have a pain in my stomach. I will get out of the way for awhile, and lay down."

He did so, amid the hisses, groan, sneers and tittering laughs of the whole regiment. The remains of an old oak tree against which rested a large haystack stood 15 or 20 yards in the rear of the regiment. Behind this bulwark the courageous little fellow crawled, almost on knees and hands, for rest, peace and safety. The next time I saw him was upon our return to Bolivar Heights. He was in a sutler's tent, squatting on an empty barrel, eating hoe, or corncake and drinking beer. We understood soon afterwards that he made tracks for Washington,[5] leaving the Army of the Potomac to fight its own battles as best it would without his most valuable aid and assistance.*

It was now about two p.m. The day was beautiful and clear. Although it was October, the weather was warm, delightful and bracing. The forests were just beginning to shed and deposit their beautiful green summer garments on mother earth. The fields, although yet clothed with verdure and freshness presented an appearance which indicated that the sweet summer of 1862 was bidding a long, sad and eternal farewell to men on earth. It was in reality autumn, the most beautiful part of the whole year, full of interest to all, to me especially. In my very early years, I read a great deal concerning the American autumn. Now I saw one in reality, a perfect one.

But what an autumn of fire and sword for the good old state of

---

* **Sutlers Note**: These were men who followed the army and sold to the troops articles of food, tobacco, and liquor. By military law at this time, one sutler, appointed by the colonel, was allowed to each regiment. In some instances, however, two or three regiments were supplied by him. His tent, or shop, was erected on or near the camp-ground of the regiment for which he was appointed. The government guaranteed him payment for goods purchased by the soldiers to the amount of one-third of their pay, which he generally received when the army was paid. The prices charged by these sutlers for goods were most exorbitant, sometimes four times over the market value. For instance, for one lb. of cheese they charged $1.50, an apple ten cents, an orange 25 cents, a small pie $1, a pint bottle of whiskey (bad at that) $2 and everything else in like proportion. Yet, had these extortioners demanded more, yes five times as much, it would have been paid. For the troops would have what their appetites craved as long as their money held out. Sutlers' supplies were purchased by their agents in the North and shipped to them at different points occupied by the army. Their profits were enormous, sometimes a fortune. I never knew or heard of any law existing to prevent or interfere with them in asking and receiving for their goods any price they put upon them. On this account, they were unfortunately a class of individuals held in contempt, almost to hatred, by the troops and even the officers of the army.

Virginia—its rivers running with human blood, its fields covered with armed fighting men, father against son, son against father, friend against friend, right against wrong, and freedom against slavery and tyranny. Oh, what an epoch in the career and history of "Old Virginia!" Well indeed might the then few remaining loyal sons and daughters of the old state have wept tears of blood over its downfall, disgrace and ruin. The Old Dominion had fallen from all that was noble, great and good to be the veriest hotbed seat and throne of disloyalty, treason, rebellion and murder. "Oh, oh, Virginia!"

A flag man, belonging to the Signal Corps attached to our brigade, was stationed on the edge of the woods a quarter of a mile to our extreme left. His assigned post of duty was on the limb of a high tree commanding an extensive view of Charlestown and the surrounding countryside. In his hand he held his little but important flag. By waving it very frequently from his perch, he kept General Meagher, who was constantly patrolling the ground on horseback between this signal station and his troops, fully informed of the movements of the Rebel force within the town and on its outskirts. From the fact that no shot from the enemy was fired at or near the flag man on this occasion, we drew the conclusion that he must have been completely hidden from the Rebels by the branches of the trees. Yet at the same time, the flag man and all his movements and actions were distinctly and plainly seen by every man of the Irish Brigade. He was keenly watched by hundreds of anxious eyes and waiting hearts. But his flag motions, or rather their meaning, were complete mysteries to all except to the chief commanding officers.

Still all watched earnestly, knowing that some signal would soon be given that meant "Forward, march." We had not long to wait. Twenty minutes later, there was a different and quicker motion of the flag than any we had previously seen. The general hastened from near the signal station where he then was to the head of his troops. Immediately on his arrival there, one consolidated stream of fire burst forth from the mouths of each gun in our battery. It was aimed at the enemy on the hill behind Charlestown. The roar of this discharge was deafening, fearful and awfully grand, shaking perceptibly the ground all around us, echoing and re-echoing from hill to hill and valley to valley for many miles all around. It could be distinctly heard for at least 30 seconds afterwards.

At this point, General Meagher, with a voice that sounded like a lion and which could be heard down the whole line from officer to officer and from man to man, gave the long and anxiously waited for command, "Attention, forward, double quick, march."*

On the command "March" being given, our whole line, headed by the gallant Meagher, sprang forward with a yell which I shall never forget. I think that it could never again be imitated, even by the same body of men. We advanced on the double-quick, as commanded, from the low ground upon which our line of battle had been formed and posted up the hill upon which our artillery was operating. Thus when we at first started, we could not see the enemy. We had no opportunity whatever of forming any idea of his numbers until we reached the top of the hill.

The summit of the hill was soon reached. We all fully expected to plainly see and meet our opponents face to face. But we were quickly disappointed. From that point we could only discern faintly in the distance, probably half a mile, a long line of greycoats which we supposed to number eight or ten hundred men just emerging from the edge of the town. The Rebs advanced on our position slowly and cautiously as if feeling their way.[6]

On we went running, passing our artillery which then had been ordered to cease firing. We passed through smoke which hung all around like clouds of thick, dense, heavy vapor. We descended the hill and reached its base. There we found an obstruction to our progress, a rail fence fully five feet high. It was solidly constructed and double the length of our entire line of battle. "Halt!" and "Tear down the fence!" were immediately commanded. The order to rip down the fence was given not only to clear the way for us but also to make a path for our artillery, who were then limbering up their guns to follow if necessary.

---

* A regiment or body of troops never advanced until the word "March" was given. The preceding words, "Attention, forward," (double-quick if necessary), were only preparatory notices to go forward. In some instances the command "March" was delayed for perhaps a minute after the command "Forward" had been given. Such was the case at this time. Just as our brigade was about to advance, General Meagher quickly turned around and in an earnest, impressive manner addressed his men, my own regiment particularly, with these words, "Now, men, steady, and do your duty." This was undoubtedly intended for my regiment, all its members being raw, green and untried men. Meagher intended to cheer and inspire us with new and fresh courage and bravery in the performance of our duty. Probably the general had fears as to the courage of my regiment when brought to confront the foe for the first time on the open field. Wisely, indeed, did he place us in a position under his own immediate eye and supervision and shoulder to shoulder with his own tried and veteran crack regiment, the 69th New York. Afterward, when asked how my regiment behaved, the general replied, "Nobly, worthy of being a part of the Irish Brigade."

The whole Irish Brigade to a man went at destroying that fence in real, downright earnest. Such cracking and snapping of posts and rails I never before or since ever heard. In ten seconds, the whole structure laid prostrate and level with the earth. Not a moment now was to be lost. The line was immediately reformed and the command given, "Forward, march." But not as before, "double quick."

In the meantime, the Rebels had halted after not having advanced more than 200 yards outside of the town. They began to show unmistakable signs of retreating without firing a shot. Still on we pressed. When almost within fair, good musket range of the Rebs, they suddenly broke, beating a hasty and confused retreat into the town. They continued through it and then headed for the open country beyond. There a Southern battery of artillery was posted, whose fire had been completely silenced by the last heavy discharge of our own. The enemy did not appear to number over eight or ten hundred men. The cause of their sudden, hasty retreat was probably due to the fact that the force which they saw coming against them was, at least in point of numbers, far superior to their own. This was true, although at the time our Irish Brigade was much reduced and weakened by severe losses in the Battles of Bull Run, Manassas, Fair Oaks, Malvern Hill, and most recently in the Battle of Antietam, where it suffered most.[7]

On this occasion, its numbers did not reach quite 1,700 men all told. Originally, the Irish Brigade numbered 3,500.[8] At this time, my own 116th was the largest regiment in the Irish Brigade, numbering as we did nearly 380 men. The other four regiments, including artillery, mustered about 1,320 men. On nearing the town and when almost upon the very ground so recently occupied by the enemy, the order "Halt! Rest on your arms" was given and promptly obeyed.

While in this position, the 69th New York marched out of the line, 20 paces in front. There the regiment halted, its soldiers ordered to re-examine and see that their arms were properly loaded and primed. After this was done, General Meagher placed himself at the head of the gallant, far-famed veterans and once more gave the marching command. He and the 69th dashed forward and into the town amid the deafening yells and cheers of the remaining portion of the brigade then left behind. With banners gaily floating in the breeze—the glorious Stars and Stripes and the emblem of the little Emerald Isle over the sea, the Green Flag so feared, dreaded, and shunned by the Rebs, the 69th entered the town. Our Signal Corps man, who had gone with the regiment, popped up suddenly on a church cupola in the town. He gave a signal with his little flag, and the remaining regiments of the Irish Brigade quietly followed and entered Charlestown.[9]

Charlestown, Virginia
October 16th, 1862

Charlestown, Jefferson County, Virginia, is a small town, some seven or eight miles southwest of Harper's Ferry on the Winchester Road. It is the county seat. Prior to the war, it had a population of 2,500 or 3,000 souls. It will be long remembered as the place where the good, but rash old John Brown of Kansas fame with six of his followers paid the penalty of Virginia law by their public execution on December 1st, 1859, after invading Harper's Ferry. The town's situation is most beautiful, being in the midst of a rich, fertile country, surrounded by gently sloping hills and lovely groves. Here and there are delightful brooks of clear, cool running water. Part of the town is composed of several fine houses, some of them superior in size and architecture to any that I had seen in that section of country. But the larger portion consisted of small buildings, many of them wooden, apparently of long standing, dirty and neglected in appearance. Among the latter were grocery, baker, grog, saddler, and blacksmith shops, and a small market house.

The town also contained two or three churches or schoolhouses, a small courthouse and a prison. We saw few of the inhabitants. All of them who could get away to places of safety outside the town did so on receipt of a notice sent to them by General Meagher that an hour later he would bombard the place. It thus gave women, children, and all who wished to keep out of the way of flying cannon balls and bursting shells a chance to do so by leaving. About two-thirds of the inhabitants left. The remaining third either would not or could not leave. They kept themselves closed up within their houses.

As our forces entered the principal, long street of the town, the Rebels were distinctly seen making their exit out at the other end of it. They climbed up the side of a long, steep hill in the direction of Winchester at top speed and in the utmost confusion. Indeed, several of the wagons of their supply train had barely got out of the town when we entered it. The drivers cut their horses fearfully to hasten their speed, fearing that our troops were in pursuit. But they made good their escape and were not followed for prudent reasons, no doubt known to our commanders. Perhaps the absence of cavalry on our side at that time frustrated the chase. Horsemen could, undoubtedly, have overtaken and captured their entire train and probably their infantry too.

Our line marched through to the opposite side of the town, then back again to near the point at which we had entered. There we joined the 69th New York which had halted without proceeding further. Adjoining this place was a plot of ground enclosed by an iron railing with two gates or entrances. In the center of the enclosure stood a neat brick church and schoolhouse. It was then occupied by about 30 Confederate soldiers who had been wounded in the streets during the bombardment.[10]

Here the Irish Brigade was again drawn up in line. Our officers assigned 300 men to picket duty on the outskirts of the town and especially on the roads by which the enemy had retreated. The required number of men being soon obtained, they were at once officered, supplied with fresh rations and dispatched to their various posts of duty for the remainder of the day and coming night. These pickets would guard us from sudden attack or surprise by the enemy should he attempt it. The remaining troops remained in possession of the town. Luckily for me, I escaped being one of the 300 men drawn for picket duty. I was tired, foot-sore and hungry.

In the meantime, our battery remained on the hill where it had been so successfully operating on the enemy, no necessity having arisen for any change in its position. The gunners lounged about the guns or laid resting on the green grass on their sides, their every movement observed by our forces in the town. Our signal man occupied the cupola of the church, ready at a moment's warning to communicate with his little flag. He could telegraph any change in position for the artillerymen which might be thought necessary by the commanding general. None, however, was made or required. The battery remained in its first position until the retrograde movement by the Irish Brigade on the next morning to Bolivar Heights, Harper's Ferry. The artillery took the head of the line bound for that place.*

---

* **"Picketing."** The simplest definition of the word "Picket" which I can give is a "watchman or guard, posted or placed in as concealed a locality as possible, at the very front of an army or even at a point beyond the front, to watch the enemy and to immediately give an alarm should he (the enemy) make an approach to his lines." Picket duty, in the early stages of the war, was dangerous. The pickets of both armies would fire at each other on duty when position and opportunity to do so presented itself. In this way, very many valuable men were lost to both Union and Confederate armies. After the Battle of Fair Oaks, a kind of "silent agreement" sprang up in many parts of the Army of

At about three-thirty p.m., after the picket guards moved off for their posts of duty, the remaining troops were ordered to stack arms, build fires, cook rations and rest. Twelve guards had been detailed for duty at the two gates leading to the church wherein lay the Rebel wounded, attended and nursed by some residents of Charlestown. Four of the guards were immediately positioned, two at each gate for two hours. At the expiration of their tour, they were replaced by two others, the second relief, for the same length of time, and so on during the afternoon and night. Fortune did not smile on me as before during the picket draft. I was one of the twelve drafted to go on duty as one of the third relief, from eight to ten p.m. and again from two to four a.m.

Curiosity on the part some of our men, including me, prompted a request to the general for the privilege of taking a stroll through the town. It was at once granted. Several other members of my regiment and I started on our little tour of inspection and curiosity through several streets and byways, witnessing as we went along sad sights, the effects of the recent bombardment.

the Potomac and the Rebel Army of Northern Virginia, that pickets should not fire ateach other while on picket duty. The agreement was well observed except on a few occasions, when it was violated by the Confederates. Picket posts extended along the entire front of the army for miles upon miles. It was called the picket line or picket tour. The posts varied in distance from each other according to circumstances, nature of the country and the position and force of the enemy, in some cases being only 40 or 50 feet apart, while in others, quite as many yards. Two men, sometimes three, occupied one post, the time being two hours on duty there and four hours off during the 24 hours' term of picket duty. In case of surprise or advance of the foe on our lines, the picket on the extreme outer post would alarm the next inner picket, both retreating to the next nearest post and so on until the whole picket line had reached the main body of the army. By that time it had been fully alarmed of the approach of the enemy and was prepared to meet him. Such was the character of picket duty in the Army of the Potomac during the fall and winter of 1862.

"The ball had struck the child on the left breast, ripping the left arm completely away. . . Must the innocent suffer with the guilty, must the mother see her own darling child turned into a mangled bleeding corpse? . . .Alas, such is civil war."

Chapter 3

**Scenes in Charlestown
and the Return to Harpers Ferry**

War is truly said to be a sad necessity. But civil war, be it long or short and under almost any circumstance, is indeed sadder and more desolating in its effects. History may record the ravages and desolations made and left in the tracks of the bloody feet of war. Even in this most unnatural contest of our own, painters of the rarest talents may one day paint the destruction in masterly styles and glowing colors. Yet, all of these efforts fall far short in showing to the eye or to the mind war's real effects upon people and country.

I proceeded along one of the streets of this ill-fated town accompanied by several members of my regiment. Our attention was attracted to a three-story house, one of the better class of dwellings there, by crowds of soldiers and a few citizens going into it. These visitors came immediately out again with dull and saddened countenances and, in not a few cases, with tearful eyes. The front door had apparently been smashed and laid about in pieces upon the cobblestone pavement opposite. We stopped and, following the example of others, entered the house and then the room on the first floor.

Merciful heaven, what a sight met our eyes. God save me the pain of another such sight as long as I live. The room was long and narrow. From one end of it to the other, regardless of those present, paced a lady, apparently not over 30 years of age. She appeared to be in terrible grief, misery and despair, refusing entirely any comfort or consolation from those of her friends and neighbors there congregated. The woman was clad in black, but in some manner her dress had been almost torn from her body. She would now and then burst out into heart-rending fits of weeping, exclaiming, "Oh, my child, my Lilly."

Not knowing exactly the cause of the lady's sorrow, I quietly inquired of an old man leaning against the door what it was. He replied that her child, her only child, had been killed about an hour ago by a ball from the Federal battery. The round passed through a window at which the child had been standing, looking down at soldiers on the street. At one end of the room, a few women and several members of our Irish Brigade were gathered around what seemed to me to be a melodeon, or pipe organ, gazing sadly and silently at something lying on its top. As soon as opportunity presented to approach the spot, we did so.

There on the top of the instrument laid a sweet little girl, some seven or eight years old, cold and stiff and dead. Except for the dead yet still beautiful, innocent pale face, all the rest of the body was covered with a large sheet, or white quilt. On this cover, particularly that part of it over the child's breast, were large spots of blood. A young colored woman was cutting the long brown curls from the child's head and perfectly saturating them with her tears.

Approaching still nearer, I asked how the child had been killed. The reply given was in substance the same as the old man's. In a flood of tears, the young colored woman laid her scissors down. With both hands, she slowly and solemnly raised the blood-stained cover off the little breast, saying in sobs as she did so, "Just look there."

My companion and I gazed for a moment at the object in horror and dismay, unable to utter a word. Then turning slowly and sadly away, we left the room. My heart was too full and my eyes positively refused to shelter any longer the streams of hot water that burst from them. The ball had struck the child on the left breast, tearing it and ripping the left arm completely away. Only a small portion of the right breast remained. It presented a most ghastly, sickening appearance. Yet, that dear little face seemed as calm and as peaceful as in a quiet, sweet slumber. Oh, cruel, cruel war! Must the innocent suffer with the guilty, yea, must the mother see her own darling child in a moment turned into a mangled bleeding corpse, for the sin, shame and rebellion of proud, haughty men and women? Alas, such is civil war.[1]

We proceeded a little farther along. Lying on a vacant space of ground between two houses, we found the dead body of a woman. The lower part of her garments were apparently burned or singed and the fragments of an exploded shell were scattered all around. Her nearly grey hair, for she had fallen with her face on the ground, indicated that she had been well advanced in years. In front of the body laid a small waiter, several pieces of broken china and some slices of bread. We inferred that she had been in the act of carrying these articles, probably to a neighboring house, when the fatal shell struck her. Turning a corner near the same place, we saw a cart or wagon on which laid the dead body of a young man, a Rebel soldier. He had evidently been placed there by some of his companions after dark. The only injury to the body visible to us was a small cut or hole above the eye. A little pool of blood had formed on the ground underneath the cart.

It was now getting near six p.m. Feeling very tired after the activities of the day and having had my curiosity to view Charlestown after the bombardment gratified, I and one of my comrades concluded to return to headquarters. This was necessary as we were hungry and had to cook our supper, take our accustomed evening smoke and enjoy a little rest before it became our turn to go on guard. We therefore sauntered slowly back, reaching our camp a few minutes after six p.m.

Our attention now was particularly directed to supplying the wants of a voracious appetite. As good fortune would have it, we were amply and liberally supplied. We boiled our coffee, roasted our fat pork, cracked our hardtack and went into them as only hungry soldiers do, in real wolf style. After partaking of this coarse but nutritious and healthy camp fare, we, as was the universal custom among the "Boys in Blue," sat down at one of our fires on a limb cut from a tree and there enjoyed an evening smoke. While sitting there with other members of our company, talking and chattering, I was somewhat surprised by the appearance of a Rebel soldier. He came boldly forward and sat down in our midst. The Reb took out his pipe, lit it and commenced to smoke. By way of introduction, he stated that he was one of five left in charge of the Rebel wounded then occupying the little church as a hospital. He had just then came out to enjoy like ourselves a good quiet smoke. Of course, we made him welcome, expecting to hear much about the strength and position of the Confederate forces. He was a young man, quite communicative. His conversation proved him intelligent and considerably experienced as a soldier in the Rebel Army of Northern Virginia.

A kind of running conversation now ensued upon the conduct of the war between those present. We had several members of the 69th New York, a few boys from the 116th Pennsylvania and our interesting Rebel visitor. It ran in something like the following strain:

Federal, "What regiment do you belong to?"

Rebel, "The 3rd South Carolina."

Federal, "How long have you been in the army?"

Rebel, "Since Bull Run fight."

Federal, "Don't you wish the war was over?"

Rebel, "Not near so much as you do."

Federal, "Don't you think the South will soon let up?"

Rebel, "Not as long as one of her men is left. You may whip us, but it will only be by unequal and overpowering numbers."

Federal, "You had better join the Union Army now."

Rebel, "Never, I will fight against the North as long as I can shoulder a musket."

Federal, "Then you don't like the Yankees."

Rebel, "Not by a damned shot. There are some pretty good New Yorkers though."

Federal, "How many men had you here?"

Rebel, "Yesterday, we had 11,000 and today only 650."

Federal, "Where did they go to?"

Rebel, "To reinforce General Lee at Winchester."

Federal, "How many men has Lee there?"

Rebel, "Between eighty and a hundred thousand."

Federal, "What is he going to do?"

Rebel, "Don't know and dare not tell if I did."

Federal, "Why did you fellows break and run a while ago?"

Rebel, "Well, I'll just tell you. Because we saw that damned infernal Green Flag of yours a coming, and knew well who was behind it. It gave us a sickening dose at Antietam."[2]

Federal, "How did you get sick?"

Rebel, "By the bayonet charge you fellows made there which broke our center. I tell you boys, we can lick you out of your Yankee shoes every day in the year with the musket or rifle, given equal numbers. But your `cold steel' and the way you wild Irishmen use it, we cannot stand."

Federal, "How is your Army on the `grub' question?"

Rebel, "Got plenty of everything but coffee. That we can't get for the blockade of our parts."

At this point, our pleasant and entertaining talk together was interrupted by the officer of the guard shouting, "Fall in, third relief." Being one of that number and having now to go on my post of duty with another comrade, I very reluctantly bid good night to Johnny, leaving him and the rest of our boys to continue the dialogue and enjoy themselves in the best way they could.[3] My post of duty, however, was not far distant, being only 15 or 20 yards away at one of the gates leading to the church.

While on duty, our instructions from the officer of the guard were to pass in or out of the church only citizens of Charlestown wishing to visit the Rebel wounded and the Confederate soldiers left to nurse and attend them at all hours of the night. None of our troops were allowed within the guard lines, except by special permission of the Union general there in command. During our two hours service at this time, we were much surprised at the number of visitors. Nearly all of them were ladies bringing large quantities of lint, bandages, delicacies, and refreshments for the wounded Confederates. The women provided hot coffee, tea, milk, and jellies, and also stimulants of wine and brandy. But the most noticable feature in the fair visitors was their silent look of scorn and contempt cast upon us and all wearing the Blue. My attention here was also directed to a Rebel general, whose name I did not learn. He seemed by his constant movements to take the deepest interest in the care and treatment of the wounded Confederates. He was without exception the most soldierly looking man I ever saw. Tall, well built, very straight, commanding in carriage and wearing a beautiful suit of fine iron-grey Rebel uniform, he won the admiration of all with whom he came in contact. At all times, while passing into or out of our lines, he did so with a graceful bow and a decidedly cultivated military salute to the guard. On no occasion did he utter a word to them. Ten p.m. now having arrived, we were relieved from duty and our places again filled by two members from the first relief.

The next thing on our program was to find a suitable place to have two or three hours of rest and sleep, having to go on guard again at two a.m. Upon our return to the campfire, which we left two hours before, we there found many of our boys fast asleep. They had spread their gum blankets on the cold, damp ground. The moon above and the starry heavens were their canopy. Nearby stood a wooden shed partly filled with hay. Quite a few of our men were quietly reposed there in slumber.

Into this place I at once determined to go. I succeeded, after considerable effort, in finding a spot to lay my weary bones for a very short time. The air in that place resounded with snores. Just as I was about commencing to aid in the chorus, my sleeping comrades and I were startled by the cry from without of "Fire, fire, git boys, git."

We jumped to our feet, half asleep and half awake. Almost stifled with smoke, we barely had time to reach the outside before the bright flames of the burning hay and shed shot like a rocket into the sky. Some of our men supposed this conflagration to be the work of an arsonist. Others disagreed. Since the hay in the shed was so near to a large, blazing fire, it had probably been ignited by a flying spark. However, be this as it may, God in his great mercy and all-wise Providence saved the lives of at least 150 Union soldiers that night. Had the shed not been open in front, the hasty escape which was made from the devouring flames would have been almost impossible.

It was now midnight. The night was clear and decidedly cold. After the excitement occasioned by the fire had somewhat subsided, all the men not detailed as guards decided to bed down on good old Mother Earth. A few fellows and I seated ourselves around a campfire which we had just been replenished with a dozen large fence rails. There we awaited the second order to return to our post of duty. We finally were ordered back to the church.

During these two hours, nothing unusual transpired. Everything was quiet and still, save an occasional moan or cry from some poor, unfortunate wounded Rebel soldier in the church. On being again relieved from duty, we returned to warmer quarters near the fire and commenced cooking an early breakfast. At seven a.m., our pickets sent out the previous afternoon came in. They reported all quiet at the front, no enemy having been seen. The guards were withdrawn and General Meagher issued an order for the Irish Brigade to be in readiness to move at ten a.m.

Having now at least three hours leisure time at hand, several of my comrades and I resolved to employ it to the best advantage in another tour of inspection. The other Irishmen conferred upon me the honor of soliciting from General Meagher a leave of absence from the ground for two hours. He willingly complied, as he always did, with any request that I ever made of him. When handing me the little written document of permission, he good-naturedly remarked, "Now, Mac, these men are in your charge."

I then thanked him and trotted off for the boys. I told the lads that I had succeeded in my mission. My comrades warmly thanked and congratulated me for the success. Some of them proposed to go one place and some to another. When my own turn came, I proposed a visit to the prison in which old John Brown and his followers had been confined and executed. I had often desired to see it. To this proposition about a dozen of my fellows agreed. All in favor of it at once started in search of the celebrated building, while those not favorable took another course. Meeting a colored woman as we turned off the ground, we inquired of her the way to the prison. Her reply was, "Golly, ge'men, don't quite know whar de prison am. Bress ye, keep a gwyn right straight up dis er street, and ye can't help seein it. Can't miss it. Can't miss it, I tell ye ge'men, can't miss it."

On we went according to the above directions. In 15 minutes, the boys and I reached a dark, dirty- looking low building. It containied a few small porthole windows in front and an iron gate at the side, perforated with little holes just large enough for an eye to peep through. No living creature was to be seen in or about the place. Its whole appearance indicated it to be in reality a dungeon. One by one, we stood and looked through the little holes into the large prison yard in which stood several old trees. While we were gaping, a young black urchin came running towards us in great haste, exclaiming with an open mouth and staring eyes, "Can't get in ge'men, can't get in. Folks all gone in the war." When I asked him if this was the prison, his reply was, "No, Sir, it's the jail."

"Did you ever hear of Old John Brown?" I said.

"O, Lor, yis. Dad told me they killed him there," replied the boy, pointing to the gate. "Where?" said I.

"Right on that big buttonball tree in the yard. Come, I'll show it to you through this hole." I looked and there stood a very large tree, the upper limbs of which had been all cut off. "Dad told us," said the boy, "that they killed Old John Brown on that very big tree." From what I had read and heard of the matter, the little fellow was undoubtedly correct. We then left, satisfied with our visit to Charlestown Prison. We had seen the very spot on which John Brown died. He, who had struck the first note of the war, had been cruelly, unmercifully and unjustly put to death on this tree.[4]

An hour of our allotted time having now nearly expired, a backward movement was begun towards camp by a different and more circuitous route than the one by which we came. We had not proceeded far on our way when we arrived opposite a brown, rough-cast house with a large orchard. The place was stocked with apple trees still laden with the tempting fruit. On the ground beneath, many fine apples laid all around. The entire place was surrounded by a low iron railing or fence, which in several parts had been knocked down. The broken pieces laid on the ground, leaving openings large enough to admit persons from the outside.

Being very fond of a good apple, which is my favorite fruit at all seasons of the year, I proposed a raid on the orchard. The plan was willingly agreed to by all, thinking that under the circumstances there could be no harm or impropriety in doing so. Accordingly, I led the way through one of the openings, followed by all of the boys except three who remained outside. They soon afterwards followed. Here the most amusing incident of my life in the army took place.

I had entered the enclosure, picked up an apple from the ground, a fine, big, juicy fellow, and commenced eating it. My left arm rested on the muzzle of my musket. A lady suddenly appeared at an open window in the house some 15 yards distant. Her hair was dishevelled and she held a comb in her hand. Upon seeing me standing there all alone—for my companions, before joining me in the attack on the apples, had gone to quench their thirsty appetites by a draught of clear, cool water from a pump which stood at the corner of the house, nearly underneath the window at which the lady stood—she addressed me in the following language, leaning out of the window: "I say, you damned, infernal Yank, don't touch one of my apples."

I, however, heeded not the order. Continuing to feast on the delicious fruit, I eyed her ladyship with silent scorn and contempt. Seeing that no respect whatever was paid to her commands, she withdrew from her position. But a moment afterwards she returned, accompanied by a large black dog who thrust his head out of the window, growling and snarling at the invaders of his territory. The beast showed a set of under and upper teeth which would have done honor to any Virginia blood-hound. Even this had no effect on me. I was determined to secure several fine apples. By this time, the angry passions of the female Virginian had reached their highest pitch. After indulging for fully ten minutes in the most abusive, obscene and blasphemous language that I ever heard, she added, "Go home, you damned, thieving Yankees to your whoring mothers in the North."

This was too much for any brave Irishman to stand, especially one clad in Uncle Sam's uniform. It made my blood boil. Dashing my musket down on the grass, I picked up the largest apple near me and shouted "Now, you get!"

I hauled off with all my force, driving the fruit through the window, smashing the glass in a thousand pieces. This caused her ladyship to beat a hasty retreat behind the wall inside. It protected her from the shower of apples which soon followed my attack on her fort.

The noise of the breaking glass, falling almost at their feet at the pump under the window, suddenly attracted the attention of my fellow soldiers. One of them remarked on seeing me throw the apple, "Look. What's the matter? Bill's got his Irish up."

But the sound of his voice had scarce died away when a shower of empty stone, porter and other bottles came down upon their heads from an upper window in the house. They cut one poor fellow's head severely and injured another. The bottles were very probably thrown by the same woman who had insulted me. This was the signal for a general uprising. Being much excited myself at the moment, I shouted to the boys, "Go at the windows with apples." They made one grand rush for the place where I still stood. Upon reaching it, they gathered up bushels of apples and then commenced a bombardment of the house. My Irish friends broke and smashed to pieces every pane of glass in the residence. They rendered its interior for the time a regular apple receptacle.

We boys then helped ourselves to the refreshing and beautiful fruit. We supplied our haversacks also without the least opposition or interference from anyone, no inmate of the dwelling attempting even to show a nose. Marching slowly out of the place on to the road, we trudged back to camp. There we divided the spoils, as far as they went, among the other members of the regiment. Our story caused much merriment and laughter throughout the Irish Brigade.

At ten a.m., the sharp, clear notes of our artillery bugle sounded from the hills, commanding all the troops to fall in line. Ten minutes afterwards, every man was in his place, ready to move. At about half past ten, the order "March" was given. By regiment, the whole brigade filed off onto the road leading up the hill to our artillery. They had awaited a junction with us. This maneuver being safely done, the entire Irish Brigade commenced its return march to Harper's Ferry. We were followed by several ambulances, some of which contained the men who were wounded in the little skirmish the day before.*

March from Charleston, on the return
to Bolivar Heights, Harper's Ferry and arrival there

Upon leaving Charlestown,[5] the heavens threatened rain. But by 12 noon, the heavy dark clouds were dispelled by the sun bursting forth in all its brightness and glory. Our line of march was over the same route. When about midway between Charlestown and Harper's Ferry, however, and while passing over a wide cleared tract of land, skirted on the left by dark, thick woods about three-quarters of a mile distant, some of our officers reported seeing a body of men in this thicket. They were thought to be a detachment of the enemy's cavalry. A halt was immediately ordered and all eyes strained on the suspicious woods. Several of my company, as well as myself, saw something very like men moving about on the edge of the woods and among the trees. But whether or not these objects really were men was never ascertained by us.

Rebel infantry were objects hard to discern at even moderate distances, owing to the dirty, earthy color of their uniforms. In several instances related by members of the 69th New York, bodies of Confederates posted in woods and thickets at distances of four or five hundred yards from Federal forces were taken as only banks of earth or rows of small trees. Thanks to this camoflauge, the Rebs frequently attacked us unexpectedly and successfully on more than one occasion. Hence, the greatest caution was absolutely necessary at all times in order to avoid surprise and loss of life. The artillerymen moved a gun off the road on

---

* It may be said that I and my companions did wrong in retaliating on the woman. But the insults and injuries inflicted upon us by her were too much to take for nothing. I was afraid at the outbreak that some of the men would use their firearms to avenge the injury inflicted on their two wounded comrades. One of our number was actually in the very act of doing so by knocking in a panel of the door of the house with the butt end of his musket. A little kind advice and entreaty on my part caused him to desist. He did so, thus preventing any further injury being done to the property. It may be somewhat out of place to state here, but I will do it, that I was a universal favorite with the members of my regiment. I wrote scores of letters home for those who could not do so themselves. I also wrote for several who could write but who preferred my style of penmanship and composition to their own. By pursuing this course towards them, I gained their respect and esteem to such a degree that my advice was often sought. The good will and regard of my fellow soldiers for me, especially those of my own company, was most fully developed afterwards on the battlefield of Fredericksburg, Virginia, Dec. 13th, 1862.

to a slight eminence. They sent two shells hissing through the air into the woods as feelers. After waiting a reasonable time for a reply, the Irish Brigade moved on without any further detention and arrived within the lines of its old camp on Bolivar Heights, Harper's Ferry at four p.m. on the 17th. We found everything just as we had left it.

Bolivar Heights
Harper's Ferry, Virginia, October 18th, 1862

The usual routine of camp duty was now resumed. It was neither hard nor laborious, drilling being the chief feature. Picketing here was not required because other regiments were already engaged in the task. My own special duties as mail agent for my regiment were resumed. Although to outsiders it might have seemed to be a soft job, it certainly was not such to me. I made it a rule to leave no part of the duty required undone. I performed fully and faithfully to the letter.

Regularly, I walked through drenching rain and over muddy roads to the division mail office in the town with letters from members of the regiment. After having made three regular daily collections and two daily deliveries, I felt that I had performed my duties. I kept constantly on the go, seldom resting from morning to night. My position was therefore not a very enviable one. But it commanded about $11 per month more than the monthly pay of the rank and file of the Army of the Potomac.

The weather began to get dreary, damp and wet. When the heavy night dew fell, even after a clear day, many men started to get sick. Several members of my regiment were soon seized with cramps, cold, chills, and diarrhea. Five or six soldiers were down in our regimental hospital tent. They had that fearful malady, dreaded by all, Camp (or Typhus) Fever. The damned disease was much more feared than Rebel bullets. Thanks to it, the Army of the Potomac lost large numbers of brave men.[6]

Two of the members of my own company were typhus victims. One of them was my most intimate, constant and confidential companion. His name was Hauck, his age 21 or 22 years. Hauck was born in Reading, Pennsylvania. In dress uniform he was unquestionably the model soldier of the regiment. His moral character, in my experience, was irreproachable. With his education and a most modest, retiring and amiable disposition, he towered far above many of his companions holding higher positions in his regiment. Hauck was attacked by this fever on a Saturday night while lying by my side in our little shelter tent, which held only two. On the following Tuesday night, the disease had done its deadly work and had claimed him for its own.

The following morning, his remains were encased in a rough, wooden pine box, the soldier's coffin. With muffled drum and the fife playing the customary "Dead March," his coffin was followed by every member of the company not then on duty. Hauck was buried in an honorable soldier's grave, over which was fired twelve guns. It was the last sad salute to all that was mortal of our dear departed friend and companion. This ceremony took place in a little cemetery roughly laid out by our soldiers which adjoined our camp. The remains of hundreds of brave men laid side by side, stricken down by disease. Many had been killed by the enemy in his attack on this place on the 13th of September, 1862. Here General Miles, commanding the Union forces, either from cowardice or incompetency, surrendered to Stonewall Jackson and a Rebel Army. In doing so, Miles was killed himself.

With my own hands, I cut out a neat, plain little headboard to mark the grave. With bristles pulled out of an old brush and writing ink, I painted the following simple inscription upon it:

Fred Hauck
Company A, 116th Regt. P.V.
Died October 1862 of disease contracted in the full discharge
of his duty as a United States Vol. Soldier
Underneath lies his Body

Owing to the dreadful character of this disease, but few of the members of our company visited Fred during his short, but severe illness. Two others and I, however, had the nerve and courage to stand by him to the last. We administered such medicine as ordered by our regimental physician and did all in our power to mitigate the poor fellow's terrible suffering. He died, almost in my hands, a few minutes after I had wet his parched lips and burning head with cold water. Hauck was delirious all the time until a few minutes before his death. When reason returned to him for a moment, I asked in a low whispering voice to his ear, "Fred, will I write and tell your Mother?"

A big tear started in his already fading and dying, but once keen, bright eye. It ran down his cheek. In a smothering, weak voice, he simply replied, "Yes, Bill, do."

Ten minutes later, his soul had taken its flight. I have no doubt that he went to a realm of bliss and peace. I wrote to his mother giving her full particulars of his illness, death and place of burial. Since I never received an acknowledgment, my letter, probably like many others then, had miscarried.[7]

Religious Services
In the Irish Brigade

An impression prevailed in many parts of the country, especially in New York and Philadelphia, that the Irish Brigade was composed chiefly, if not altogether, of men of the Roman Catholic faith. This, to my own personal knowledge, was not the case. The men had a perfect right to worship the Great Ruler of the Universe according to the dictates of their conscience. But in no other organization of the same number of men in the Army of the Potomac were there fewer Roman Catholics. Nevertheless, it was true that several of the commanding officers, including the Chief himself [Meagher], were of that persuasion. But they were Catholics only by profession, certainly not in practice.[8]

In the few religious services held during my time in the Irish Brigade by its chaplains, some of whom were Roman Catholics and others Methodists, I can safely say that twenty attended the Protestant services for every two who went to Mass. Services were held always in the open air for one hour each Sabbath evening. These meetings were exceedingly interesting, heavily attended and very orderly, respectful and quiet. The services consisted of singing, prayer, and plain, practical remarks on portions of Scripture, familiar, or supposed to be, to all. The singing, however, was the most attractive feature and was truly grand.

It was led by a choir, consisting of three very fine singers from my own regiment, two from the 28th Massachusetts and the bugler of our attached artillery. Their hymns produced a profound effect on all those present or within hearing distance. Pen and ink cannot describe the beautiful harmony. When it came to the grand old doxology, "Praise God from Whom All Blessings Flow," oh, what a thrill it sent through every heart. I never heard such strong music since then. Think of it—14 or 15 hundred men all in the uniform of United States soldiers, raising their voices in such a place and under such circumstances to the throne of God.

Nor was this all. These voices were accompanied by the sweet, silver tongue of a bugle in the hands of a perfect master of that instrument. This soldier produced soft, sweet heavenly music on his instrument. It was truly wonderful and grand—at times in tones scarce audible and at others, almost in the same breath, in tones sharp and shrill, echoing from hill to hill for miles around. But my powers to do justice in describing these meetings and their effects upon the troops come far short of what is necessary. I may, however, note that they were a source of much comfort and encouragement to myself and others.[9]

Flags

A few days after our return to Bolivar Heights from Charlestown, the 116th Pennsylvania received a beautiful new silk regimental flag, heavily fringed with golden tinsel. It was presented to our regiment by Adjutant General Thomas, I think, after a fine patriotic speech. The colors were a gift from the lady friends of the regiment in Philadelphia. Our colonel accepted the flag with fitting terms, amid rounds of cheers and patriotic airs by the Irish Brigade band. It was a most beautiful and appropriate gift from the fair and loved ones then far away.[10] Each man there and then renewed his pledge and determination to "Stand by that Flag," the glorious emblem of his country's nationality, to the last or to perish beneath its folds.*

Letter Writing

Absence makes the heart grow fonder. This old saying particularly applied in the 116th Regiment, Pennsylvania Volunteers. Expecting to remain on Bolivar Heights for some time, the boys, with lots of free time at hand, wrote long letters to loved ones at home.

Consequently, as I expected, many demands were made upon me to write letters. Oh, what long and tiresome ones I wrote for those members of my own company especially and also for some of other compa-

---

* The flags of the Confederate Army changed over time. In March 1861, the Confederate Congress adopted the so-called "Stars and Bars," composed of three horizontal bars of equal width, the middle one white, the others red, with a blue union containing nine stars which were white, arranged in a circle. The resemblance of this to the "Stars and Stripes" led to confusion and mistakes in the field. So in September, 1861, a new battle flag was adopted. This flag had a red field charged with a blue saltier and a narrow border of white, on which were displayed 13 white stars. In 1863, the "Stars and Bars" were supplanted by a flag with a white field. The flag of 1863 was found deficient in service, it being liable to be taken for a flag of truce. On February 4, 1865, the outer half of the field beyond the union was covered with a vertical red bar. This was the last flag of the Confederacy and alike perished with its downfall.

nies. I wrote for some who could not write themselves and occasionally for others who could. My special duties as mail agent had to be faithfully performed every day to the entire satisfaction of the whole command. After this, my volunteer duties as letter-writer commenced, occupying nearly every moment of my leisure time. It left me scanty time for moderate and necessary rest in sleep. But I never regretted any sacrifices made. I often realized the fact that in helping and obliging my brothers I was doing good to and helping myself. Truly, it was then more blessed to give than to receive.

On one particular occasion when three important letters intended to enclose money to needy ones had to be written, our ink ran out. For love or money, no ink could be had. Here was trouble. But being somewhat of an inventive genius, especially in times of difficulty or scarcity, I put my powers of invention into operation. I produceed a substitute for the much desired fluid.

Having observed in my duty travels a little brown berry about the size and appearance of our Northern currant growing along the roadside, the thought struck me that its juice might make a substitute for ink. Accordingly, I collected a number of the little, apparently good-for-nothing berries and pounded them up with a spoon in my tin cup. I then strained the juice through a thin rag into a little bottle, which I still have, and tried it with a pen. Much to my agreeable surprise, the fluid proved to be equal, if not superior, to the best red ink I ever used. I used my berry ink to write many scores of letters for my companions and me. My friends seemed much puzzled to know where or how I got the ink. I kept the secret for a long time afterwards. I retained several letters of my own written at that time and place with this berry juice. Although considerably faded, they can still be read.

Night Scenes on Bolivar Heights
October, 1862

Nature is diversified in her scenery. The beautiful and serene landscape observed from Bolivar Heights on a fine, clear day was most extensive and grand. Tall, grim old rocks lifted their bald heads far, far towards the heavens in solemn grandeur. Distant lowlands were also visible from this point. The scene was so breath-taking that it made one conscious of nothing but the panorama of loveliness stretched out below. Far away in the distance could also be seen the grand old Potomac, winding its peaceful way through little valleys and woods of living green.

The river joined and mingled its waters with its modest little sister of the Shenandoah Valley almost at our feet. Indeed, it seemed to me as if Nature had selected and placed her hand upon this region. Here she displayed her fantastic powers in uplifting the earth and giving it strange shapes and startling contrasts.

While the view in daytime from those heights was truly grand and impressive, the scenes at night were no less wanting in grandeur, interest and even solemnity. I often delighted to stand on the bold and rugged cliffs overhanging the Shenandoah when it was very dark. I could see scattered all over and around Bolivar, Loudon and Maryland Heights hundreds of fires lit by our brave army. We numbered at this point some 30,000 troops of all kinds. The view presented to the eye a night scene of military life which could not fail to animate and cheer the heart. Yet as my comrades and I stood and gazed in silent and sad admiration upon such night scenes, our hearts could not help but go up to Him who rules the Universe with the earnest petition, "God save our bleeding and distracted country, in this the time of her terrible and pressing need."

Another attraction at Bolivar Heights was the drums beating at night. They produced pleasant and exhilirating feelings among many of the troops. This drum beating, or to use the military term, "tattoo," sounded every night at nine p.m. throughout the whole army. It was the signal for all troops not on duty to put out lights and retire to their quarters for the evening. It commenced at division headquarters and was taken up by regiments or brigades for probably ten miles all around, until every soldier knew that his hour for rest and sleep had arrived. Tattoo generally lasted about ten or fifteen minutes and was a merry and gay little season. After it ended, all was as still and quiet as death in that brave and powerful army, save for the tread of the sentinel as he paced his lonely midnight beat. Our picket line here, consisting of about 1,600 men, was generally formed and sent to the front at four p.m. each afternoon on 24 hours' duty.

But the most beautiful scenes I ever witnessed were those of a clear, moonlight night on Bolivar Heights and vicinity. On several occasions, the moon shone so clear and bright at night that the smallest footprint could be easily read by any person of ordinary eyesight. On the evening of the October 20th, I wrote seven letters for members of my company by moonlight alone. I was sitting at my usual writing desk, the head of a cracker box, with the ink manufactured from berries.

The appearance of the country all around on this night was most interesting, beautiful, enchanting and awfully grand. The scenery elevated one's thoughts and aspirations from earth to heaven—from war to peace and rest. With awe as well as admiration did I often gaze on these most beautiful night scenes. The bright, full, clear moon poured all the lustrous light and sympathy which she could give to that pretty country. However, the land was covered with a host of armed men ready for war, ready to shed the blood of their fellow men.

Far, far away up on Loudon and Maryland Heights, almost touching the clouds and along the Charlestown and Sheperdstown Roads could be seen portions of the picket guard. Soldiers variously leaned against rocks, stood behind trees, or moved about on open ground. As they moved to and fro, their shining bayonets could be distinctly seen, although miles away. At the midnight hour, blades flashed in the moonlight in an eery silence almost like the stillness of the grave. Such a sight was truly one of awful grandeur and beauty. My heart and thoughts rose to heaven. The experience deepened my religions convictions and fully convinced and persuaded me that the deeper those feelings became, the higher would rise my heroism and love of country. But my descriptive powers are too weak and entirely inadequate to do anything like justice to these moonlight scenes on Bolivar Heights near Harper's Ferry, Virginia. I do not believe it to be in the power of man to describe them as they appeared to my view. The experience caused my mind to revert to the sweet inspired words of the Psalmist when he said:

> I, to the hills will left mine eyes,
> From whence doth come mine aid.
> My safety cometh from the Lord,
> Who heaven and earth had made.
>
> Thy foot he'll not let slide, nor will
> He slumber that thee keeps,
> Behold, he that keeps Israel,
> He slumbers not, nor sleeps.
>
> The Lord thee keeps, the Lord they shade,
> On thy right hand doth stay.
> The moon by night thee shall not smite,
> Nor yet the sun by day.

The Lord shall keep they soul, he shall
Preserve thee from all ill,
Henceforth thy going out and in
God keep for ever will."[11]

*"The Rebel's body turned and rolled over and over down to the
Earth through the branches and foliage of the tree, chased by his rifle.
We really had to laugh hearty because of the curious way he fell."*

Chapter 4

Chasing the Rebels:
The Fight at Snicker's Gap

Little hard work needed to be done by my regiment at this point.
Consequently, nearly everyone enjoyed a good time of rest and amusement. I was an exception. Due to my duties as mail clerk, I had no time
for recreation. I was so busy that I could barely satisfy the demands of
nature for rest and sleep. But this season of military inactivity ended
shortly. On the morning of the 21st, a rumor circulated that a powerful
body of Confederate cavalry and infantry, the former commanded by
General Stuart of Rebel notoriety and the latter a portion of General
Stonewall Jackson's command, were advancing up the Shenandoah Valley. The story proved true. The Rebels captured an entire Union provision train consisting of 14 wagons.

On receipt of this news, General Slocum of our army sent out an
expedition of 2,500 men to that area. Our troops returned the next day
after having encountered a body of Rebel cavalry in the Valley. After a
short engagement, three were killed and 19 wounded on the Rebel side.
Our men took 35 prisoners. The remainder of the Johnnies made their
escape with the contents of the train after setting the wagons on fire.
This rendered the wagons useless for army service afterwards.[1]

On the afternoon of the 25th, a general order was issued from headquarters for all troops to be in readiness for a forward movement the next day. Each man was to be provided with three days cooked rations and 40 rounds of ammunition. This looked like business again. It pointed to another collision with the enemy in some quarter then unknown in the near future. That night was one of unusual activity and bustle in the various camps all around.

Large fires illuminated the heavens as far as the eye could reach in all directions. These bonfires blazed and crackled on hill and in vale, illuminating a scene in military life full of animation, industry and beauty. Whole droves of cattle were knocked down by musket balls. They fell prey to the tender mercies of the butcher's knife. Each regiment received its allotted portion of the butchered carcasses. These were speedily consigned for boiling into large camp kettles filled with water. Orderlies on horseback bearing dispatches from headquarters dashed to and fro until nearly midnight. Privates busied themselves in cooking rations, packing up clothing, cleaning firearms and doing a hundred other things incident to breaking camp. That night no "tattoo" sounded. Few men sought rest or turned in to their tents until long after midnight.

At daybreak on next morning, while the stars were yet shining, the long roll of drums and the shrill, sharp notes of cavalry and artillery bugles broke upon the ears of the sleeping soldiers. We were aroused from refreshing slumber and pleasant dreams. After rollcall and a hurried breakfast, the preparations commenced the previous evening were completed. By ten a.m., the tents were all down and on board our army wagons. Artillery horses stood harnessed, pawing the ground with their hoofs, ready to be hitched to their guns. Every man was ready for the command "Fall in." However, the order was not received until later.

At eleven a.m., the troops at Loudon Heights on the other side of the river started to stir. They went into motion, ascending those heights, beyond which lay the Shenandoah Valley in Virginia proper. Although at a distance, their long blue lines could be distinctly seen winding their way to the summit by a hundred different routes. Upon reaching the top, they soon disappeared from our view behind the distant hills. From this movement and the direction in which it was made, we inferred that our part of the army would soon follow them. At 3:30 p.m., cavalry regiments passed close to our camp. Some of our men asked one of them, "Where bound?"

He replied, "The Shenandoah Valley."*

As we stood or lounged upon the green earth waiting for the signal to "Fall in line," some ten or twelve batteries of artillery and another regiment of cavalry passed by following those that had already done so. It was not until seven p.m. that we received marching orders. Then the Irish Brigade, my own regiment honored by being the advance, was on its way. We took the same road taken by the troops before us. It was time to bid goodbye to Bolivar Heights, Harper's Ferry, Jefferson County, Virginia.[2]

On the March from Bolivar Heights near Harper's Ferry, Virginia, commencing October 26, 1862

Upon descending Bolivar Heights on the way to Harper's Ferry, the head of my regiment had almost reached the foot of the last hill at the entrance to the town when a halt was sounded. We heard the order given to "Rest in place, upon your arms." This delay in our progress was caused by two artillery horses and a gun falling overboard from the narrow pontoon bridge crossing the river, then only a short distance ahead. It was the only way for the troops behind to proceed. The efforts which were then in progress to save the horses and the gun occasioned the temporary halt of our brigade. Only one of the unfortunate animals was saved, the weight of the gun and carriage dragging the other one so deep down in the water that both horse and gun were lost.

The night was a delightful one, one of those clear, quiet moonlight nights that I loved so much during my life in the army. I was in the front rank of my regiment. I could see a splendid moonlight view of the whole brigade extending back up the hill. Seventeen hundred clear, glistening bayonets sparkled in the moonbeams, presenting a real grand military appearance. At the same time, it made the blood run cold contemplating those terrible instruments of war and death.

While in this position, I heard the faint, hardly audible sound of singing. It originated in the rear of our column. Upon listening attentively, I found that it was the tune sung to the words "John Brown's body lies moldering in the grave."

---

* The army route from Bolivar Heights to the Valley of the Shenandoah was through the town of Harper's Ferry and then across the pontoon bridge spanning the Potomac. On the other side, we had to ascend Loudon Heights, already crossed by the other troops.

The chorus was immediately taken up by every man in my regiment, producing a most invigorating, cheerful and happy effect upon the troops. Soon afterwards, we moved on. The singing continued, keeping time to the heavy tramp, tramp, tramp of the regiment, while the pale moon seemed to look down in sympathy and love from her high and heavenly sphere. And as we passed through the little battered, burnt and nearly desolate, but once beautiful, town of Harper's Ferry, the troops persisted in singing the touching and appropriate melody:

> *John Brown's body lies moldering in the grave,*
> *John Brown's body lies moldering in the grave,*
> *John Brown's body lies moldering in the grave,*
>   *As we go marching along. (Chorus)*

> *We'll hang Jeff Davis on a sour apple tree,*
> *We'll hang Jeff Davis on a sour apple tree,*
> *We'll hang Jeff Davis on a sour apple tree,*
>   *As we go marching along. (Chorus)*

> *John Brown's knapsack strapped upon his back,*
> *John Brown's knapsack strapped upon his back,*
> *John Brown's knapsack strapped upon his back,*
>   *As we go marching along.*

>   *Chorus: Glory, Glory, Hallelujah,*
>   *Glory, Glory, Hallelujah,*
>   *Glory, Glory, Hallelujah,*
>   *As We Go Marching Along.*[3]

The few remaining inhabitants, chiefly colored, warmly greeted us when they herad their favorite song sung by Union soldiers as they marched along. They waved handkerchiefs and cheered from the windows of their little houses. They poured their earnest and ever welcome blessings upon our heads. "De Lord bress ye. De Lord bress Uncle Sam's boys and good old Fader `Abe,'" they shouted.

The Irish Brigade now proceeded on its way across the bridge in safety. We halted on the other side for a few moments, waiting for the 69th New York Regiment bringing up the rear. It was now nearly ten p.m.* We climbed to the top of Loudon Heights with considerable difficulty. The men were loaded down with their equipment and the road was very narrow, winding and rutty. Then the brigade descended to a level piece of ground on the opposite side. Fires were started and we encamped for the night. The troops preceding us had advanced about two miles farther and were also resting for the night.

Next morning, the march of the Irish Brigade continued. All the other troops remained on the ground on which they had encamped the night before. We passed them and halted again for the night at about five p.m. We built fires in thick woods. Here we were entertained by General Meagher. He gave a short speech, politely informing us that we were now the advance for our entire division. Two hundred-fifty pickets were immediately thrown out. I was one of them. But the night passed by quietly along the lines.

We were now fairly deep into the ever memorable Shenandoah Valley, expecting to meet the enemy in heavy force at any minute.** The Valley was the key at this point in opening the door to the march of our troops south. The Confederate leaders very naturally used every means and effort to hold it and prevent its occupation by Union troops. But General McClellan was determined that such should not be the case now. The war had to be prosecuted. No obstacle would impede the march of McClellan's Army towards the Capital of the Southern Confederacy. The movement just now commenced was only the beginning of the plan of our Commander-in Chief to defeat and to drive the

---

* Owing to the construction of pontoon bridges, large bodies of troops in crossing them must do so with the greatest caution for their own safety. If crossed quickly by troops on one and the same step, the bridge will swing to and fro, causing men to tumble overboard. If crossed too slow, the boats underneath are liable to sink or break away from their moorings. Therefore, just as the troops were about going on the bridge, orders were given to break step and cross at moderate speed. This was done, resulting in the safe arrival of the troops on the opposite side in one half of an hour.

** This Valley runs through parts of Jefferson, Clarke, Page and Warren Counties Virginia. It was a remarkable place throughout the war, especially in the earlier part of it. The Valley was the scene of many a hard and stubborn fight. It was there that General Patterson commanding a Union Army was defeated by the Confederates under General Johnston in July, 1861, and driven out. It was in this Valley that a splendid Federal Force under General Banks was obliged to flee before the advancing legions under Stonewall Jackson in the summer of 1862. It was here that General Pope, commanding another fine Northern Army, was compelled to retire after his sad defeat and pursuit by the Rebel Army under General Lee in September, 1862. At least for a short time, the Valley remained in undisputed possession of the Confederate forces.

enemy out of the Valley. Its capture would open up the way for the advance of the Federal forces on Richmond.

On the morning of the 28th, the army again was in motion, proceeding down the Valley. During the three succeeding days, nothing worthy of special notice transpired. Our Irish Brigade still continued to be the advance. On the morning of November 1st, it was reported at headquarters that a heavy detachment of Rebel infantry, cavalry and artillery, under the ever active and restless Jackson, was running a race with us in the same direction. But the Rebs were on the opposite side of a range of hills. These were probably four miles distant on our right, entirely hidden from our view. The information had been brought by mounted scouts who had been sent out the night before.

What with the advance of our army, no one knew exactly what was going on. It was, however, supposed that McClellan's object was to beat Jackson. General Jackson's intentions were to flank or turn suddenly upon our forces, meet them fair in the teeth and bring on a general engagement.*

A regular daily march of from ten to fourteen miles was kept up by our forces, every precaution being taken by our generals to guard against a surprise attack by the enemy. Mounted scouts by day preceded our advancing columns. At night, an unusual strong picket line was thrown out far in front and around the various camps. No sign of the foe was found until about noon on the 4th of November.

The mounted scouts came hurriedly to our column just as we had halted for to take dinner. The horsemen reported that the Rebel Army

---

* In reference to General Stonewall Jackson, as a soldier, I will here state that according to statements made by some of his own men, afterwards prisoners in our hands, he was an active, thorough military man, and the most successful general in the Confederate Army. Indeed, these statements seemed true from my own personal observations of the movements and manuverings of the troops under his command. General Jackson was also distinguished for the great and wonderful ability which he possessed of moving or marching large bodies of troops from one point to another in the shortest possible space of time, far outstripping that of any of our Union generals. He would be here today with his men and 30 or 40 miles distant tomorrow. In the morning we would find him in our rear, harassing and perplexing us. And in the evening he would be at our front, provoking an engagement or an advance. As a Christian man, General Jackson stood high in the estimation of his soldiers. The people of the South, as well as many at the North, respected his devoutness to God. It was truly a pity and a shame that such a character should ever have espoused the Cause of the Southern Confederacy or have been in any way connected with those who were then endeavoring to destroy our glorious Union and country.

was advancing. All now was bustle and activity. But there was not the slightest confusion. We had just at this time reached a point within a mile of Snicker's Gap. The enemy had more than once before entrenched himself there. The gap is in the Blue Ridge Mountains, which runs from Loudon County to Clarke County, Virginia.[4]

Our artillery was at once posted upon eminences within easy range of the gap. The infantry was drawn up at various points on the side of a low range of hills at supporting distances. A heavy force of cavalry was posted a mile in our rear, ready for any emergency. The position of my own Irish Brigade was the nearest to our artillery on the left, while General Caldwell's brigade, another Irish organization, was the nearest on the right.[5] At about three p.m., we could see in the distance dark masses of Confederates approaching.

Our guns opened a furious fire upon them. The Rebel gunners soon replied and, for one half of an hour, a most vigorous cannonade was kept up by both sides. At this stage of the action, which was expected to become a general engagement before night closed upon the scene, my own regiment was for the first time in its history deployed as skirmishers. Skirmishing was the most unpleasant, most dangerous and most trying of all army duties. Men were shot down while out skirmishing from every imaginable, hidden, covered position.

We advanced under cover of our artillery fire, in squads of from three to five men each. The skirmishers cautiously and slowly approached the Confederate position. With me were two men from Company B and one from Company G. A clump of long but narrow woods laid right in our front some four or five hundred paces distant. The enemy was massing troops there behind the trees. Several of his sharpshooters were supposed to be hiding in the greenery.

We could not then see them but knew that they were there. Two skirmishers had already been shot down a few minutes before by rifle balls coming from that direction. This place was now made the chief point of attack by my own squad on the right. We were joined by another on the left. Other squads advanced by various routes against similar places.

We proceeded at a very slow walk, sometimes stooping or crouching low down with musket loaded and primed to see some particular object in the distance. Sometimes we stood still to listen. At other times, we advanced quickly, watching for Rebel skirmishers.[6]

We had just gained the edge of the woods when "bang" went a rifle. The ball sung its usual little song in my ear as it passed close to my head. It startled me considerably, being so sudden, yet not quite unexpected. Another "bang" and down went my nearest comrade, wounded in the foot. I stood in amazement, wondering where on earth these shots came from, for I saw nobody but our own men. By this time my wounded companion had crawled behind a bank of earth for safety. When he raised his head up to see where we had gone to, another ball cut part of the regimental number off his cap.

I immediately stationed myself behind a large tree. My two remaining companions did the same, some 20 or 30 yards to my left, remaining there very quietly and watchfully. We all searched for the position of the Rebel sharpshooter. Directly, I heard a rustling noise among the branches of a high tree a little to my right. Upon looking up there, I saw Johnny sitting on one of the branches. He had his rifle in hand, ready to blaze away again. I motioned to my companions, "I've got him, look out."

I quickly left my then dangerous position for a safer one. I soon found a new hiding place behind another tree. As soon as I got over my excitement, which I did in a minute, I said to myself, "Now, Johnny, I'll bring you down soon from there."

I raised the hammer of my musket, looked over at my two companions who by that time had got a glimpse of the Reb, and beckoned to them that I wanted the first shot at him. They agreed, bringing their pieces to an order arms and stood watching me. I then shifted my position from tree to tree to get a good side sight on my mark. As soon as I found one, which was not long, I placed one knee on the ground. I rested the butt end of my musket on the other knee for steadiness. Then I shouldered my gun and took deliberate aim at my adversary perched in the tree. I don't think he saw me. While I felt reluctant to fire at him slyly or from under cover, I knew that it was either my life or his. Preferring my own and acting to a certain extent upon the maxim that "anything is fair in war," I pulled my trigger. I sent the whole charge crashing and cutting through the branches of the tree. But I never even got close to hitting my object. My shot was a complete failure.

Johnny was left no time to retaliate. One of my companions, upon seeing my lack of success, immediately fired. He had no better result. After this double failure, there came the chance of the third man. He took steady aim from beside a tree. When he pulled, he brought the Reb to the earth as a bleeding corpse. This normally would be no sight to laugh at. But the Rebel's body turned and rolled over and over down to the earth through the branches and foliage of the tree, chased by his rifle. We really had to laugh hearty because of the curious way he fell.

It was now nearly five p.m. and darkness was coming on. No advance of the massed forces of either our own army or the Confederate had yet been made. Away far to our left could be seen the remaining squads of our skirmishers, moving here and there over the ground. We heard an occasional shot between them and the Rebel skirmishers. No farther advance of my own party having been ordered, we stayed put. Remaining on the edge of the woods, we waited for orders to return to the main body of the army. We did not encounter the enemy's skirmishers there again.

At about 5:30 p.m., we were ordered in. By six p.m., the whole regiment had arrived within the lines again, having lost only five men wounded and none killed. A picket line was then thrown out, extending three miles along our entire front and consisting of 1,800 men from various regiments. But daylight next morning revealed that the Confederate army had "dusted" (retreated) during the night. The enemy was said to have there numbered 35,000 men. But where they went remained a mystery. Our whole column then resumed its march in the direction of Warrenton, Virginia, headed again by the Irish Brigade.[7]

General George Brinton McClellan
as Commander-in-chief of the Army of the Potomac

While the operation just described and others similar were going on in the Shenandoah Valley, General McClellan was relieved and was superseded by General Ambrose E. Burnside of Rhode Island. McClellan was ordered to report at Trenton, New Jersey. This was on the 5th of November. It was indeed a sad and heavy blow for McClellan's brave soldiers by whom he was loved, honored and almost idolized.

But why was General McClellan relieved of the command of the noble Army of the Potomac? Was he incompetent or was he unsuccessful in his military operations? Let the Battles of Cedar Mountain, South Mountain, Malvern Hill and the bloody plains of Antietam answer. Were his pitiful, constant and earnest pleadings for reinforcements to meet the almost overpowering Armies of Rebeldom complied with? Such requests were immediately granted to his successor. Let the Congress of his country explain. When his half-fed and suffering troops were dying at the very gates of Richmond, what aid was given him? Mothers, sisters and wives in the North, answer. Was he a kind, open-hearted, benevolent and modest Christian gentleman, not only in the midst of active military duties but also before he assumed them and after his release from them?

In losing General McClellan, the Army of the Potomac lost its best commander, a man of no ordinary military ability. The soldier, the common soldier, especially lost his best and most faithful army friend. God bless him.[8]

The March to Warrenton, Virginia

Nothing of special interest occurred during our march from Snicker's Gap to Warrenton. The enemy put in only one appearance in our front and in our rear. This was in the form of small squads of raiding cavalry, not sufficiently strong to induce an attack. The march was a rough one. We took a circuitous route, sometimes along hilly, narrow and uneven high roads and at other times through brush and along the edge of streams. We passed through several small villages or settlements, or rather their ruins, including New Baltimore and Piedmont. The latter had been evacuated by a small Rebel force upon our approach.

At this point, our division forded a stream 15 or 20 yards wide. It was not deep, but the men sunk nearly up to their waists in chilly, freezing water. We arrived on the afternoon of the 9th of November, 1862, at a point within a mile of Warrenton. There we halted and awaited orders. The town had been held only a short time before by the Confederate troops.[9]

Warrenton, Fauquier County, Virginia

Warrenton is a small town, between 50 and 60 miles southwest of Washington. Prior to the war it had a population of about 2,000 souls. The town sits on high and commanding ground. Yet at no time during the war did it elicit any special attention from either the Union or the Confederate Armies as a military post worth holding. It contained some quite neat and comfortable houses, at least from outside appearance, as well as a church. I noticed these structures while passing through the town. We were ordered not to occupy the place. Its inhabitants, like every other Virginia town that we saw, consisted of women, children and old men only.

At 3 p.m., we were again ordered forward. After marching through the town to a spot one half mile south of it, we were ordered to break ranks, stack arms and pitch tents. This was joyous, glorious news for the poor, footsore, weary and downright tired soldier. Everyone was covered and pasted from head to foot with mud, dust and dirt. Thus, after two weeks of roundabout marching from Harper's Ferry to Warrenton, we were again permitted to enjoy a few days of rest and repose.

But before quitting this little Virginian town, I must relate the kind of greeting or reception extended to our troops by its inhabitants. Our reception in Fairfax Courthouse and in Charlestown was anything but cordial and agreeable. But our reception in Warrentown took the premium, laying the others "right out in the shade." As we filed up the main street of the town, my own regiment in the lead, we were greeted with hisses and groans from women standing in doorways and crowding the windows of houses. They yelled as we passed along, "There goes the damned Abolitionists. Kill them."

Nor was this the worst. Upon reaching the center of the town, we were assailed by a shower of missiles, including stones, brickbats, chunks of firewood, bottles, shoemaker hammers, and pieces of coal. They were all thrown at us by the hands of these fair Virginia damsels, aimed from windows.

The men fairly boiled with rage. But we dared not return the insults under penalty of imprisonment by court martial. This we received due notice of before entering the town. We were further instructed that should any of the inhabitants go even so far as to fire upon the troops, the fire could not be returned without orders from the commanding general.

Before reaching the end of the town, several members of my regiment had received severe cuts and bruises from these flying missiles. My colonel [Dennis Heenan], riding at the head of his regiment, narrowly escaped stopping a shoemaker's hammer thrown at him from a window. The hammer struck his horse, nearly knocking out one of its eyes. I was struck on the back of the head myself with a lump of coal. It severely cut me, leaving me with a sore head for ten days afterwards. We, however, pushed on and reached open ground. After pitching our tents, we rested, recovering from the painful experience of the "Secession ladies" in Warrenton, Virginia.

Appearance of the Shenandoah Valley

Our line of march took us through the heart of this beautiful, fertile and picturesque valley. It was called "the Garden of Virginia." The journey revealed to me in a most painful and impressive manner the ravages and desolation of this terrible and cruel war. The farms and fields were much larger and appeared to have been better cultivated than any other in Virginia. But the fields that formerly had borne millions of sheaves of golden waving grain laid blank and bare with scarce a vestige of verdure or vegetation visible. Beautiful orchards of Virginia's choicest fruit trees laid prostrate, cut down by the axe of the soldier or torn to pieces by cannonballs. Fire, that ever constant and faithful ally of bloody war, had left his mark at almost every step. Heaps of ruins and burned, blackened walls marked the sites where beautiful country residences and peaceful homes once stood. During the entire march, I only saw three decent houses which bore no mark of injury. From one of these we received the first friendly greeting or evidence of friendship and goodwill from white people.

This house or cottage, for such it really was, presented a remarkable neat, comfortable and quiet appearance. It sat about 20 yards off the road where our troops were passing. It was surrounded by a porch, in front of which was a tastily laid-out little lawn and garden containing small trees and blooming autumn flowers. The sight reminded many of the boys of their own sweet homes and friends then far away in the North.

As the regiment approached this place, two apparently young and pretty women, clad in black (I saw nothing else in Virginia) slowly emerged from the door. They supported between them an aged and very feeble-looking lady wearing the old-fashioned Scotch or Irish widow's white cap. They advanced to the edge of the porch and, as regiment after regiment passed by, the young ladies gracefully greeted them by waving their white handkerchiefs, while the old lady could be distinctly seen weeping.

This was a most touching scene, something so unexpected in a country where the Union soldier was so much despised and hated. Yet even here, away down in the "Garden of Rebel Virginia," we had friends who cheered for us. Thank God for it, although it was the only thing of the kind that I ever saw in the enemy's country during my life in the army. These kind ladyfriends received a warm response. Seventeen hundred heads were at one time uncovered—seventeen hundred caps waved in the air, and from seventeen hundred loyal hearts and mouths went up cheer after cheer, accompanied by the roll of our drums, for our isolated well wishers. The occasion was one ever worthy to be remembered by every member of the Irish Brigade. I frequently think of it with unmingled pleasure and inexpressible delight.

In Camp near Warrenton, Virginia
November 9, 1862

Upon arriving at camp, we found some eight or ten regiments in the vicinity. They had arrived the day before by a different route. Like ourselves, these boys were pretty well used up by a long and fatiguing march and were now enjoying a short season of rest. Fresh troops, including artillery, cavalry and infantry, arrived hourly all night and through the next day. At this point, the Union forces numbered about 80,000 men. General McClellan's Farewell Address had just been issued. The day after our arrival at Warrenton, it was read publicly by General Meagher to the Irish Brigade. It created among the troops universal feelings of the most profound sorrow, sadness and gloom.

On the morning of the 11th, the entire army numbered close to a 100,000 men. We were notified to appear in full dress uniform, fully equipped (except knapsacks) at the various headquarters of our regiments or brigades. We were then ordered to march at seven a.m. to designated places. The troops were to line both sides of a highroad near the town. General McClellan was to pass on this road on his way to Washington. We had been given the chance to offer a parting salute and last, sad farewell to our beloved, honored, respected and noble commander. Everyone was eager to stand test. The order was promptly and most willingly obeyed.

At ten a.m., the troops were all in position, lining the roadside and awaiting the coming of the general. They presented a most magnificent, grand and dazzling military appearance. It had never been equalled on the American continent. The infantry by brigades lined the sides of the road in close mass. In their rear were posted the cavalry and behind them the artillery. The Irish Brigade was located somewhere near the center of the line.

In half an hour, cheering and the booming of cannon could be heard far away down the line, indicating the passage of General McClellan. He neared and rode past our own position at a very fast trot with several members of his mounted staff. Cannon after cannon belched forth from their iron mouths a thundering, deafening roar. Cheer upon cheer rent the air as he bid us goodbye with uncovered head and cap in hand. Nor did these manifestations of our regard for our brave old commander cease until he had completely passed beyond our view. He received similar salutes as he passed through the rest of the line. Orders were soon given to return to camp. The return march bore more resemblance to the "Dead March" at a soldier's funeral than the movement of live and active men. All appeared dejected, lonely and lost. Hundreds wept bitterly. The few who had life enough to converse upon the situation of military affairs asked, "What next?"[10]

General Ambrose E. Burnside

General McClellan was short in stature, mild and pleasing in manner, and could easily be approached by any of his men. He had an open, fair and inviting countenance and quick, bright, blue eyes. In contrast, General Burnside was tall, stoutly built, and had a dark, frowning face. His eyes were black and piercing. The common soldier was afraid to approach him because of his strict manner and bearing.

The Army of the Potomac was now under the leadership of its new commander. I do not know if General Burnside's abilities as an experienced or successful military officer entitled him succeed General McClellan in the management and direction of such an organization as the Army of the Potomac. One thing, however, I do know. As the army's leader, he never gained the confidence and love of the men. While commander-in-chief, he never struck one important, successful blow against the Rebel Army in Virginia. His character, however, for loyalty, honesty, sobriety, good intentions and earnest effort to crush the Rebellion was well known. It entitled him to the esteem and respect not only of the army but of all good Union men. It was probably owing to these good and noble traits in his character, not his military greatness or experience, that raised him to the position which he then occupied. He was soon-after obliged to give up his command because of the sad, terrible Union defeat at Fredericksburg, Virginia, on Saturday, the 13th of December, 1862.[11]

Upon returning to camp, all troops, except those on the picket line and on guard duty, were allowed to rest. On the next day, the 12th instant, nothing important took place. The only business transacted was a dress parade and an inspection of arms for about an hour in the early part of the afternoon. At four p.m., it commenced to snow, the first that we had seen in Virginia. By six p.m., the ground was covered with snow to the depth of two or three inches. At eight p.m., quite unexpectedly and for reasons not explained, my entire regiment was ordered out on picket duty. We were posted about two miles southwest of Warrenton on the side of a long range of hills. After remaining there on duty until midnight, we were recalled. We arrived back in camp again, having suffered from the exposure to the storm for four hours and a march through the drifting and blinding snow. The 13th of November was bright and clear. At noon, the snow that had fallen the night before had almost disappeared. But it left the ground damp and wet. Water soaked through our small shelter tents. It rendered them almost untenable. Thanks to huge, roaring fires kept burning all day over our campground, we succeeded in drying our clothing. By evening, our comfort had decidedly improved.

At six p.m., the guards, as was the custom, were doubled. I was detailed as a guard for second relief. I was scheduled to go on duty at eight p.m. that night.

Our brigade headquarters, including the tent of General Meagher, was located on an eminence near some woods. It was fully one quarter of a mile outside of the camp lines. At this place, two guards were posted day and night, their beat being from a point 20 yards below the general's tent to another at about the same distance above it. Consequently, in patrolling his beat here, the guard passed and re-passed in front of the tent. An immense fire was always kept burning. It threw out a heat which was felt for a considerable distance all around. On this post I was placed that evening, isolated from my companions in camp.

At eight p.m., General Meagher and several high-ranking officers assembled in the tent. The entourage included the new commander-in-chief, General Burnside. The officers consulted, as I soon afterwards found out, with reference to another important forward movement of the army, the particulars of which were then roughly written with pencil. Forty-two plain copies of the document were ordered to be written with ink and addressed to that number of distinguished officers. Two parties were detailed on the following morning to copy these papers privately in General Meagher's tent. By the general's recommendation, I was one of the scribes. A lieutenant of a New York regiment was the other. We each wrote 21 copies, the contents of which were under no circumstance to be divulged to any of the rank and file, nor even to officers other than those to whom the documents were addressed.

It will be remembered that in my sketch of General Meagher, I alluded to his sad, most unfortunate, intemperate habits. Sad indeed, for he was a whole-souled and perfect gentleman, this weakness excepted. I saw at last the evil effects of liquor upon him while on guard duty that night.

I had been on my post for probably an hour. While passing over my beat opposite General Meagher's tent, I noticed an officer standing in the doorway. I could not see plainly see who he was because the flyleaf of the tent covered him. I proceeded to the end of the beat. Upon returning and when within a few yards of the tent again, the same person was still there, but farther out holding on to the center pole and acting in a strange manner. I stopped and, by the light of the fire, discovered it to be General Meagher. He was very drunk, looked strangely wild and only prevented himself from falling down by his grasp of the center pole. His position was a dangerous one. Only a few yards in front of him on slightly descending ground burned an immense fire. He would undoubtedly have tumbled headlong into the blaze if he let go of the pole.

The occupants of the tent did not seem to notice or to realize his danger. They made no effort to get him inside. I stood with eyes fixed upon him, trying to figure out what was best to do. I hoped that if he did fall down, which his body movements indicated would soon happen, he would fall against the tent. I did not want to create any unnecessary alarm or even to signify in any way to his brother officers my knowledge of his sad condition. It was a fearful, trying moment to me. But thank God, He gave me presence of mind to keep cool and collected and enabled me to successfully meet what followed.

Three minutes later, to my horror, Meagher suddenly let go of the pole. He ran or rather plunged forward towards the fire. Upon seeing this, I immediately rushed towards him. With the bayonet on my musket, I stopped his progress and threw him back on the ground. I had to use my bayonet because he would have fallen into the blazing logs before I could catch him with my hands. He was only a few feet from the fire. Perhaps he would have even been roasted alive. In rushing forward to save General Meagher, I excitedly exclaimed in a loud tone, "My God."

The inmates of the tent quickly appeared upon the scene. At a glance, they took in the situation of affairs. We raised the general, then unconscious, upon his feet. In helping him into his tent, one of the highest officers, both in rank and age, remarked to him, "General, you owe your life to that man," pointing at me.*

During my excitement in preventing this accident and while helping to raise the general off the ground, my musket accidentally fell upon the fire, causing it to go off. The report of the discharge caused considerable alarm and curiosity in the camp among the boys. They wanted to know the cause of a single shot from such a quarter at night. The musket was damaged in the stock from the fire. But next morning, upon arriving in General Meagher's tent to copy papers, a beautiful new musket with new bayonet was there given me. This presentation occasioned no little curiosity among my comrades. They wanted to know why and how I got the weapon. But I resolved to keep "mum" upon that point. To this day, none of my in the army know how or under what circumstances I came into possession of the new musket and bayonet at that time.

General Meagher never made any direct allusion to this incident. But from his conduct and actions, every time I was in his company after the event, I plainly saw that he felt deeply mortified. But at the same time he was truly grateful and thankful to me. To his honor and credit, I never saw General Meagher intoxicated again.[12]

On the 14th of November, 1862, the announcement was officially made that the head-quarters of the Army of the Potomac was then at Warrenton, Virginia. On the same day, the army was divided into three grand divisions—the right wing, consisting of the Second (my own) and Ninth Army Corps under General Sumner, 30,000 strong; the left wing, consisting of the First and Sixth Army Corps under General Franklin, 45,000 strong; the center, consisting of the Third and Fifth Army Corps under General Hooker, 40,000 strong; the Eleventh Army Corps, 15,000 strong under General Siegel to act as a reserve. Total strength was about 150,000 men.[13]

It was about this time that our beloved, honored and good President Abraham Lincoln issued his ever memorable proclamation directing the United States forces to properly observe the Sabbath.[14] The news was hailed with no small delight by the troops. But I am sorry to say that for a variety of reasons, probably none or few of them good and sufficient,

---

* I am sorry to state here that "drunkenness" in the army, especially among its officers, at this time, was alarmingly prevalent. To that fact, I think I am not wrong in saying, the lack of success experienced for some time afterwards by the Union Army might to some extent be traced.

the proclamation did not receive the consideration and obedience to which it was so justly entitled.

There was little or no change made in the regular daily work and duties of the troops—certainly none as regards making the Sabbath a day of rest and divine worship.*

On the night of the 14th, marching orders were again issued for the whole army to be in readiness next day to move towards Fredericksburg, Virginia, some 35 or 40 miles distant.[15] This city was then held by the Confederates. It was one of their most important depots for supplying the Southern Army—with clothing manufactured there and food from northern and western Virginia. The sooner the city was taken out of Rebel hands, the better it would be for the United States. One day's rations and 20 rounds of ammunition per man next morning were issued. One half of the army commenced the march that day at ten a.m. They were followed by the other half at daylight next morning, my own Irish Brigade at this time moving forwards. By ten a.m. the same day, Warrenton had been evacuated by the Union Army. The foul-mouthed and treacherous hordes of female, Secessionist murderers were left to themselves undisturbed.

The whereabouts of the Rebel Army that had confronted us at Snicker's Gap was unknown. Whether or not any of our commanding officers were acquainted with its position, I was never able to ascertain. In connection with this, I may here say that for some unexplained reason the common soldiers were as a general rule kept in total ignorance of the position of the enemy until the very eve of a battle. In some few instances, we did not know of his approach until actually fired upon. It is a fact worthy of notice that people at home, hundreds of miles away in the North, knew more about a battle, its casualties, positions of the contending forces, the victors and losers, than the men actually engaged in the conflict. It was solely through newspapers received by our troops from their friends far away, from Philadelphia and

---

* In connection with the formation of the Army of the Potomac at this time into three grand divisions, I can say to my own personal knowledge (for I saw the official documents, offer and reply) that General Meagher was offered the command of one of the divisions. He was even urged to accept it. Meagher positively declined to do so saying that when he entered the service of the United States, he determined never to accept of a higher position than that of brigadier general. General Meagher in his early years had the advantage of not only a first-rate English and Classical education, but also a thorough military training according to the British Army system, well fitting him in connection with his other fine soldierly qualities for the highest position in the United States Army.[16]

New York especially, that they learned the particulars of some hard-fought field, perhaps one upon which they themselves had struggled and bled.

On the afternoon of November 9th, the day of our arrival at War-renton, an incident occurred in my own regiment which I have omitted to relate. Our march on the 9th commenced at early dawn. It was a long and fatiguing one of nearly 21 miles. The weather was warm and sultry, although it was late in the fall. Several of our men fell down by the way or had to leave the ranks for the road side from pure exhaustion.

In my own Company A was one John Major, a Philadelphian, a large, powerful man in appearance capable of standing any amount of fatigue or exposure which light, thin, wiry men would not be supposed to be able to endure. Major, with much difficulty, held out till reaching camp where he immediately sank down on the ground and complained of cramps in the stomach. The regimental doctor was at once summoned. He administered a dose of medicine which seemed to have a good effect upon the sufferer. But Major, a few moments later, with one piercing cry fell back on the ground in violent convulsions, foaming at the mouth. Five minutes afterwards, he was dead.

Another companion and I dug a shallow grave. Some of the others rolled the body of our dead comrade up in his blanket closely. We consigned it to its freshly made house of clay, over which was fired the sad farewell and parting salute of 12 rounds of musketry. Thus, another of our number filled "an honorable soldier's grave."*[17]

---

* Thin, lean and even delicate men were found to generally endure the long marches and fatigue of army life better than many strong and healthy-looking men.

Falmouth. Stafford County. Va.
November 17ᵗʰ 1862.

Falmouth, was a small town almost deserted, its only inhabitants at this time, being women and children, (generally of English origin) and men, too old to perform military duty. Here, we learned the curious fact, that when hostilities commenced, nearly all the young, and middle aged men of the town, volunteered their services for the war, and strange to say, that about half of the number advocated the Union Cause, and joined its Army, while the other half, sympathizing with the South, went into the service of the Confederacy. "Verily, this was a town divided against itself."

Falmouth is one of the oldest towns in Virginia, being settled many years ago by the English, and deriving its name from the town of the same in England. It is situated on the northern side of the Rappahannock, at the base of the elevation of land extending for miles above and below the town, and skirting the river, known as the "Stafford Hills." These

"Standing upon Stafford Hills on the clear, cold afternoon of November 22, 1862, I looked over the scene before me. Two immense armies were assembling and marshalling their hosts, ready to again drench Virginia's sacred soil with blood."

Chapter 5

The March to Fredericksburg and Service Along the Rappahannock

The weather was now getting quite cold and winter-like, threatening another fall of snow or rain. At about noon of the first day of the march from Warrenton to Falmouth, a light, cold drizzling rain set in, which soon increased to torrents, wetting completely through the clothing of the troops. It was of the utmost importance for the men to keep their firearms dry, ready for use at a moment's notice. This was accomplished by each man tieing his India rubber or gum blanket tightly around the lock and barrel of his musket, thereby shielding it from the pelting rain and keeping the weapon in good servicable condition. On this occasion, the first day of our march, my Irish Brigade was detailed as a guard for a drove of 700 head of cattle accompanying the army. Our progress was very slow, owing to the rugged and uneven face of the country over which our route lay, as well as the wild and almost unmanagable condition of the animals. The beasts had recently arrived from the mountains of Texas.

It rained hard and constant from two p.m. on the 16th. As darkness approached, no indication of clearing was visible. The troops were all soaking wet long before a halt for the night was made, the water running out over the tops of their boots in streams as they marched along. At about five p.m., when darkness only compelled a halt and prevented a farther advance that day, a cavalry bugler announced the end of the day's march. We had just reached a point ten miles distant from our place of starting in the morning. Several other brigades of our division had in the same time and on the same route passed us by. They had reached a point fully seven miles ahead.

Our slow progress was, however, unavoidable. We were cursed by the care required to guard and to drive the large number of cattle in our charge. It was a task most trying, provoking and harassing the patience and tempers of the men detailed for such duty. As for me, I felt absolutely wicked. I had broken my bayonet over the rump of a little unruly steer while it cut up in one of its highland flings. But such work had to be done. Otherwise, the men would have starved. We were afterwards complimented for the progress which we had made, slow as we thought it was. We had gone considerably beyond the expectations of our commanding general.

After halting, quarters for the cattle were the first thing to be provided. We drove the animals into a large clump of woods nearby. A long rope was then stretched around the outer trees of these woods, encircling them and the cattle within. In this way, together with a guard of 100 men placed around the enclosure, the cattle were kept safely together until the next day. In the morning, a New Jersey brigade came up. These soldiers were entrusted with the care of the cattle for the balance of the march to Falmouth.

After fencing in our charge, the cattle, quarters for ourselves were the next thing in question. We were now at a point ten miles southeast of Warrenton, in a dreary, desolate, and wasted country. It was very hilly and more thickly wooded than any other place in Virginia through which we had previously passed. It was raining fearfully, so common at this season of the year in this part of the Old Dominion. How to get fires kindled was no easy problem to solve. Everything on the troops was soaking wet with water. The lucifers positively refused to emit a single spark of fire. The wood was in a condition almost past ignition.

However, after feeling and fumbling for a while in the darkness, we succeeded in finding a few comparatively dry leaves and branches of trees which were then collected together. With the aid of a flint and steel, this fuel was at least coaxed to burn, shedding a light which enabled us to fell several fir and pine trees. Other fires were started. At 9 p.m., some 18 or 20 other fires blazed and cracked through the woods, our resting place for the night. It was, however, only with constant attention and nursing that the fires were prevented from being extinguished by the rain. It still continued to pour down in torrents.

By this time, hunger was tightening its hold upon every man in camp. The day's trying and irritating march seemed to stimulate the appetites of the troops. They devoured long before night the rations issued to them in the morning and intended to last until the next day. A little "salt horse" was all that still remained. Only a few men still had even this in their haversacks. Coffee, the soldier's greatest luxury on a hard march, was all used up. No more of it would be had until our supply train arrived. The wagons were still several miles distant in our rear. Whiskey was then issued to us as a ration. In no instance to my own knowledge had it ever been given or allowed before, except when ordered or prescribed by a surgeon or doctor for men stricken with chills and cramps. Even then, it was seldom administered, quinine being the medicine generally used under such circumstances. Immense quantities of quinine were consumed in the army about this season of the year. On this occasion, however, the general rule was a little deviated from. I suppose it was due to the inclement weather, miserable condition of the troops and their poor prospect of a night's rest. Some few of our boys managed somehow or another by "hook or by crook" to get away with much more than the allowed ration of whiskey this night. It was about five tablespoons full. The consequence was a free fight, black eyes and bloody noses. These drunk fellows were immediately arrested and placed under guard of a company of other soldiers. This broke up the liquor business for the time being, at least so far as the rank and file of our division was concerned. But I am sorry to say that it still flowed in super-abundance in the officer's quarters. [1]

Some time between 11 p.m. and midnight, our provision train arrived within one half a mile of our campground. It halted for the night in a valley. Between the supply train and our men laid a long track of marshy, wet ground and a shallow, muddy, narrow stream. The night was pitch dark. The rain, now accompanied by sleet freezing as it came down, caused both the air and the ground to feel most uncomfortably damp and biting cold. No issue of rations was to take place till morning. The condition of the troops from hunger, especially from the absence of hot coffee on this fearful night, was truly sad and deplorable. To lay down was only to add misery to our condition. To sit up or stand up all night without hot coffee was thought by some to be almost impossible.

But then, how was the so much craved and indispensable beverage to be obtained before morning?

A plan presented itself to my mind. If successful, its completion would be perhaps the greatest and most acceptable service which I had ever rendered my companions in arms. I put this scheme into operation. Its object was to secure for my own company, if not the entire regiment, a supply of coffee, as well as a ration each per man of sugar, hardtack and pork.

I had become quite intimate with the commissary of the regiment, having on several occasions rendered him service. I thought that I could reach him, then with our provision train one half a mile away. He might, if it was in his power to do so, issue to me food for my company. But the night was very dark, wet and freezing. My route would be over marshy, sinking ground, through which extended a muddy ditch, some five or six feet wide at its widest part. This ditch had to be crossed to reach the supply train. It was now midnight, probably a little later, and the weather unchanged. Sergeant Stretchabock of my own company volunteered to accompany me on my hazardous and uncertain expedition. Taking it for granted that we would be successful, we took with us our two army woolen blankets in which to carry the provisions back to our camp. Nothing ventured, nothing won. So off we started.

We proceeded very cautiously, feeling the way as we advanced. Heading for the dim flickering lights of our supply train in the distance, we trudged forwards. With considerable toil and difficulty, we reached the ditch and commenced a search for its narrowest and safest part to cross. Upon finding a ford, we passed safely over and soon arrived at the train.

After some searching and directions from the wagoners, we found the commissary. I at once made known our errand. "I would like much," he said, "to fix the boys up before morning, but dare not do so without authority." He proceeded, "Did you see the general?"

"No," I replied.

"Well," he said, pointing to a wagon some 50 feet away in which a very dim light was burning, "go over there. He is in that wagon. Ask him and report to me what he says about it."

We proceeded at once to the wagon. Upon reaching it, we heard several voices from within, one of which I at once recognized as General Meagher. The wagon was a covered one. It was then completely closed all around and on the top to keep the rain and sleet out of it. I raised the end covering, where I found the general and three other officers. I saluted them all and asked to speak with the general. He immediately complied. After relating my story to him, he put on his cap and accompanied me back to the commissary. On the way, he remarked that his orders were not to issue rations until seven a.m. But under the present pressing circumstances, he would assume the responsibility in ordering them now.

He then directed the commissary to deliver to my partner and me a full supply of the needed food for our own company. Meagher also bid me to notify the other companies of my regiment upon our arrival in camp again to report at once to the commissary's quarters for their share of provisions. He then said farewell and hurried away to the wagon. After moving several boxes and bags, we received an abundant supply of the good things, in fact a double share. We deposited these supplies in the center of our blankets, tied the four corners of each together, slung them over our shoulders and started our return to camp. Stretchabok and I were fully satisfied, our expedition having been a complete success, at least so far. It was now after one a.m. No change for the better had taken place in the weather.

We reached the ditch again, but not without stumbling over large stones and occasionally plunging into mudholes with which our route abounded. In vain did we seek our previous crossing place, owing to the darkness. We concluded to cross at the point at which we then had reached. This was perhaps the widest part of the ditch. It was roughly and apparently newly bridged over by three or four small branchless trees. They were stretched across and laid close together, known then in our army as a "corduroy" road or bridge. The makeshift bridge was very narrow. Owing to the rain, it was slippery and dangerous to tread upon. I, however, proceeded in passing over safely. But my companion not so fortunate. When he had almost gained the opposite side, he slipped and fell into the muddy ditch below with his load of provisions on top of him.

He, like a good fellow, shouted lustily for help as he held on to his precious burden with one hand. With the other, Stretchabok grasped the weeds growing along the edge of the ditch to prevent himself from sinking head and ears in the water and mud into which he had been propelled. I at once deposited my load on the ground and reached out to help him. Instead of doing so, I found myself dragged down into the mud and water with Stretchabok. He, a large, powerful, heavy man, had pulled me into the ditch. It was a pretty kettle of fish. We scrambled and splashed there for a minute or two. But at length, we succeeded in gaining the bank, considerably more scared than hurt. We two presented roughly used specimens of humanity in the shape and garb of soldiers.

We then went "fishing" for his blanket containing the rations. Stretchabok let go of the supplies when I fell into the ditch with him. We finally hooked them with a tree branch. The contents were much damaged. But after the supplies were washed well, they were very welcome and most acceptable to the hungry and voracious appetites of the men in our company.

We soon afterwards reached camp and immediately communicated General Meagher's message to the weary and hungry troops. They at once responded. Long before daylight, our camp resounded with shouts and songs of joy and good humor, proceeding from men with full stomachs and merry hearts. Afterwards, my comrades imposed upon me the title of "Angel Gabriel." I was the recipient of many tokens of marked love and regard afterwards. At daybreak, it ceased raining; the dark clouds commenced to move farther south before a stiff breeze which had sprung up. The indications were that we would see fair, bright and milder weather.

The line of march was again taken up a little before eight a.m. on the morning of November 17th. The weather was clear and cold. The troops, notwithstanding the previous day's trying and fatiguing duties and a night of torture, unrest and fasting, were in excellent spirits. They commenced the march by singing the ballad, "Jordan's A Hard Road to Travel." Their physical condition, considering what they had experienced already on this march, was by no means despicable. In fact, it was good.

The Irish Brigade on this occasion moved forward by regiments, starting at intervals of one hour between each. My own regiment [116th Pennsylvania] was the third on the program. Owing to disease, death, a few desertions and other causes, my regiment was reduced down to about 350 men all told. Nothing of special interest occurred until the afternoon. At 12 p.m., we reached a place where only a few days before a body of Union cavalry, a part of General Siegel's Command then in the vicinity of Culpepper Court House, had an engagement with a force of Rebel infantry. The skirmish resulted in the defeat of the enemy. The Rebs retreated towards Fredericksburg, Virginia. The woods in this vicinity had been fired. Whole acres of valuable timber lay charred and destroyed. The country for miles around bore unmistakable marks of a severe struggle. At about 2:30 p.m. after a march that day of 13 or 14 miles, we arrived at a point three miles northeast of Falmouth, Stafford County, and there were ordered to halt, stack arms and rest.

We had scarce been here one half an hour when the bearer of a dispatch from General Sumner, our division commander, came dashing along a road on our left. The man rode up to General Meagher and delivered to him a sealed envelope. I knew from my own short experience among army documents and papers that it was another order respecting some further movement of the Irish Brigade. I had a good view of the paper, being only eight or ten yards distant from the general when he received it. After reading it, Meagher quickly mounted his horse, rode hurriedly to each regimental commander and gave them some private instructions. Then he consulted with the chief engineer of the brigade artillery force.

This artilleryman, after his short interview with the general, at once ordered forward his battery. He posted it on an eminence about one quarter of a mile then in front of our infantry. We all knew by his movement that something important was at hand. The troops very naturally manifested much curiosity and even uneasiness to know what it was. A few minutes later, the bugle sounded, calling all the men into line again. In a very short period of time afterwards, the Irish Brigade, tired and weary as it was after the day's march, was ready for the word "Forward," eager to meet the enemy in any quarter.

We were then within one quarter of a mile of the far-famed and beautiful Rappahannock River, only three and one half miles from the city of Fredericksburg. It was said to be garrisoned by strong detachments of Rebel infantry and cavalry numbering 4,000 men. Several batteries of heavy artillery were rumored to be mounted upon Marye's and Fredericksburg Heights in the rear.

It was now in the neighborhood of four p.m. General Meagher, riding to the center front of the Irish Brigade, told the troops that they were about to make a most important movement. He addressed his soldiers, saying something like the following: "Men of the Irish Brigade of the Army of the Potomac, you have been selected by our chief officer, General Sumner, to ford yonder river. We are to capture the Rebel artillery on the opposite shore. Follow me, I lead the way. Be brave, courageous and unflinching. Victory will be ours."

The Irish Brigade then moved quickly forward towards the river, headed by its noble commander. The men cheered and indulged in the wildest expressions of delight as they neared the ford in the stream over which they were then expecting to cross. A moment later, a courier galloped to the side of General Meagher and handed him another written message. Upon reading it, Meagher brought the Irish Brigade to a halt. He ordered us to fall back to the point from which we commenced the movement to the river.

It was then learned that the message received by Meagher was from the commander-in-chief, General Burnside. It countermanded the order previously received from General Sumner to ford the river and capture the Rebel guns. General Burnside deemed it inexpedient to attack the enemy on the southern side of the Rappahannock before his own communications were thoroughly established. At that time, many thought our communications sufficiently perfected to warrant the attempt.[*2]

After the Irish Brigade retired from the river, it marched to a place in the midst of extensive woods about a mile north of Falmouth, Stafford County, Virginia, where it camped, expecting to remain there during the inclement weather and to erect winter quarters.

Falmouth, Stafford County, Virginia
November 17, 1862

Falmouth was a small town almost deserted, its only inhabitants at this time being women, children, and men too old to perform military duty. Here we learned the curious fact that when hostilities commenced, nearly all the young and middle-aged men of the town volunteered their services for the war. Strange to say, about half of the number

---

* In regard to General Burnside countermanding the order given by General Sumner for our Irish Brigade to cross the river and capture the Rebel guns, I am of the opinion and I am not alone in it that General Burnside, notwithstanding his alleged unprepared condition to attack the enemy, committed the saddest blunder in his whole military career. At that time and place, there were only two Rebel batteries posted on the southern side of the river, unsupported as far as was known or seen by us, save by about 200 Rebel infantry. These troops seemed to be only pickets along the river's front between that point and Fredericksburg, some three and one half or four miles below. In this state of affairs, it is my firm belief that the Irish Brigade would have succeeded in taking the Rebel guns. If then reinforced by say another brigade from the 50,000 Union troops then within supporting distance, the Irish Brigade might have marched along the southern side of the river to Fredericksburg, surprised the garrison and captured the city. In this way, a victory might have resulted to Union arms. Not, however, without some loss of life, but with little when compared with the wholesale sacrifice and slaughter of Federal soldiers at the same place not a month after. On the 17th day of November, the day on which the blow should and could have been successfully struck, the Confederate Army around Fredericksburg did not number quite 5,000 men.

advocated the Union cause and joined its army while the other half, sympathizing with the South, went into the service of the Confederacy. Verily, this was a town divided against itself.

Falmouth was one of the oldest towns in Virginia, being settled many years ago by the English and deriving its name from a village in England. It was situated on the northern side of the Rappahannock at the base of an elevation of land extending for miles and skirting the river. The area was known as Stafford Hills. These hills rose high above the river, commanding an extensive view of the surrounding country and the city of Fredericksburg on the opposite shore. This was the position chosen by the Union Army for the bombardment of Fredericksburg. The sides of these hills above Falmouth were dotted here and there with woods from their top to the water's edge. In contrast, the hills below the town presented a barren, bleak appearance, destitute of vegetation of any kind.[3]

The country running north and north east from the town was generally level. But it was thickly and heavily covered with timber. Once in a while a cleared spot could be seen. There usually stood a farmhouse, built in Virginia's style of architecture, rough but strong, seldom over two stories in height. These houses invariably had beside them a dirty, black looking slave's hut or log house. Poor, unfortunate, downtrodden and abused menials found shelter and rest at night in these hovels. They lived lives of bondage and cruelty.

Our Irish Brigade now camped in a woods near a clearing. The place was high above the Rappahannock. Water was abundant and communication with Washington was clear and open by way of Aquia Creek, then our base of supplies. The men anticipated spending what many of them termed "a gay and happy winter in Dixie's land." But alas, poor fellows, hundreds never left the place. Such is the fate of war.

Surrender of Fredericksburg Demanded
November 21, 1862

On November 21, General Sumner sent a written communication to the mayor of Fredericksburg, whose name was Slaughter. Our general demanded the unconditional surrender of the city to our Federal forces. Sumner asserted in his demand that the city authorities had given aid and comfort to the enemies of the U.S. government. He also stated that the Confederate troops in the city fired upon Yankee men from the roofs and shelter of the houses. If refused, General Sumner warned that he would immediately shell the town, after allowing its women, children, sick and aged inhabitants 24 hours to leave it.

Mayor Slaughter replied that the citizens were not responsible for firing on General Sumner's forces. The mayor also noted that the Confederate general then in command of the troops garrisoning the city would not allow surrender. He stated that it would be impossible to remove the non-combatants within the 24 hours named by General Sumner and requested longer time.[4]

General Sumner replied that the Union guns would not open on the city at the hour named in his first message.*

The Army of the Potomac was now fairly in front of Fredericksburg. It being conceded that the city would not be surrendered without hard and stubborn fighting, preparations for the conflict were at once commenced and carried forward in downright, real earnest by our army on the northern side of the Rappahannock. The Confederates on the southern side were no less active. The passage of the river by the Federal troops could only be effected under the heavy and constant fire of our entire artillery force. Consequently, that valuable and indispensable arm of the service at once commenced operations in hurrying forward their terrible instruments of war and destruction. The position selected for the artillery to open fire in the bombardment of the doomed city was the summit of the Stafford Hills. From there, every part of the town could be shelled, the distance being somewhere in the neighborhood of twelve hundred yards. The city's elevation was below the hills.

The roads, as all Virginia roads are in the winter season, were in horrible condition, almost impassable. Yet notwithstanding this, heavy siege guns and artillery of almost every caliber rolled along, each gun being dragged to its position by the power of from four to six and, in some instances, eight horses. Sometimes as many mules were used. Pontoon bridges were required for our troops to cross the river, since the bridge connecting Fredericksburg with Falmouth had been burned by the Rebels in the Spring of 1862 to prevent passage of Federal troops. Boats for these bridges were being built rapidly at Aquia Creek and hurried forward by land to the present position of the army. Their

---

* The troops referred to by General Sumner as having been fired upon were a portion of his own division of the army. I think it was the infantry brigade of General Burns. These soldiers had reached Falmouth ahead of us. Upon attempting to cross the Rappahannock, they were repulsed and driven back by musketry from Confederate troops occupying the houses near the riverfront and concealed in positions on riverbanks.

transportation, like the artillery, was an exceeding tedious and difficult matter. They were dragged along by mules on trucks made for the purpose or on large, heavy army wagons. The pontoons journeyed from the terminus of Aquia Creek and the Fredericksburg Railroad. They were dragged onto covered positions as near the river as practicable, there to be in readiness for launching when the army was prepared to cross and seize Fredericksburg.[5]

While these war preparations by the Union Army for the siege and capture of this important town were in progress on the northern side of the Rappahannock, the Confederates on the southern side were daily and nightly busily engaged in fortifying the town against the anticipated Federal advance and attack. From the top of the Stafford Hills, we witnessed them mounting battery after battery on Marye's and Fredericksburg Heights. These eminences soon bristled with cannons. Near the southern side of the town and along the riverfront, hundreds of Rebel soldiers busily plied the spade, shovel and pick, throwing up breastworks and digging rifle pits in broad daylight under our very noses. At night, their camp fires illuminated the heavens for 25 miles around. The low, rumbling sound of moving artillery could be distinctly heard rattling over the rough streets of the ill-fated town. The shrill, sharp whistles of locomotives sounded plain and clear as trains brought up more Rebel troops. The enemy plainly had determined to contest every inch of ground when our army advanced.[6]

It would be hard to describe the feelings of our boys in contemplating these gigantic preparations for the bloody and terrific contest which soon followed. Suffice it to say that the almost general feeling among the Union troops was one of gloom and great depression. They saw before them the strong, almost impregnable position of the enemy and knew about his resources behind. They were not inspired with the same confidence and courage which they experienced under the leadership of their old commander [General McClellan]. Indeed, while all hoped for a victory, few, very few, dreamed about gaining it here. After looking at the Rebel works over the water, one officer remarked, "No competent, sane commander would attack that place from this side of the river."[7]

Another exclaimed, "Boys, this will be no popgun practice like at Charlestown."

Camp One Mile North of Falmouth,
Stafford County, Virginia
North Side of River Rappahannock
and behind Stafford Hills
November 22, 1862

My regiment, while camped here, spent the time in company drill and picketing the Rappahannock. We picketed north of Falmouth for about a mile. Upon two occasions, we did our guard duty under moonlight. We cooperated with other troops in throwing up earthworks on the summit of a hill between our camp and Falmouth. It was known by the name of Roundtop Mountain. The hill stood all alone and its summit was the highest point of land near the river in Stafford County. Roundtop Mountain was then being prepared to receive some of our heaviest guns and mortars for the bombardment of Fredericksburg.

On November 21 after our arrival in this camp, General Hancock, who commanded my division, issued an order for all troops to be ready for inspection on the next day at nine a.m. Morning came, dark, gloomy and threatening rain. At the hour appointed, Generals Sumner, Hancock and Meagher appeared on horseback. This was the first time that I had the pleasure of a close, good look at Hancock and Sumner. I heard them converse together, talk to the troops and issue orders. Their words and actions left an indelible impression on me.

General [Edwin V.] Sumner

General Sumner was a man apparently well advanced in years. He had a medium height and build and long, white hair. Sumner appeared calm and quiet. In manner, the general was very reserved. I saw him afterwards on several occasions in the company of other officers of high rank. While they sometimes seemed considerably excited and perplexed, General Sumner was cool and collected; he seemed the perfect master of his business. His word was law in the Army of the Potomac. He enjoyed the fullest confidence not only of his government and country but also of every officer and private soldier in the army.[8]

General [Winfield Scott] Hancock

General Winfield Scott Hancock was about 35 years of age and five feet ten inches high. He had a heavy build and red, sandy hair. Hancock wore a short military moustache of the same color. His whole manner and bearing indicated him to be what he really was and had been from a boy, a soldier of the Regular Army of the United States. Unlike Sumner, General Hancock was fiery and excitable, iron-willed and, in many instances, harsh and tyrannical to the volunteer troops under his command. He expected that they, men who had temporarily abandoned civil life to aid their country's armies in the time of danger and need, should already have attained that perfection in military discipline and drill which only regular troops by lengthy experience reach.

On one occasion, I understood that he was severely reproved for just such conduct to his volunteer soldiery. While intoxication to a sad and alarming extent prevailed now, not only among the rank and file but also among a large number of officers, the still greater and more heinous sin of profanity knew no bounds. I would be sorry indeed to cast the shadow of a stain or reproach upon the character of the brave, indomitable Hancock, or to pluck from his manly brow a fragment of the laurels for which he fought so valiantly. Yet I cannot hide the fact that General Hancock reached the highest degree of perfection in cursing at his volunteer troops. In giving orders to his men on the march, drill, parade, or even the battlefield, he seldom did so without an oath of the most unpardonable nature. Indeed, he seemed to have got into such a habit of indulging in profane language that he could never address the troops without taking God's name in vain. General Hancock in this respect, however, was not an isolated character in the Army of the Potomac.

He was fully equalled by Generals Hooker and the deceased General Kearny. I had the privilege, I mean pain, of hearing Hooker a few days before the Battle of Fredericksburg. Together with General Hancock, General Hooker seemed to have received an extensive education in profanity. Generals McClellan, Burnside, Sumner and Meagher never gave in to this mean, low, contemptible and damning vice. At least none of them used profanity when I was in hearing range.[9]

On the morning of November 22, the Irish Brigade was in line and ready for inspection as ordered. The work was commenced by General Hancock. He personally inspected the firearms and uniforms of my own regiment and the 28th Massachussetts. Other officers inspected the remaining regiments of the Irish Brigade. In my regiment, Company C, was a man who went by the name of "Richmond Dick." He was characterized by his laziness, indolent habits and utter disregard for neatness of military dress and the common army rules for cleanliness. The regiment now for the first time was being closely inspected by a disciplinarian second to none in the American army. Those of our number who knew about Hancock felt satisfied that when the general reached Dick in his round of inspection there would be music. As usual, Dick's dress and uniform were in no way reasonably clean. His appearance would never satisfy the keen, piercing eye of our division commander.

The 28th was the first regiment examined. With the exception of a slight reproof to two of its members for dusty coats, it came off with flying colors. Next came my own, Company "A." All right. "B" the same. "C." Oh, no! Stop, watch the fiery eye of Hancock as it catches the first sight of something down the line, stowed away among the men of Company "D." It was no less a personage than "Richmond Dick." Nearer and nearer the dreaded inspector got to him. Now Dick was reached. He presented a dirty musket to the chief, who took hold of it, looked at it suspiciously, then stared at its owner, scanning him for a moment from head to foot. The other troops stood at attention in unbroken stillness and silence. Half a minute later, the clear, loud voice of the general, was heard, "What in the devil are you doing here?"

Then the weapon was dashed to the ground. The dirty, slovenly soldier was seized by the coat collar and dragged out of the line by the powerful arm of Hancock. This scene caused a tittering laugh by all the troops there. The offender now received one of the general's not to be forgotten tongue-thrashings, never lacking in profanity. Dick was then sent spinning towards his quarters by a kick on the posterior from the toe of one of the general's heavy-soled army boots. Hancock warned Dick that if he was ever found again outside of his own company during drill, parade or inspection or caught in such a slovenly condition, he would be tied up by the thumbs for 24 hours without food and water. This must have scared poor Dick. For next morning, he could not be found anywhere within the Union lines in the vicinity of Falmouth. The supposition was that he had either hid himself away in some part of the dark woods or forded the Rappahannock and entered the Confederate Army. He was by birth a Welshman, but for many years had resided in Richmond, Virginia. At outbreak of the war, he was a resident of the Southwark District of Philadelphia.*[10]

---

* Punishment in the Army—Punishment was inflicted upon all who violated the rules and regulations of the army. The following are some of the ways in which it was administered—for "desertion," or being found "asleep" on guard or picket duty, which was the highest crime known in the army, the penalty was "death" by shooting. The

Picketing the northern shore of the Rappahannock now commenced. A strong force of pickets performed that duty day and night. My regiment formed part of the picket tour, guarding the river's front from Falmouth north for about a mile. During our encampment here, we spent nearly every alternate day in the performance of picket duty. A mail agent for the regiment was not now needed owing to the irregularity of the mail service from the North. Mail seldom reached us more than once a week. So, I returned to my original place in the ranks.

The time allotted to each regiment for picket duty now was 24 hours. At the expiration of this tour, the regiment was relieved and returned to camp. A fresh regiment took its place on the picket line. Picket posts were very near to each other there, owing to the close proximity of the powerful Rebel army. It would have been almost impossible for even a single man to cross the river without attracting the attention of Union pickets on this side of the river or Rebel pickets on the other. The Rebs had a force equally strong and as watchful as our own. These enemy pickets were within speaking distance of our men. The river was only about 200 yards wide there.[11]

Standing upon Stafford Hills on the clear, cold afternoon of November 22, 1862, I looked over the scene before me. Two immense armies were assembling and marshalling their hosts, ready to again drench Virginia's sacred soil with blood. How could I refrain from wishing and praying that this cruel, unnatural and devastating war was at an end forever? But the war could not be wished away. It was a sad, terrible reality, a reality well calculated to fill one's heart with horror and dismay. I was, however, more convinced than ever that the cause for which I fought was truly the cause of God and humanity. I felt confident that in endeavoring to perform my duty faithfully, God would give me the

---

condemned man was compelled at the time of execution to sit on his coffin (generally a rough pine box purposely made for him) while, at a distance of several yards, a platoon of 12 men fired one concentrated volley of musketry into his body, killing him instantly. For offenses of a less serious character, men were required to carry water for the use of a whole regiment for a day without receiving food. Extra guard or picket duty was another mode of punishment. Sometimes, offenders were compelled to stand in one position against a tree for a number of hours or forced to carry a log of wood on their shoulders from one specified place to another without stopping or laying the load down for a certain length of time. Men were also suspended by a rope tied around the arms, hands and, not unfrequently, the thumbs, to the limb of a tree for two hours. Their feet barely touched the ground to relieve the weight of the body. In the majority of cases, where offenses were of a light or trivial nature, the punishment was imprisonment for one, two or more days in the guardhouse. This was a Sibley canvas tent erected for that purpose in nearly every regiment or brigade camp.

necessary strength and courage and enable me to meet every danger and trial.

On the night of November 22, there was clear moonlight. At nine p.m., the regiment, with two others, was ordered out to assist in the construction of earthworks on the summit of Roundtop Mountain. The regiment as it marched out of camp presented rather an unusual appearance, the men looking more like a band of uniformed farmers going to work in the fields than soldiers. Each man was armed with a pick, spade or shovel instead of a musket. The change seemed agreeable, for all marched along in the best of good humor. Upon reaching the working ground, operations commenced immediately.

Immense banks of earth were thrown up to serve as a protection for our gunners against an anticipated artillery fire from the Rebel batteries on Fredericksburg Heights. The work of piling up these earthworks was always performed by night to prevent enemy observation. The boys worked faithfully till near daylight when they ceased their labor and returned to camp.[12] Four hours were allowed for rest and sleep. After which, roll was called and breakfast, consisting of a cup of water and a small portion of hardtack without coffee, was consumed. During the remainder of the day, no special duty being assigned to the regiment, the men amused themselves in various ways around their quarters. Many devoted the time to card playing, others to reading or writing, while others slept and rested. Not a few sat or lounged around campfires, smoking, chatting, or singing, while others indulged in different kinds of short hunting excursions.

Our rations at this time were again nearly exhausted. Of dear coffee there was none, owing to the non-arrival of a supply train overdue from Aquia Creek. We had only a bite for dinner. Afterwards, our colonel [Dennis Heenan] came around among the men and told us that the train in question had fallen down an embankment. It was stuck fast in the mud some five or six miles northeast of our camp. He asked for ten men to go to the place and help to dig out the train, or at least to save some of the supplies then so much needed.

The number required at once volunteered, including me. A large uncovered army wagon and four strong mules were placed at our service. We jumped on board. In a short time, we were dashing along at a fearful rate of speed through woods, over ditches and down and up rough, rocky and precipitous hills. Our driver, William McCarty, was a reckless, daring devil, and a good soldier, regardless of danger. As he wildly drove past the camps of other troops on the route, our little party was frequently complimented. We heard shouts like "How are you 116th?" "There goes the bloody 116th!" or "Here comes Heenan's Regulars of Philadelphia."

About two p.m., we reached the wagons, three in number. They had capsized and fallen down into an embankment fully ten feet lower than the narrow, muddy, rut-filled road which bore the traffic there. We at once saw that the wagons could not be extricated by the force at hand. It had commenced to rain one half hour before. The ditch in which the wagons laid was fast filling up with water. Soon afterwards, the water reached over the floors, damaging and destroying everything with which it came in contact. The flood finally carried away the boxes, barrels and bags of provisions with which the train was loaded. One of our number, much against the advice of the rest, attempted to lay hold on a floating box of crackers. He slipped and fell into the now rushing water and was only rescued from drowning by a rope thrown to him from the wet, slimy bank above. It continued to rain in torrents. Seeing that any effort on our part to save even part of this government property would be fruitless, we returned to our four mule wagon. We started on the return trip to camp. It was now between three and four p.m.

As we passed along, the storm seemed to increase. It was accompanied by sharp, vivid flashes of lightning and deafening peals of thunder. The country all around was deluged with water. This was the severest storm, especially of constant, heavy, battering rain, that I ever saw. Our progress towards camp was slow, having for a time lost our way. Exposed without the slightest covering or protection from the fury of the tempest, we were soaking and floating in water. But this was not the worst. Upon arriving in camp at about seven p.m., we found nearly all the fires extinguished by the rain, many tents blown down by the wind and the ground flooded with water. Confusion reigned supreme. By the kindness of some members of the regiment whose tents had not been blown down and who had built small fires within them, we were provided with shelter and a little warmth. We were then informed by them that orders had been received for the regiment to go on picket duty next morning at nine a.m. on the Rappahannock.

Our little party, who had suffered so much from the storm, were now separated. Each man sought and fortunately found a standing tent where he was made welcome. The occupants made us welcome, even at the sacrifice of their own personal convenience and comfort. I was in just such a tent at eight p.m. with its owners, two members of Company G. I crouched, shivered and shook over a few dying embers of a wood fire, feeling for the first time in my army experience really sick, chilly and cold.

There seemed to be no relief at hand. Complaining would not alleviate my condition. I had no dry clothing to exchange for the soaking wet garments on my body. I was sitting in this condition, fearing an attack of the dreaded army chills and fever, when I heard the voice of the regimental commissary outside. He was looking for the men who had been on the expedition to the wagons. I jumped to my feet and answered, "Here's one of them."

"Go right to my tent," said he, "and wait there on me."

I did so. In ten minutes he arrived, accompanied by the other nine. "Boys," said he, "the colonel has ordered you two rations of whiskey per man. To warm you up, for you can get no coffee before morning. The colonel has made a requisition on the citizens of Falmouth for one ration of bread and coffee per man in the regiment. He will pay for them in the name of the United States. The bread and coffee are to be delivered here before the regiment goes on picket. Also, the colonel has telegraphed to Aquia Creek for fresh supplies for those lost. They are expected here by noon tomorrow."

Each man then received two-thirds of an army tincup full of whiskey, which he soon swallowed. Then we all returned to wet, unhealthy quarters for the night. If not benefited in reality by the liquor, our drooping spirits were raised by it. I do not and would not advocate the use of intoxicating liquor under any circumstance. But I must and do conscientiously say that the liquor I drank on that night prevented an attack of chills and fever. Perhaps the liquor even saved my life.

A most uncomfortable night was passed by all in camp. But with morning came clearer weather and indications of a fair day. The ration required from Falmouth arrived in due time for an early breakfast. The so-called coffee, much to the disappointment of the men, turned out to be only roasted again. After some necessary duties and preparations for the front, the regiment marched out of camp at eight a.m. At nine a.m., the picket posts on the shore of the Rappahannock opposite Fredericksburg and north of Falmouth were fully manned.

Picket Duty on the Rappahannock
Commencing November 23, 1862

The distance from camp to the picket lines was about two miles. The route laid through woods touching the base of Roundtop Mountain, then over a cleared, but uneven and marshy tract of land into Falmouth. From there we marked to the river and the bluffs bordering it, north of the town. That part of the line assigned to my regiment commenced at a burnt bridge and extended for about a mile northeast. There were three picket lines, the first or front close along the edge of the stream; the second or center, halfway up the sides of the steep and thickly wooded hills skirting the river; and the third, an inner line, extending along their summit. The front was exposed to full view of the enemy on the opposite shore. But the center and inner lines, owing to the trees, were nearly hidden from them. Two men occupied each picket post for two hours at a time. At the expiration of their shift, they were relieved from duty for four hours by two others called the "relief." Upon being relieved, pickets retired to some convenient place within the lines where fires had been built or temporary shelter found.

There were three reliefs for every post, consisting of two men each, all under command of an officer of the regiment and his subordinates. Thus, each member of the regiment performed eight hours of picket duty out of every 24 hours assigned to the regiment. I was attached to the first relief. With my partner, a member of my company, I was placed at Post No. 1 near the burnt bridge and opposite the Confederate pickets on the Fredericksburg side of the river. All the other posts of our front line along the Rappahannock were placed opposite posts occupied by Rebel pickets.

Here was a good opportunity for target practice between the pickets of both armies. But not a trigger was pulled on either side. From my post of duty, I beheld a scene which I shall never forget. The early part of the day was bright, clear and cold, with scarce a cloud visible in the blue sky. A strong northwester prevailed. The beautiful Rappahannock rolled along at my feet, crested by thousands of troubled, little white-capped waves. The surrounding scenery presented a picture worthy of undying remembrance. Behind me on the hills skirting the river floated the glorious Stars and Stripes and 100,000 Union soldiers. Before me laid historic old Fredericksburg with scores of Rebel emblems waving in the breeze and 80,000 Confederate troops behind its fortified hills. The sun shone full and bright. With the aid of a small field glass borrowed from an officer friend, I saw endless lines of Rebel heavy artillery far away up on the heights behind the town.

Nor was this all. Nearer the city and thickly dotting the lower highground, including Marye's Heights, were countless rows of breast-works and rifle pits. Here and there among these works were batteries of light field artillery. With the assistance of my borrowed glass, I saw the Rebel artillerists changing the positions of guns or inspecting them. Rebel cavalry dashed from one place to another. Rebel infantry with bright shining muskets and bayonets suddenly appeared in some ravine or opening between dark and distant hills. Just as suddenly, they disappeared again.

I frequently stood near the bank of the river and watched whole companies of Rebel infantry drilling. I must confess that from what I saw, they appeared to be far ahead of many Federal regiments as far as the manual of arms was concerned. Their movements were also quicker. I witnessed hundreds of Rebel cavalrymen leading and riding their horses down the streets of the city. The cavalrymen brought the horses into the Rappahannock to drink, not 200 yards from my post. I watched the Rebs indulging in such games and amusements as shinny, playing ball, running races and jumping. They always presented not only a gay and happy appearance but also a most defiant one. Upon one occasion, 50 members of my regiment and I stood for half an hour on the northern side of the river watching the progress of a regular ring fight between two Confederate soldiers surrounded at least by 300 of their comrades.[13]

It was now nearing 11 a.m., the time at which the second relief was to be posted, relieving my comrade and me on Post No. 1 for four hours. At the appointed hour, the officer then in charge of Posts No. 1 to 10 appeared at the head of his little band of 20 men. The usual salutes were given between the relievers and the relieved. The officer instructed the relief how to act and new pickets were placed on duty. The men relieved then fell into the places of those who had relieved them in the line and so on from Post No. 1 to 10. The 20 men of the first relief marched back to the regiment's temporary quarters in Falmouth.

Thus ended my first two hours of this dangerous service. Although much exposed, I liked picket duty and found the position and time spent profitable for reflection, study and observation. Not a moment was wasted.

"It was not uncommon in this section of Virginia for Federal soldiers to be made prisoners and sometimes even to be murdered while taking shelter in private houses or foraging."

Chapter 6

Picketing and Foraging in Falmouth, Virginia

The command post for the picket relief was in an unoccupied brick building at the extreme end of Falmouth near the river, about 30 yards from the burnt bridge. This building had been used as a flour mill before the war. But in the spring of 1862, it was partly destroyed by the Rebels. Its machinery, which seemed to have been both extensive and valuable, now laid in heaps over the partly torn up floors. It always afforded shelter to the troops while on the picket line.

At eleven a.m., my companion, Pvt. Foltz, and I were relieved from duty on Post No. 1. We retired to the quarters in the brick building where we spent the time as pleasantly and advantageously as possible. At three p.m., we were again on post. We had pretty empty stomachs, the rations expected from Aquia Creek not having arrived. I never experienced such acute hunger as on this occasion. When my post comrade shared with me a large raw turnip which he received from a member of a neighboring regiment, it seemed like a feast of good things. Nothing unusual transpired during this term of duty until relief time, five p.m., had nearly arrived.

Standing carelessly with both hands leaning on the muzzle of my musket, I watched a squad of Rebel pickets marching along the opposite side of the river. Suddenly, I heard a noise resembling the paddling of a boat on the stream. It was then getting dark. I could with difficulty see the opposite shore and the enemy's pickets. Thinking that the strange sound I had heard might be imaginary, I called to my companion a few yards distant. I asked him if he heard any peculiar noise on the water. He listened attentively but said, "No."

I, however, continued to hear it. Nor was it imagination. A few minutes afterwards, a dark object neared us. It proved to be a splendid, large, brown horse, saddled and bridled. The animal apparently had tired of his Rebel master and was swimming the river towards, perhaps, more agreeable quarters and treatment within the Union lines. The horse continued his progress to the shore, coming nearer and nearer to my partner and me. At this time, a Rebel picket over the water who had been watching the horse shouted lustily across, "Shoot that damned horse."

Not seeing any disposition on our part to comply with his command, he raised his own musket as if to fire at the horse then almost within our grasp or at us, I don't know which. One of our pickets on Post No. 2, some 25 yards above us on the river, had been quietly watching the proceedings from a concealed position. He sprang forward to the edge of the water and leveled his rifle at the Reb. This man threatened that if the Johnny pulled a trigger on either my companion and me or the horse, he would, "Blow the Reb's whole damned head off of him."

Johnny took the hint and wasted no powder. By this time, the animal had nearly reached the shore, so close to it that I once attempted to catch the bridle which floated on the water. But suddenly, as if scared by something, the horse gave a snort, wildly tossing his head. The beast immediately commenced re-crossing the river. The last I saw of him, he was on the "double-quick" down the stream, apparently heading for Fredericksburg which he so very recently had taken the notion to evacuate. So my companion and I lost the prize. At one time I thought for certain that we were sure of at least a Rebel horse as a trophy. But such is life, full of uncertainties and disappointments at every step. Ten minutes after, the relief came around and, as before, we returned to our quarters until again summoned to duty.

About six p.m., the wind, which had been blowing fresh all day, increased to a gale. It knocked things about in no very agreeable manner and created a solemn, mournful, melancholy sound through the leafless forest trees. The sound was similar to the noise produced by the rigging of a ship in a storm at sea. The heavens looked black and wild—not a star could be seen. The picket on the Rappahannock saw before him a stormy, dark, and bitter cold winter night. The rations fortunately had arrived during our absence on post. They aided very materially in fortifying and strengthening the men against the fierce storm of cutting wind, sleet and rain that prevailed.

At 9:50 p.m., the familiar voice of the sergeant of the guard sounded the call, "Fall in, first relief."

Five minutes later, the men, headed by an officer with his little dark lantern in hand, again took up the round of march for the various posts. The wind blew a perfect hurricane and the angry waters of the Rappahannock beat wildly against its dark and gloomy banks. Here and there, moving along the opposite side like us, could be indistinctly seen the small, glimmering lights of dark lanterns in the hands of the Rebel pickets. The only sound heard was the voice of the storm and the raging, roaring waters. It was in reality to me a solemn, terrible scene. It forcibly reminded me of the truth of the beautiful lines:

> "God moves in a mysterious way,
> His wonders to perform,
> He plants his foot-steps in the sea,
> And rides upon the storm."[1]

It was intensely cold, bringing tears to the eyes and sharp cutting pains to the ears. I entered upon my trying and lonely duty with a fear which I cannot describe. I never before or afterwards experienced such fright and I hope that I never will. This fear was not caused by my close proximity to the front picket line of the Confederate Army or of the duty to be performed on my post. Not being physically one of the strongest of men, I was afraid that the severity of the night and my exposure to it would prove fatal. I truly feared that I would be frozen to death on my post.

My comrade and I were now left all alone. We used every conceivable means to keep warm, but in vain. The blood seemed to stop circulating. Being limited to the short bounds of our post, little exercise was had in the way of walking and moving around. One of the abutments of the bridge at which the post commenced afforded slight shelter from the fury of the howling northeast wind. We eagerly availed ourselves of its protection. My companion soon began to suffer intensely from the cold. But probably no more than me. We stood close together, leaning against the abutment for probably three-quarters of an hour, discussing in a low voice the severity of the Union Army Rules then in force. They prohibited the kindling of fires for the men on the outer or front picket line. The enemy's pickets on the opposite shore had built hundreds of them which burned bright and high as far as the eye could see.

While thus engaged, my partner ceased conversing. He remained silent for a time, apparently deaf to what I was saying. A moment later he exclaimed in a husky, hoarse voice, "Bill, I'm freezing. I can't stand this. Let us go and warm up somewhere in the town. We can be back on post before the second relief comes around again and no danger exists at this point." I told him, "No."

He might do as he pleased, but as for me, I would stick to my post until relieved. I reminded him of his obligations and the penalty for breaking them. I used every effort to cheer him up, but in vain. He then left, saying he would return soon. He requested me not to give him away in case the officer of the night came around in his absence. I assured him that I would not. Away he sailed. He was a first-rate fellow, a good soldier and a warm-hearted friend to me. For these reasons, I would have proved ungrateful had I exposed his conduct on this occasion, induced only and entirely by the severity of a cold, dark winter night.*

I was now entirely alone, stiff with cold. I soon felt an unusual sleepy sensation creeping over me and a desire to lay down on the cold, wet ground. It was with great difficulty that I did not do so. I drew the large cape of my overcoat over my head, covering it all except the eyes and tied it on with a string. I stationed myself partly under the arch of the bridge which broke the force of the wind. With my hands in my pockets and my musket at my side, I determined, sink or swim, to perform my duty until regularly relieved.

The next thing I remembered was waking up from sleep on the top of a bale of cotton, covered up with army blankets in the picket headquarters. A huge log fire blazed nearby. Upon coming to life again,

---

* The punishment for leaving the picket post until properly relieved or for being found asleep upon it while on duty is the same as for desertion—namely, death by shooting.

several thoughts rushed upon me, "Where am I? Where have I been? What has happened to me? Is this a dream?"

I got up on my feet, rubbed my eyes, and then sat down again upon my bed of cotton. My limbs were stiff and painful. My ears seemed dead to feeling and touch. One of my comrades sitting at the fire then brought me a brimming tin cup full of strong, hot coffee. He said that it had been made for me "if I would ever awake again." I drank it all. Oh, how good and reviving. It was now seven a.m. With reference to what had befallen me the night before, the following statement was made to the officer of the night. He exonerated me from all blame and expressed much feeling and sympathy for me upon hearing the facts.

The sergeant of the guard stated that he arrived at Post No. 1 to relieve it at 11 p.m. He discovered me leaning against the stonework of the bridge in a stooping, bent-forward posture. He spoke several times to me, but no reply or movement was made by me. One of his men then held a lantern to my face. Turning around, this soldier suddenly exclaimed, "My God, sergeant, that man's frozen to death."

Two men then laid hold of my arms, shook me, and called me by name. After repeating the operation the third time, signs of life appeared. I opened my partly closed eyes and was carried to headquarters by the same two men, accompanied by the sergeant. I was carefully deposited on the cotton bale. The regimental doctor not then being on the ground, one from a neighboring regiment was brought to see me. He gave me some medicine and ordered that I be covered up with blankets. When the doctor left, he said to my comrades, "Had he been exposed 20 minutes longer, he would have been brought in a frozen corpse."

I was perfectly unconscious of everything that happened to me from the time I covered my head with the cape of my overcoat until I found myself lying on the cotton bale. I then learned, much to my surprise and horror, all that had happened to me on that fearful night on the banks of the Rappahannock. Half an hour later, I witnessed the arrival of an ambulance containing the bodies of two dead members of an Ohio regiment who had been frozen to death on picket duty. They were at a point on the river some two miles north of my own post. One of them was found standing against a tree dead stiff, the other lying lifeless on the ground. An hour later, the dead body of a member of a Connecticut regiment was also brought in. The arrival of these corpses created feelings of sorrow and melancholy in all present. I was particularly affected when I reflected upon my own narrow and providential escape from a similar death. It was truly a terrible night, large numbers of the Union troops being so badly frozen that they were unfit for duty for several days afterwards.

The regiment was relieved from duty at nine a.m. when the 28th Massachusetts arrived. Returning to camp, we performed only such duties as were absolutely necessary. The main order of business was rest.

Before starting for camp, however, Captain C of my own regiment[2] tendered me the privilege of remaining at rest in my tolerably comfortable quarters at Falmouth until evening. He said I could leisurely return to camp if better. By his request, I was placed in charge of the officer commanding the 28th [Colonel Richard Byrnes] who treated me in the most hospitable, kind and gentlemanly manner. He ordered me plenty to eat, lots of strong, hot coffee and piles of covering, as well as a little smuggled brandy of his own.

All that day I lived like a "fighting cock," attention and kindness heaped upon me by the men of my sister regiment. They were comparative strangers to me. Why did they treat me so well? It was certainly for nothing that I had done. It only could have proceeded from the mercy and loving kindness of God, in whose hands are the lives and destinies of the whole human race. To Him alone I ascribe this wonderful treatment.

At three p.m., my limbs feeling less painful, I thanked my benefactors. I asked for and received a pass from the commanding officer to get me through our lines between Falmouth and camp. With my constant companion, my musket slung over my shoulder, I started on my journey. I reached camp a little after five p.m., having traveled at a speed of about a mile an hour. I need hardly say that I was made welcome by the members of my own immediate military family.

At nine p.m. on the morning of the 25th, the regiment was again on the picket line. We occupied a position about a mile north of that held on the 23rd. The storm had spent itself and was followed by a delightful calm. Although the cold had but slightly abated, the weather was clear, bright and cheerful. The wet, soft ground had become dry and hard. The river which so recently had presented such a scene of turmoil and wild confusion now flowed peacefully and quietly along. Our position on this occasion was better sheltered, being along the edge of a thick woods extending back from the river's front for fully three miles. One man only was now assigned to each post, the posts being nearer to each other than before. The pickets were almost within speaking distance of each other. I was placed on Post No. 7 and assigned as before to the first relief. My post commenced at the water's edge to a point ten yards back from it. The position suited me well with the condition of my frost-bitten ears and limbs, being well sheltered by trees.

During my two hours of morning duty on post, nothing worthy of special note transpired. The weather was very clear. It afforded me an excellent opportunity to make close observations of the Confederate works over the river. The scene was truly grand and warlike. There was lots of activity, showing that the enemy had the fullest determination to resist any advance of Federal troops beyond the Rappahannock.

The headquarters of the pickets were some 300 yards back from the river and behind a low range of hills hidden from the Rebel view. The men, being without tents, improvised shelter. They divided themselves into groups or squads of from ten to fifteen men each. They then fastened together their gum blankets and suspended them overhead between trees, forming a rude kind of awning under which fires were built for the comfort and convenience of the men not on duty.

Upon coming off post at five p.m. with wolfish appetites, we found rations scarce. Seeing no near prospect of relief from Uncle Sam, four of my comrades and I determined to go on a foraging expedition. We had observed a fine-looking large farmhouse on a bluff near the Rappahannock about half a mile distant. So we started with muskets shouldered for that point. Our program was to gain admittance to the house, peacefully if possible or forcibly if necessary, after which food was to be asked for. If refused, we would seize provisions, each man agreeing to pay the owner of the property full value in greenbacks. This would be done to avoid the penalty of an army law then in force. It forbade all United States troops from seizing or appropriating private property in the enemy's country without official authority or paying its equivalent in United States money. The troops had been paid off only a day before. Consequently, each man was flush. It was nearly six p.m. and dark when we reached the place. The sky was spilling snow.

Two of the boys marched up to the door where they brought their muskets to order arms. The others, including me, kept at a distance to watch the progress of events. The door soon opened. Inside stood a rough, powerful woman, apparently of English or Irish birth. Upon seeing uniformed men, she fled out of sight and into some back apartment. The pioneers then gave us the signal to advance. We quickly obeyed. Five armed men entered the building without the slightest opposition.

Upon entering the dwelling, we proceeded along a narrow hall. It was dimly lit at the back end by a dirty oil lamp suspended from the ceiling by a small iron chain. Opposite this lamp was a closed door. It led to a room which was immediately occupied by the foragers. There we found an old man comfortably reclining on a rude wooden bench. He was quietly smoking his long pipe. The whereabouts of the rough specimen of humanity in the shape of a woman who first admitted us to the house remained a mystery.

The room was rudely furnished but warm, a large log fire roaring up a chimney of sufficient dimensions to admit two flour barrels abreast. The old Englishman, for such he turned out to be, quickly abandoned his pipe, laying it down on the seat from which he had just risen. Approaching us as we entered the room, he saluted us with, "Well, lads, what's yer will at this time a night?"

Our leader replied, "Don't get scared, dad, we're only after `grub.' That's all. Got any cold victuals about? We're damned hungry."

"Blast it," said the old man as he turned to leave the room for something to quiet our voracious appetites. "I'll see, warm yerselves, and I'll tell Peg. But make no noise, yer in dangerous quarters. The people up above," said he, pointing to the upper parts of the house, "don't like a hair on a Yankee soldier's head. All their boys are in General Lee's camp over the river. Keep quiet now, till I come back. I'll try and get ye a bite of something."

After saying this, he left the room through a door which he locked behind him. It forcibly impressed upon our minds the fact that we were caged, caught in our own trap. At least for a time, we were prisoners in the hands of our bitter enemies.*

Being now left to ourselves, our first and very natural thoughts were to form some plan by which to resist an attack. This matter, however, was easily and satisfactorily disposed of by our chief, a cool, collected, far-seeing and daring soldier. He was afraid of nothing, as he often used to say, except women and sometimes not even afraid of them. The old man had been absent probably ten minutes when our ears were greeted by the sound of heavy footsteps descending stairs. The sound came from the back part of the building. At almost the same moment of time, another and a more startling noise was heard proceeding from a room

---

*It was not uncommon in this section of Virginia for Federal soldiers to be made prisoners and sometimes even to be murdered while taking shelter in private houses or foraging.

right overhead. It sounded like a stack of arms falling down in confusion. Silence for a second or two reigned among our little band, each one looking at another in amazement.

A moment passed. In a low tone of voice, our chief gave the order, "Attention, men. Look to your pieces."

The command was quickly obeyed. The room was divided into picket posts and each man immediately went upon post duty, fully prepared to give a warm reception to anything in the shape of an enemy who would put in an appearance. By this time, the tramp of feet had died away. Not a sound was heard outside of our prison. Five minutes later, footsteps were again heard coming down a narrow flight of stairs to a little door opening into our room. The door was behind a partition not noticed before by any of us. The little door opened and our old Englishman friend again made his appearance, looking somewhat frightened and very nervous. "What's the matter?" cried one of our boys.

"How are you on the `grub' question now?" shouted another.

The old man replied in a trembling low tone of voice, evidently afraid that the people above would hear what he said. "Bad luck, boys, bad luck. They say no cursed Yankee can have a bite here. I would willingly give you all something myself, but I'm, I'm, I'm, a—afraid ye see. I'm am old, helpless man living here with my two married daughters. They are strong Secesh and both of their husbands are officers in the Rebel army. They're in General A.P. Hill's division just over the river there."

"Well, my old friend," said our chief, "that may do well enough as far as you and your folks are concerned, but it won't fill our empty stomachs. Look here, have you enough victuals to spare in this building? That's what concerns me and my men most. Answer candidly, or—."

"Plenty," returned the old man, "plenty in the cellar." He pointed to a door in a corner of the room, apparently leading to that place.

"All right," said our commander. "If you are afraid to help us, we will help ourselves." Going to the door indicated, he tried to open it but found it locked. Just then, the confused voices of women scolding and wrangling were heard from an upper room. A little later, the small door behind the partition opened. A ghastly, pale lady dressed in black stood before us, holding a small burning oil lamp. She looked at us cooly. In a perfectly composed and very ladylike manner, she addressed us saying,

"Soldiers, have you not mistaken the place? I wish you would." As she said the word "would," she burst into tears, exclaiming, "Oh, my God!"

Our leader then walked up close to her and spoke to her in a quiet, gentlemanly manner. No one could do it better than him. He said, "Madam, do not be alarmed. We only came here for something to eat, not to plunder and destroy. You know it's hard to suffer hunger when there's plenty at hand. We know you can supply our present wants without injuring yourselves. Therefore, if you do not do so, we are bound to take it forcibly. Now, what say you?"

"Well," she said, after a moment's reflection and having gained her self-composure. "I suppose we must obey the Bible's command to `feed our enemies.'"

Having said this, she drew a key from her pocket and handed it to our commander. In a gentle and feeling manner she pointed to the cellar door, saying, "Go down there and take enough to feed your men. But please don't destroy or burn anything."

Our man then went to the door. While he inserted the key in the keyhole, we heard a loud coarse voice and the hurried, heavy tramp of a woman coming down the stairs. "Don't let them, don't let them, the thieving murdering blackguards," shouted the woman, still invisible to us.

In another moment, this woman appeared. She was a sight. Her hair was disheveled and she had a face totally void of the slightest trace of her sex or intelligence. This woman was fearfully excited and bore marks of having broken away from some person endeavoring to hold her back. Her appearance was the signal for immediate seizure by our party. Another fellow and I, letting our muskets drop, sprang forward, catching her by both arms. We dragged her to the wooden bench and for a time succeeded in holding her down there. She kicked, attempted to bite, cursed, swore, cried, laughed, sent us and the whole Union Army to hell a thousand times and made every effort to break loose. The crazy woman failed for awhile.

In one of her hands, she clutched with an iron grasp which we could not break a rolling pin. It must have weighed about two pounds and was 15 or 20 inches long, the kind bakers use in rolling dough or pastry. By some sudden jerk, she broke my partner's hold of her arms. She hauled off and dealt me a blow on the mouth with the rolling pin. It drew the claret so freely that blood stained my uniform from head to feet. The rolling pin knocked out one my front teeth. I never saw or heard tell of that tooth afterwards. While all this was going on, the lady in black and the old man stood looking on in silence and amazement, all the life and excitement apparently then in the house being concentrated in that one room.

Two of our men then proceeded to the cellar. I, my mouth bleeding, was relieved from my dangerous position with the crazed woman by one of the strongest of my comrades. Our chief placed me on guard at the cellar entrance. In a very few moments the men returned, bearing in their hands and arms six large Johnny or hoe cakes. This was a kind of bread very common in Virginia. The loaves were delicious and healthy, composed of Indian meal, mutton suet and sugar. Our men had also filled two haversacks with raw potatoes. Additionally, they foraged a large, dried codfish and a glass jar full of fine mixed English pickles.

The men, without saying a word, deposited the victuals on a wooden table in the room. They winked at us. One of them quickly turned around and glanced at the woman still confined between two of our companions. He said to her, "How's that for high, old gal?"

She fairly boiled with rage, but it was of no use. "Now, madam," said our leader, addressing the lady in black, "got any pork about?"

"Nothing but livestock," replied the lady.

"Where is it?" asked my comrade.

"In the rear of the building," said the lady, "close to the edge of the woods."

"Well then, madam, we want a hog, dead or alive. Have you any objections to our killing one?"

"None now," replied the lady with a sigh. "It would be useless for me to protest against it. Take all you want. Then please, oh do please, take your departure."

Having now secured nearly all that we needed, two volunteers were called upon to go in search of the hogs. We wanted to kill a small one and bring it back to the house. Our leader and I at once responded. The remaining three men were to remain in the building until our return, one of them as guard at the rear door. The other two needed to keep the still wild, unruly and homicidal female Hibernian in proper and safe subjection until we were ready to leave the house. This being now arranged, the lady in black retired up stairs, promising to see us again on the return of the hog-hunters. The old man seated himself quietly on his bench. The guard took his post at the rear door. Two men still restrained the dangerous woman from violence. My companion and I who volunteered started down through a long, narrow hall as directed by the old man on our "pig-hunting tour." It was now seven p.m. or probably a littler later. It was absolutely necessary for us to report at camp at 8:45 p.m., ready for picket service again.

Upon emerging from the hall, we found ourselves on the edge of a large lot surrounded by thick, heavy woods. After considerable hard tramping and much seeking, owing to the darkness of the evening, we at last discovered our prey. The hogs were housed up for the night in a little enclosure near the woods. Had it not been for the kind of light which the snow, then about an inch deep on the ground, was giving us, we probably would have failed in finding our game.

But fortune smiled upon us. We approached the pen cautiously, relying upon the bayonet and butt end of the musket as the instruments for slaughter, for we dare not shoot. Gunfire would have alarmed other camps in the neighborhood. We pulled open the small door of the pen. Immediately out bounced four or five large hogs, followed by an innumerable family of youngsters, squeaking and grunting at every step, terribly frightened and running pell-mell between our legs. They knocked my companion and me down. We, however, soon regained our feet again and then commenced the chase.

After considerable racing and plunging through snow and low brushwood, my companion, whose powers of endurance in running were decidedly superior to my own, at last succeeded in cornering a fine young pig. It weighted about 40 pounds. One plunge of the bayonet pinned the pig fast to the ground. I hurried up to the spot. With two well directed and telling blows on the head of the dying little animal with the butt of my musket, I ended its suffering. We allowed it time to bleed freely, after which the pig was carefully wrapped up in a gum blanket. With our muskets in one hand and two corners of the blanket containing the dead hog in the other, my comrade and I commenced our return to the house to join our companions. We had been absent on our pig hunt probably 40 minutes. It was now nearing eight p.m.

As we entered the house with our precious burden, the guard at the door, faithful to his trust, passed us through the lines. He warmly congratulated us on our success. We walked along the hall and entered the room which was our unofficial headquarters. My companion and I deposited our load upon the floor. Matters there were pretty much the same as we had left them, the old man quietly occupying his seat before the fire and "Biddy" closely guarded by two soldiers. Our leader then announced to our old friend, the Englishman, that we were ready to leave. He requested the Englishman to call his daughter, the lady in black, so that she might receive proper compensation for the provisions about to be carried off. She soon appeared and addressed us saying, "Well men, you have succeeded."

"Yes," replied two or three voices. "Ready to settle our account with yourself or the old gentleman here. What are the damages?"

"Well," she said hesitatingly, "what kind of money have you got?"

"Greenbacks," replied our leader.

"Ah," returned the lady, "no good here."

At the same moment, the loud angry voice of "Biddy" from another part of the room was heard. She shouted, "Trash, trash, throw it in their faces, mistress. Let them wipe their asses with it, the damned Yankee murtherers and thieves."*

The violent conduct of this woman seemed now to cause much annoyance to the lady in black. She appeared considerably agitated and frightened, not knowing whether to accept greenbacks or not. There was little time to lose. Acting upon this, our leader again addressed her politely, "Madam, our time is nearly up. Will you accept our money for these articles or not? If you do, ten dollars are ready for you, what we consider fair market value."

"The imps o' the Devil, oche, listen tay them," ejaculated the woman still under guard. But no notice of her interruption being taken, the lady soon replied, "I accept your offer, the `paper' may be of some value to somebody. But pay Father and please excuse me."

She then made a graceful bow and beckoned to the dangerous domestic to follow. Both left the room. The latter heaped curses upon us and, as she termed it, bad luck to every "bluecoat."

Our business now here being ended except paying for the provisions, I walked past my companions and close up to the old gentleman. Laying my left hand upon his shoulder, I said, "Friend, what's the damage?"

"Well, lad," he replied, "it's so long since I bought or sold anything that I caunt say. Whatever the lads say themselves."**

---

*Before entering the premises, our little party agreed that we would pay $10 for provisions. Each man subscribed $2 and placed the money in my hands.

**The provisions, including the dead hog, had been placed all together on a table in the room. Judging from the looks of the pile and having some experience in the market value of such articles, I concluded that what we had now confiscated was honestly worth from $12 to $15.

"Now, boys," said I, addressing my comrades, "I want another dollar from each man, with one from myself. Out with the cash. No time to lose."

This, I suppose, took them rather by surprise. But I was fully determined not to aid in carrying away anything not paid for. Feeling sure that $10 was not a fair and just compensation for what we had ready to be removed, I concluded to pay the old man $15. Consequently, I demanded five dollars additional. My order was instantly and willingly obeyed, each man placing a greenback in my hand. I raised the amount in my possession to the required sum of $15.

I handed the old man $15, stating that the boys at first intended to have paid $10 only. He received the money thankfully, stuffing it into a breast pocket in his old coat. Going to a closet in the room, the old man brought from there five large plugs of fine Virginia tobacco, each piece nearly a pound heavy. He handed each man one of the plugs. We thanked him, after which the fruits of our foraging expedition were equally distributed among our little party for transportation. Shaking our old, kind-hearted English friend warmly by his hand, we wished him good luck and that the war would soon be over.[3]

We left the building, no doubt much to the relief of its inmates, the female portion especially. We commenced the return march to our picket relief headquarters. It was now a little after eight p.m and snow continued to fall. In order to reach headquarters in time, we found it necessary to take the shortest possible route. Accordingly, we passed through woods in the rear of the second picket line, crossed over the remains of fences, waded ditches, and frequently stumbled over piles of stones. The rough terrain, added to the state of the weather, the darkness of the night and the burdens carried, made this little march one never to be forgotten. I wished that some of our Philadelphia friends whom I had often heard say that the soldier's life in America was one of "ease and pleasure" had seen our little band returning to headquarters that night. I feel confident that such a statement would ever after be foreign to them.

We arrived at our destination about ten minutes before the first relief was ordered to "fall in." Five men who composed the squad to which my four of my companions and I were attached sat around a large log fire awaiting the summons to duty. They had been ignorant of our whereabouts and had felt anxious for our safety. The fellows were much pleased at our return in time to enter again upon the duties of the picket post with them. In a few words, we told them the cause of our absence and laid down before them the fruits of our expedition, much to their delight and joy. Knowing that only a few moments remained to us, we concluded to hide the spoil until our return from duty at 11 p.m. We carried all the articles of food into a patch of brushwood nearby and covered them over with branches and the needles from fir trees. We were just returning to our fire when the well-known voice of our post commander was heard calling, "Fall in, first relief." The command was promptly obeyed. Ten minutes later, every man was again on his post on the dark banks of the Rappahannock.

Nothing unusual occurred during this term of picket service from nine to 11 p.m. The night seemed to be unusually quiet and still on both sides of the river. The only sound heard by the sentinel on his lonely post was the distant, rumbling noise of railroad cars behind the heights of Fredericksburg. These trains were hurrying up reinforcements for the Confederate army there. It again reminded me of the gigantic preparations being made to oppose the advance of Federal troops in that direction.[4] The river too, as it hurried along peacefully to be lost in Chesapeake Bay, shared in the stillness of the night. The flowing waters were only heard only where they rushed among a few isolated rocks in the center of the Rappahannock. This sound was both pleasing and melancholy to the attentive listener.

Upon coming off duty at 11 p.m., we had as usual ravenous appetites. But fortunately this time we had something good and choice to fall back on. We first built a scorching fire of pine logs which reflected light and heat all around. The food hidden away was next brought forward and the hog was prepared for roasting. This was done in a style novel to the majority of my companions and me. The cook was a certain officer of my own company. He performed the work in a manner which excited my greatest curiosity and admiration. It proved to be a valuable lesson.

The officer first prepared a paste of moist earth and clay. This paste was placed two or three inches thick all around the hog in its natural state. The whole was then laid in the middle of the fire. The mud-covered pig was blanketed over with hot ashes and burning wood. About an hour after, it was drawn out. The coating of clay, then burnt to a crisp, fell in pieces. It revealed roast pork. For flavor and whiteness, I never tasted anything as good. This mode of cooking was not only easy. The entire juice and flavor of the meat thus cooked was retained and not allowed to escape as is the case in boiling or frying. I often afterwards saw chicken cooked in the same way. I heard several months after leaving the army that the style of cooking meats which I have just

described had become very general among all the troops and their officers.

A little before nine a.m. on the morning of November 26th, the
regiment was again relieved by the arrival of the old and famous 69th
New York of our Irish Brigade. After nearly an hour's march through a
dry snow and keen, sharp air, we arrived in camp and built rousing fires.
Fresh rations being issued, the men anticipated another day of rest and
good living. They were not disappointed. A gay and happy time was
enjoyed by all in many different ways, not ceasing till long after dark.
Then, as was expected, notice was given for the regiment to report again
to Falmouth next morning for picket duty.

For two or three days previous to this time, occasional cannonading
was heard at this place. It came from a southerly direction. Various
rumors floated about as to its cause but nothing definite could be
learned until some time afterwards. Later it was announced officially in
camp that heavy detachments of the Confederate army had been driven
back by a portion of General Siegel's command at United States Ford.
The Rebs made several attempts to cross the river at that point, in the
hope of getting at our rear and flanking our army on this side of the
river. If successful, this maneuver would have placed the Union forces
between two terrible fires, namely from a Rebel army in the rear and the
Rebel batteries on the heights of Fredericksburg in front. But Siegel, ever
on the watch, drove them back after several artillery skirmishes and
prevented their passage of the river.[5]

November 27th, 1862

The morning of the 27th was in reality a grand and glorious one.
The ground, which the day before had been damp, muddy and slippery,
was now hard and comparatively dry. It was lightly coated with snow
made crisp by the previous night's freezing. Not a breath of wind was
heard among the trees of the immense forest in which our camps were
located. Owing to the good weather and an abundant supply of fresh
rations, including plenty of newly killed beef, the troops were jubilant
and seemed to have forgotten past hardship and suffering.

At eight a.m., our bugle called "Attention" and then "Forward,
march." The regiment was again in motion towards Falmouth. The
little town was reached forty minutes afterwards. At nine a.m., every
picket post assigned to the regiment was fully manned. Our principal
posts on this occasion were on the edge of the river, immediately oppo-

site Fredericksburg. They were occupied by two men each. Other posts of less importance were occupied by one man each. The picket line extended for a quarter of a mile above the ill-fated city. Our picket relief headquarters was in an old, unoccupied frame house on the top of a bluff overlooking the Rappahannock, nearly opposite Fredericksburg, and a mile or so south of Roundtop Mountain. About 300 yards back from this building stood a neat, large farmhouse surrounded by tall trees. It was occupied, as we afterwards learned, only by a few female slaves, their children and Massa Turner (or Toner) as the slaves called him. The house and indeed all around it bore the marks of good care. It obviously was the home of someone in the upper and higher walks of life. This we found out to be the case. We also discovered that "Massa," although of Southern birth and parentage, was a thorough and true Union man. He was a zealous advocate of the Union's causes and principles, something rare indeed to find in this part of old Virginia. Later that day, Turner himself informed us that his wife and grownup sons and daughters, whom he termed "Redhot Secesh," had deserted and left him and their home because of his devotion to the Union.

"And all," he said, "for my fidelity to our country's cause."

Another member of my company and I were assigned to the third relief on November 27th. We went on duty at one p.m. at Post No. 4, which was located in a thick woods running from the very edge of the river several miles back into the country. The post was on the brink of the stream opposite the most compactly built part of Fredericksburg. Rebel picket posts extended along the shore as far as the eye could reach. Here I saw a Confederate picket arrested by his officers and marched back under guard for discharging his piece at a duck or some other fowl in the water.

Nothing unusual transpired here during daytime. The weather was truly lovely, bright, bracing and cheerful, so mild that many of our men not on duty could be seen reclining on grassy mounds behind our picket lines. The atmosphere being so clear, I enjoyed a more extensive and grander view of the Rebel works and fortifications than upon any previous occasion. I became more and more convinced that any attack made upon them by the Union forces from the northern side of the river would only prove a terrible disaster and defeat.[6]

It was custom in the Army of the Potomac to provide a guard of two to five men for any house or building of value within Federal lines. Such was particularly the case when the property belonged to a Union man or one reputed to be such. This was done to prevent vandalism by a certain class of Federal soldiery. I am glad to say there were few of them. These tramps seemed to care little about the abuse which they gave other people's property.

Sometime during the day, the occupant and owner of the Turner farmhouse made a request for two men of our regiment to guard his house and property during our short stay of only 24 hours. The application was soon granted. After coming off duty on Post No. 4 at three p.m., my companion and I were privately informed by our commanding officer, Lt. Nolan of Co. G, a Philadelphian with whom I had lately become very intimate and friendly, that we would protect the house. We of course replied at once that we would. He then directed us to follow him as we were required to go on duty at once. Obeying his order, we soon arrived at a little gate through which we passed. Then we walked along a wide gravel walk to our destination, the house of Mr. Turner, where we were met by that gentleman himself at the door. Our commanding officer introduced us as the guard requested. The officer then left after instructing us on our duty. Lt. Nolan ordered us to report at picket headquarters next morning at 8:45 a.m. and to return to camp with the regiment at nine a.m.

Mr. Turner now invited us into his house. There he made known to us his recent difficulties with his family on account of his Union principles. He introduced us to the only inmates of his dwelling, three female slaves and their children, some ten or eleven in number of the genuine ebony hue. Turner made known to us fears which he entertained. He assured my companion and me of his implicit confidence in us both as men and as soldiers of the Federal army. Turner proffered us free access to all parts of his house and ground at any hour of the day or night while on duty. He instructed the slaves to supply us liberally with the best cooked provisions within his home, as well as splendid cider with which the cellar was well stocked. Turner also informed us that our colonel had kindly consented to reinforce us at eight or nine p.m. with two other reliable men. He then bade us goodbye, saying that he would retire and seek a little rest and sleep which he had been denied for the last three days and nights. The master left himself and his entire premises under our care and protection. It was now nearly five p.m. and almost dark.

Upon being left alone, my comrade and I, acting on Mr. Turner's recommendation and also feeling very tired because we just came off picket duty, walked into to his parlor. It was a large and most comfortably furnished room. There we found half an hour's rest and ease upon

soft, cushioned lounges and chairs. Oh, what strange luxury and indescribable ease when compared to our soldier's bed in the field. This
parlor brought back memories of our own comfortable homes far away.
Perhaps at that very hour, our families were praying for our safety.

Soon after entering the room, I sat down on a lounge near a window. I had a beautiful view of the surrounding country, although it was
desolate and wasted. I could also see many of our principal picket posts
in the distance on the bluffs overhanging the Rappahannock. My companion occupied another seat of the same kind nearby. Although not
intending to sleep, slumber stole a march upon me. The next thing I
heard was my partner shaking me violently and shouting, "Bill, wake
up, don't leave me all alone."

I quickly obeyed the summons. I was somewhat mortified and
surprised that my fatigue had so far overpowered me. It was now close
to six p.m.

My companion and I were ravenous, ready to eat anything. It was
not long before our appetites were appeased. At half past six, one of the
black women entered the room with a joyful, happy, smiling face. I can
still see in my mind today the delight on her countenance. She addressed us, saying, "Now, Honeys, come to supper. Come. De Lor bress.
Oh, De Lor bress Massa Lincoln's men."

She then conducted us into a neat, though small, dining room. In
its center stood a table, fairly groaning with the weight of the good
things upon it. It was covered with a snow white table cloth, the first
thing of the kind that I had seen in Virginia. The food was coarse and
plain, but plenty. It consisted of small roasted pig, two or three boiled
rabbits, hoe-cake, white potatoes and an immense apple pie. To wash all
these down, there was an enormous quantity of cider. Oh, what living
for soldiers in the field, I thought to myself, in the very heart of the
enemy's country. As my eye scanned the grand and plentiful layout, I
felt satisfied there were yet left some good things in Old Virginia.

Our colored waitress now handed forward two chairs and invited us
to sit down and eat. She said, "Now, Honeys, guess yer hungry. Massa
telt me to git de sodgers plenty to eat for de wer a fiten to free our people
down South. Gemen, I tried my purtiest. Sit down, gemen and eat
hearty. Plenty more in de kitchen if ye need it. Plenty more, gemen.
Massa telt me, Massa telt me, gemen." Bounding forward, she spoke
again, "De Lor bress Massa Lincoln's men." Then she disappeared,
closing the door behind her, leaving my companion and me to enjoy the
feast.

Soon after finishing the bountiful meal, our colored friend again appeared. She carried in her arms a long box containing tobacco, the genuine and unadulterated Old Virginian, and pipes. She deposited both the pipes and tobacco on a little table near my comrade's side. Then she said, "Guess de gemen likes to smoke."

Of course, that was just "our style." Especially at that particular time, right after eating. We unhesitatingly replied, "Yes, certainly, Aunty."

She then was again about to leave us to enjoy a quiet smoke when I stopped her. I said, "Look here, Aunty, this won't do. Can't you let us smoke in the kitchen?"

"Bress ye, yes, honey. But I did not like to ask ye out there."

"Just the thing for us, Aunty," I replied, "please pilot us to it."

At once complying, she conducted us to the kitchen. It was a large, long room with a boarded floor and low ceiling, liberally stacked with kitchen furniture and cooking utensils. It had a fireplace fully eight feet long. Large hearths were common in Virginia for burning huge logs of wood. An immense fire on a cold winter night not only made the room in which it was built exceedingly comfortable, but also bright and cheerful. I have often wished that such fireplaces were as general in the North as they were in this section of the South.

"There, geman," said the woman as we entered the kitchen, pointing to a long bench near the large log fire. "There's Massa's seat, jist sit ye down on't an' make yerselves comfortable." We did so. How comfortable, how homelike it was. What a jolly, old-time smoke we enjoyed. During our term of duty at Mr. Turner's house, we made this room our headquarters. Mr. Turner's slaves heaped one kindness after another upon us. Those poor, downtrodden, dark people of the South treated us like kings.

My unexpected visit to this place afforded me the opportunity of observing how a Southern female slave family lived. The children of the three slave women, whose ages varied from five to 13 years, and the parents themselves seemed to me to be the happiest, healthiest and most contented people I ever saw. Their modesty was beautiful and commendable. Much to my surprise, their intelligence, particularly in religious matters, was far beyond that of thousands of the opposite color in the free North. The little darkies appeared to vie with each other in attending to the wants and requests of "Uncle Abe's" men, as my comrade and I were called. Their love, honor and quick obedience to their parents was singularly pleasing and attractive. It brought to my mind the Divine Command, "Honor thy Father and thy Mother."[7]

I wanted to learn something more in regard to these interesting people. I determined to seize the first opportunity to ask the woman a few questions on that subject. It was now eight p.m.. The promised two men to reinforce us for the night had arrived. They joined my partner and me on the bench opposite the roaring fire. The children had noiselessly left the room for bed. The women, having finished their work for the day and, being smokers of tobacco, were invited to seats beside us to smoke their pipes before retiring. They accepted the invitation thankfully. They thought it an honor conferred upon them.

It was the time for me to ask them a few simple questions. I wish that some of my Philadelphia friends had seen that group. In that cozy, bright, warm room filled with tobacco smoke, there was nothing but good humor and goodwill towards one another, black and white. We enjoyed ourselves on that bitter, cold December night, literally within the range of 400 Rebel guns.[8]

Four prominent generals of the Army of the Potomac (upper right, clockwise): George McClellan; Ambrose Burnside; Winfield Hancock; and Edwin Sumner.

"I was again favored with a most commanding view of the Rebel works, which impressed me even more than before of a unanimous purpose and determination on the part of the Confederates to fight to the last."

Chapter 7

Fredericksburg: The Eve of Battle

At last an opportunity presented itself to ask a few questions of the three slave women. I certainly made the most of it. I first asked them where they had been born. Two of the women answered that they were natives of Louisiana, where they said they had a good "Massa" who treated them well and taught them to read and even to write. But soon after the outbreak of the war, their "Massa's" plantation had been burnt and destroyed by both Union and Confederate soldiers. Desiring to escape North, fearful of capture by the Rebels, they had entered the Union lines near New Orleans. Reaching this part of Virginia, they had met Mr. Turner. They volunteered their services to him. He took the two of them into his house. They had lived with him for 14 or 15 months.

Their children had accompanied them on their journey, some of them sharing the hospitality of Mr. Turner and the rest that of a neighboring planter. Their husbands, they stated, had entered the Union Army about the same time that they sought protection of the Union lines on their way northward. The other woman, who was much the older of the three, stated that she did not know her exact age, but thought it to be about 63 years. She had been born in Georgia and there sold when a mere girl to the father of Mr. Turner. After his death, she became the property of his son, her present owner. To use her own words, she was "considered one of the Turner family." She was the mother of four children, all residing with her there, her husband having died several years ago. When I asked her if she was satisfied with her condition as a slave, she seemed astonished at the question. She replied, "Yes, I guess I is. Da good Lor gives me all I want."

I asked, "Would you not like to be free?"

Her reply was, "Why, child, what do ye mean? Free, free. I could not be freer than I am here. De good Lor has given me and my children de best Massa in de South. Got all we want, I tell ye ge'men, got all we want, all we want."

I then inquired of her if she would not like to see her less fortunate people in slavery set free. I told her that Mr. Lincoln and his army were now trying to liberate the slaves. This seemed to touch her heart and feelings more forcibly than any of the previous questions, for lifting up her hands, with tears plainly visible in her eyes, she said, "Honey, de Lor bress good Massa Lincoln and all his men. I pray de Lor for them every day. Ye see, I was only telling ye about myself."

I then asked her how she and her children got the education which they had, to which she replied, "Massa Turner taught me reading and writing 20 years ago. Now he sends the children to school in Falmouth every Saturday and Sunday and lets me go to bible schooling once a week."

First-rate old gal, I thought to myself. Slavery after all, at least in this case, was not so bad as it was invariably represented by people in the North. This conversation proved to me that, in some locations of the South, slavery existed only in name. Some, if not many, of the so-called slaves preferred their kind of life to a free one in which permanent employment and even tolerably comfortable homes or places of abode might have been uncertainties to them.[1]

At ten p.m., the women retired, leaving my three companions and me in sole charge of the house and premises. Before leaving the room, however, the eldest woman went to a large closet and brought from there a quantity of cold roast pork and bread and butter. She deposited them on the table, after which she brought up from the cellar a bucket full of cider, setting it near the table. "Now, ge'men," said she, as she modestly bade us goodnight with a blessing truly rich and beautiful, "Now, just help yerselves when ye feel like eating."

We said that we certainly would. And we most certainly did. Strange as it may appear, at least half of the cider was still in the bucket next morning, although none of our party were temperance men. We preferred our favorite army beverage, strong, hot coffee. The old woman had also most liberally supplied us with this nourishing drink. Such good living and comfortable quarters in the very face of the enemy were almost too much of a good thing to endure.

Our picket headquarters was in a log hut formerly occupied by slaves, situated about 300 yards south of Mr. Turner's house. Because of the rotation by pickets, this hut was normally occupied by from 20 to 30 of our men not on duty. At eleven p.m., my companion who first went on guard with me at Mr. Turner's house and I decided to make a short visit to the hut to see how the boys were getting along. The two companions who had recently reinforced us agreed to take good care of the Turner home while we were gone. We started our journey.

The night was still, dark and cold, the only attraction to the eye of the soldier being the innumerable campfires of the enemy on the opposite shore. Here and there we could see the glimmering light of a small fire along the Union lines. We approached the headquarters hut as noiselessly as possible, not wishing to be seen until we saw what was going on inside. We went round to the south side of the structure. There we found a small window about three feet square, out of which poured a glare from the fire within. For brightness and dimensions, it would have made three respectable locomotive headlights. "A fine target for the Rebs," I whispered to my companion, "if they should feel inclined to send over a few feelers in the shape of shells and cannon balls."

"Ditto," said he.

We then peeped through the window and saw several of the boys seated around a fire. The blaze was so large that it seemed like a whole cord of wood had been ignited. Soldiers laid upon the floor in all conceivable positions, a few sleeping, others silent and thoughtful, and, as usual, many smoking and telling yarns. The scene, although a rough one, was to me a most beautiful one. It presented at almost the hour of midnight, a real picture of the soldier's life in time of war.

Satisfied with what we saw from outside, we entered the hut by a door on the opposite side. We were made welcome and invited to seats near the fire. I sat for a few moments in silence, scanning every face, nook and corner in the little enclosure. I wondered if the danger which I had seen had not been thought of by any of those present. Much to my surprise, I soon discovered that just such ignorance prevailed. Rising up, I inquired quietly for the officer of the night. I was was told that he was in Falmouth and expected back in time to post the third relief at three a.m. "Well," said I to my nearest neighbor, "please loan me your blanket, I left my own behind."

"Yes," he said, "but what the devil do you want with a blanket here?"

"No matter, you'll seen see," I replied.

Taking it off his shoulder, he handed it to me. At the same time, he eyed me rather suspiciously. Pulling two nails out of a board, I made my way among the men scattered around in all directions to the window. The stream of dangerous light was still pouring out. I nailed the blanket up against it, completely hiding from outside view the glare of the fire within.

"What's that for?" asked one in astonishment.

"What does he mean?" said another, and so on.

"Oh, nothing in particular," I returned, "but you see that fire there, don't you?"

"Yes, what of it?"

"You see that window?" I asked.

"Yes."

"And you saw those `shooting irons' over the river today?" I queried.

"Yes."

"Well, now I'll tell you exactly what I mean. I thought that some of us might get our heads knocked off in time enough without coaxing the Rebs by the light of that fire shining in their faces."

The hint was taken at once. "By damn, Bill, we never thought of it. Good for you, old boy," said one fellow.

"Now, boys," I said, "douse the glim." This was slang for put or let the fire go out. "Don't put another stick on it tonight."

We then retired to an adjoining clump of woods, there to await developments. The hut was dangerous ground since the fire had burned so bright and long. Everything on the Confederate side of the river, however, continued quiet for some time afterwards. No demonstration of any kind was made by the enemy against the hut. Yet something told me that there was "music and mischief" in the air. I said so to some of the boys. I also said that it was impossible for the hut to have escaped Rebel observation. I predicted that the hut would be shelled before morning's dawn.

My guard companion and I returned a little later to Turner's house to see how matters were progressing there. As before, all was serene and lovely in that place. After telling the two men on guard in the house what had happened on our visit to headquarters, we returned to the boys still in the woods. We were informed by them that nothing alarming had as yet occurred. At about one a.m., an hour after the second relief had been posted, we again took possession of the hut. We thought that it was now comparatively safe. We kept up a low fire sufficient to counteract the chilling effects of the cold, damp night. But we stopped up every hole and crevice through which the faintest light might reveal our position to the enemy.

An apparently old and well-used bedstead stood in one corner of the hut. Upon it laid a mattress, bolster and counterpane. Feeling somewhat sleepy, I slipped over and laid down upon it. I stood my musket against one of the posts close to my head. I requested my companion to wake me up in an hour, in time for the posting of the third relief. Before laying down, however, an object which seemed to have been carelessly thrown or kicked under the bed attracted my attention. I picked it up and found it to be an old Bible. It had the name of Sallie Jackson or Johnson written on the flyleaf and an illegible date. I tore the leaf out and put the book into my haversack. I intended to keep it and take it home, should I live, as a memento of this terrible war.

On the inside cover, I wrote a plain inscription with pencil. The following is an exact copy:

"William McCarter,
Company A,
116th Regiment Pennsylvania Volunteers
Found in a Negro's hut, near Falmouth, Virginia
while on Picket duty in the Rappahannock
on the night of Thursday, November 27th, 1862"

In a few moments I was fast asleep. The boys sat around the little fire spending time in their usual manner. Oh, how I must have slept! But I did not enjoy it long. In about half an hour, just as I had commenced to play some beautiful tunes on my "nasal organ," I suddenly found myself caught by the leg and jerked out of the bed. I sprawled on my back on the floor.

I soon, however, jumped upon my feet. Matters were in terrible confusion. The boys were rushing pell-mell out of the little door, calling to me as they went, "Get, Bill, get, quick, quick."

I was soon on the double-quick too, knowing that such a hasty retreat could only be caused by most imminent danger. We ran to the woods and I there learned its cause. A shell, notwithstanding the tacit agreement existing between Rebel and Union pickets, from a Confederate battery had been thrown at the hut while I slept. Fortunately, it missed and burst fifty feet away without injuring anyone. We waited for more of the deadly messengers while standing behind trees for protection. Nor had we to wait long. We were evidently marked by the enemy or at least the hut was. Judging from the shots fired, the Rebs had made decent progress in getting our correct range. In about ten minutes, another missile came hissing over the tops of the trees and fell between the hut and Mr. Turner's private house. It burst with a frightful noise, injuring none of us who were considerable distance away. But the shell killed a cavalry horse tied to a tree. The shell broke the leg of another horse, which next morning had to be dispatched with bullets to put it out of pain.

At almost the same moment, another shell came along. Falling far short of its mark, it buried itself without exploding in the side of a bluff in soft earth. Nor had the Johnnies done with us yet. Oh, no, indeed. In a very short space of time, bang went another Rebel gun and over came another shell. It swept through the air like a fiery tailed comet, eliciting the cry of "Look out there" from us all. Hitting a barrel used for a chimney top on the hut, the missile shivered it to pieces, together with portions of the wooden roof nearby. All fell down on the fire below, igniting the whole woodwork. In five minutes, the entire structure was wrapped in flames. "What about my prediction, now?" I said to a comrade.

"Right again," replied he.*

The hut was now in flames and illuminating the sky. The night was pitch dark, so the flames appeared even brighter. Our little party retired deeper into the woods, fearing that the light would reveal our exact position to the enemy. The Rebs would undoubtedly have thrown

---

* Persons who have never seen artillery firing are apt to suppose that a cannon ball or shell after leaving the muzzle of the gun cannot be seen passing through the air. Such is not the case. It can be followed without difficulty with the eye. A person standing in its track, if at a reasonable distance from the gun, can dodge the ball or shell if he is watchful and quick.

shells among us. But, fortunately, we escaped such a catastrophe. The hut soon burned to the ground. The bright light which had shone gave place to total darkness and a death-like stillness all around.

Fears were now entertained by some of our men that Mr. Turner would hold us responsible for the destruction of the hut. It too was his property. I said that I did not see how he could. However, my companion and I started again for his house to break the news to him, leaving the rest of the boys shivering and shaking in the cold, dark woods. We had not proceeded far before we met the gentleman himself, half dressed, coming over to see. He asked, "Has anyone had been killed or wounded?"

Upon our informing him that there were no casualties whatever among the troops, which we considered almost miraculous, he seemed much relieved and thankful. Addressing us, he said, much to our gratification and considerable surprise, "Well, can't help it, damn the old place. It was about time it was out of the way anyhow." Continuing, he said, "The boys will have no shelter now. Just go back and tell them that when not on duty to make my house their headquarters until morning."

Of course we obeyed this order immediately. I need hardly add that it was news entirely unexpected by the boys and most welcome to them. Soon afterwards, the cozy kitchen in Mr. Turner's house was occupied by some 28 to 30 members of my regiment. We stayed there until break of day, the jolliest time with plenty to eat and drink. It was the best time we men ever spent in the Army of the Potomac.

Nothing worthy of note transpired during the remaining few hours of service at Turner's house. At five a.m., the slave women were again about. Pursuant to Mr. Turner's orders, they provided our entire party, although a large and unexpected one, with breakfast consisting of good hot coffee, salt fish and cornbread. All the men excepting three companions and me specially detailed as guards at the house left afterwards for other parts on the picket line. At half past eight a.m., we bade Mr. Turner and his household goodbye, thanking him and his slaves for their hospitality and kindness. In return, we received from Mr. Turner his thanks for our services and from his slave women a "blessing." That benediction certainly followed some of us afterwards.

We reached the regiment partly drawn up in line, ready to move at the appointed time. At half past nine a.m., our pickets all being called in from the front, the entire command commenced its return march to camp. A Michigan regiment took our place on the picket line.

In Camp near Falmouth, Virginia
Friday, November 28th, 1862

Notwithstanding almost daily picketing by our regiment, the 116th was again ordered out on the following morning. We were ordered to a point on the picket line some two miles east of our position on the 27th. Nothing particular occurred on the march. The weather, although cloudy and dark, was not unpleasantly cold, at least while the troops continued in motion. I was attached as before to the first relief, and, with another comrade, went upon duty at nine a.m. on Post No. 13 near the river.

I was again favored with a most commanding view of the Rebel works, which impressed me even more than before of a unanimous purpose and determination on the part of the Confederates to fight to the last. Little, however, did I think that this was to be my last day's experience of picket service, but it was.

While standing on my post a little after ten a.m., I observed a mounted horseman, accompanied by an officer on foot, slowly approaching my position. Upon coming closer, I at once recognized General Meagher's orderly, my friend Lt. Nolan. Nearer and nearer they came, until the horseman brought his bearer to a halt at my side. The lieutenant addressed the rider and pointed at me. Nolan said, "Here's your man, orderly," in a very jocose manner. He then drew from his pocket an envelope containing a paper and said to me, "Here's a warrant for you. Consider yourself under arrest." Then handing me the enclosure, for he and I were quite intimate at this time, Nolan said, "Here it is, read for yourself."

I did so. I found as near as I can recollect, for I had no time to take an exact copy of the paper, the following: "Look up McCarter, a young Irishman of Company A of your regiment and send him with bearer forthwith to my tent. Fill his place in the line with another man, Signed, T. F. Meagher."

"All right," I said, somewhat curious to know what the general wanted with me. "Shall I go now, Lieutenant?"

"Oh, no," he replied, "remain on your post until I send you a substitute. The orderly will wait on you till then."

He then left, saying that another man would be on hand in half an hour to take my place when the orderly and I could start for the General's headquarters in our camp. I then inquired of the messenger if he knew why I was wanted. He replied, "No," stating that he did not know what the envelope contained until it was opened by the commanding officer at picket headquarters.

In a little more than an hour later, the orderly and I reached and entered General Meagher's tent. We found that officer dictating an army document to his adjutant, who was writing it on his desk. Upon entering, the usual military salute passed between both parties. General Meagher said, "Glad to see you, McCarter." He then took me by the hand and continued, "Didn't expect you so soon. I like promptness." Turning round to the adjutant, who, by the way, was staring at me with open mouth and eyes, Meagher said, "Adjutant, this is one of Colonel Heenan's men of the 116th, the best penman in the brigade. Here," he continued as he opened a portfolio, "here is some of his writing, just look at it and see if you can beat it."

The adjutant took a sharp, scrutinizing look at the written paper, then at me, and asked how I did it, if with plain pen and ink. I only replied with a nod. "Well," he said, "I have been among some of the best penmen in the city of Boston for the last seven years, but I'll be hanged, General, if any of them could touch that. I don't wonder that the general wants you here. But instead of coming as `my' assistant, I must ask to become `yours.'"

General Meagher smiled. "I told you so," he said. "But come, let us finish up the work now in hand. Mac will copy it afterwards in this style," pointing to the portfolio. "It will tickle Hancock, since he wants it to be forwarded to Washington tonight."[2]

The general requested me to take a seat at the fire until the paper would be ready, which I did. Drawing from my blouse pocket my old and faithful army pipe, I double-charged it with the real Virginia weed handed me just then by the general. In a short time, I was enjoying a smoke from a pipe which seemed to be going by steam.* I had been seated by the general's fire for probably an hour, waiting upon him and the adjutant to finish the document then in their hands which I was to copy, when the cook, an old Irishman of the ranks, announced that dinner was ready. It was most welcome news to me in particular as I expected to be a sharer.

---

* For the information of any of my readers not knowing what the duties of "adjutants" were, at least during my life in the army, I may state that the Adjutant-General was the official dispenser of all military orders and the receiver of every species of military report, document and suggestion. Assistant Adjutant-Generals of equal or proportionate rank were assigned to every corps, division and brigade. All of these formed an independent roll in the lists of the army, having its own fixed duties as well as its own system

"Shall I bring it in, General?" politely continued the man with the apron.

"Certainly, Joseph," was the reply, "and set an extra place for another."

"Good boy," I said to myself, "that's the talk."

In a very few minutes the cook returned, carrying the victuals, consisting of salt-broiled salmon, potatoes with their jackets on, fresh army biscuit, butter, hot coffee with condensed milk and a metal pitcher of cold water. A small camp table covered with an India rubber blanket was set in the center of the tent. Upon the table the feast was placed, together with three tin plates, three tin cups and three knives and forks. All now being ready, the general arose. In his usual gentlemanly manner and Irish way, he invited the adjutant and me to join him in campfare, saying, "Now, my boys, help yourselves to whatever is before you."

I need hardly say that there was at least one in that little party who did ample justice to the eatables and who seemed to be made most welcome to them. After dinner, the work on the document was resumed. But, before it was completed, a dispatch was received from division headquarters asking if the paper was finished as it had to be mailed at four p.m. for Washington. It was then after three p.m. General Meagher replied verbally, noting that it would be sent over in due time, but he also said, "Tell the general for me to excuse its roughness as the time was too limited to get it up otherwise. I intended to have sent him a decent paper but cannot now, under the circumstances, do so."

Thus, I got out of one job of writing which, judging from its length and careless penmanship, would have been no easy one for me. The document, I afterwards learned, related to serious charges against a certain officer. It also covered the erection of winter quarters by the Irish Brigade in this vicinity and a few other military matters of less importance.

of promotion. Every document intended for the perusal or approval of the commander had to ascend regularly from its starting point through the line of adjutants and be first read or approved by each general to whom one of these adjutants was assigned. If any of them disapproved of it, its upward course was not always stopped but the hopes of its final approval were not very flattering. Every military paper was, or should have been signed "By order of General A.B.C.D.; Assistant Adjutant-General." The "adjutants" were simply the secretaries and clerks of the army, keeping its records and account and performing other military duties, a description of which would occupy too much space and time to narrate, and in such a position I now found myself placed.

The paper now being finished and sent away, General Meagher remarked that he had hoped "this day's scribbling" was ended. He never had been a good "quill driver" and never expected to be. "Now, Mac," he said, "I have a private matter of my own which I would like you to attend to at your convenience. I want you to get it up for me in your very best style _ something like this," opening his portfolio and laying his hand upon the verses there, copied by me in Philadelphia. "It is a poem of some 37 or 38 verses, of my own composition. It is titled, `Midnight on the Potomac.' I wish it written in this book," he said, unlocking a tin box and taking therefrom the most beautiful scrapbook I ever saw, labelled in large fancy guilded letters: "Thomas Francis Meagher, from his Friends in Ireland, January 1st, 1862."

"You are relieved of all regimental duties and I have notified your colonel to that effect. Consider yourself, until otherwise notified, my own private secretary and attached to these headquarters," stated Meagher.

I was so completely overcome at this that I burst into tears. All that I could say at the moment was, "Thank you general, I certainly never dreamed of this." The incident when I had saved General Meagher from the campfire flashed like lightning upon my mind. The honor which he had now conferred upon me was an unmistakable proof that he had not forgotten me. I was convinced more than ever before that the simplest act of kindness or assistance extended by man to his fellow man, although for a time may seem to be forgotten, will undoubtedly be remembered and rewarded so at some time and in some way or another.

Soon after dispatching the paper to division headquarters, General Meagher notified me that he was going away for a few hours and would leave everything within his tent under my care. The guard outside would see that no one should enter it unless properly authorized to do so. I was, therefore, soon alone. Having no writing of an official character to do then, nor until next day, I embraced the opportunity to commence writing the poem by General Meagher. I had just finished the fourth verse when the General returned. He seemed highly pleased with my work and passed some very handsome compliments upon the penmanship.

"But, General," I said, " it will appear to you to better advantage when it is finished. I would prefer you not to see again till that time."

"All right," said he, "just as you wish." He then unbuckled his sword and hung it upon the center pole of the tent. Meagher lit a cigar, pulled off his long army boots and sat down at the fire to warm his feet, saying to me as he did so, "Now, Mac, I am here. If you feel inclined to take a stroll over among the boys, you are perfectly at liberty to do so. But," he continued, "be here again at eight p.m. Joseph will have supper ready then. Have you received the countersign for the night?"

"No, sir," said I.

"Well, you may need it," he said, whispering to me the words, "Forty-Four."

"Thank you, General," I returned. After again lighting my pipe, I sallied forth into the woods, beautifully illuminated by hundreds of bright campfires. Around these fires the boys were whiling away yet another dark night in the Army of the Potomac. All is well, I thought, as I slowly sauntered along, having no one particular point in view to visit. Reviewing General Meagher's kindness to me, I concluded that it was no wonder that the Irish Brigade was so devoted to its commander. It has been said that our boys would fight "through seas of blood" if ordered to do so by Meagher.

I need hardly say that my return to headquarters was at the specified time. With General Meagher, I partook of another hearty meal. It consisted of coffee, roasted potatoes, hardtack and butter. Supper over, the general and I vacated the tent for the outside, he with his cigar and me with my pipe, filled at his expense with prime cut and dry Virginia tobacco. Seating ourselves at the large log fire close at hand, around which some 12 or 15 officers and privates were resting and warming themselves, we enjoyed a quiet evening smoke. We joined in with our companions in usual campfire talk. At nine p.m., "tattoo" sounded on the drums all around. This being the signal to retire, the bustling and living campgrounds of 200 regiments soon became as still and silent as a churchyard, not even the tread of a sentinel being heard owing to the softness of the ground.

The general, however, did not retire to sleep, but merely reentered his tent, beckoning me to follow. I did so while he lighted two candles, placed them on his desk and commenced to write. "Now, Mac," he said, pointing to a rude but not uncomfortable couch in one corner of the tent, "you can `bunk' any time you wish. I must remain up for several hours yet as there is to be a special meeting here tonight at eleven p.m. of distinguished officers."

It was then half past nine. "All right general," I said, "but will not my presence be objectionable during the meeting?"

He smiled as he replied, "Oh, no, I'll fix that. Sit down, however, for a while and look over some newspapers here and keep me company."

I at once obeyed while he went on writing. Time passed quickly. Before I knew it, 10:45 p.m. had arrived with the general still busy at his desk. Not wishing to interrupt him by asking him whether I had better retire to my couch or to the outside when the officers began to assemble, I quietly arose. Approaching him closely, I said, "General, it's near eleven p.m. and the meeting hour. With your permission I prefer going outside until it is over."

"Certainly," he returned, "if you prefer doing so. One of my orderlies is afloat yet in his tent and you can spend the time with him. He is a first rate fellow. In the meantime, please go over and tell him that I wish to see him for a moment immediately."

After notifying the orderly whom I found fast asleep in his tent, I returned to my retreat at the campfire. The orderly took his post at the general's tent door, ready to usher the expected visitors into his presence upon their arrival. Being somewhat curious myself to see who they were, I took a position such as would permit of a good view of them in passing into the general's quarters.

About twenty minutes past eleven they arrived, but who they were I did not know, nor could I afterwards find out. However, I am almost sure that of the five who constituted that meeting, two of them I would not be far mistaken in saying were Generals Burnside and Hancock. I had more than once or twice met and seen Hancock and Burnside before. Owing to the darkness of the night and the close manner in which they were muffled up with their big, heavy army coats while passing by me, the officers were not perfectly recognizable. Their build and carriage, however, were familiar to me, having been a close observer of these men when opportunity offered. It brought me to the conclusion now that they were the distinguished men whom I have named.[3] The meeting closed at 12:30 p.m. and the officers returned quietly to their quarters. The general then invited me to retire, first handing me a glass of old brandy. Hoping to find me well and ready for work next day, Meagher said, pointing to several loose papers on his desk, "Here's plenty for you to do."

I pulled off my boots and cap, bade him goodnight and jumped into my new bunk. I slumbered like a "Know-nothing" until the bugle sang and drum rolled at five a.m. in the morning. These notified me that it was time to become a "Know-something."

Saturday, November 29th, 1862

The morning of the 29th indicated rain or snow, causing our camp to present a gloomy and uninviting appearance. At eight a.m., the regiment again moved for the picket line. The absence of my friends still more increased the dismal look of the grounds, producing within me feelings of loneliness. The only occupants of our camp that day and night, since the regiment left early in the morning, were General Meagher, his visitors, eight or ten camp guards, provost marshals, and me.

I commenced my allotted day's writing of official documents at 8:30 a.m. A little before two p.m., I had them finished and on their way to Gen. Hancock's headquarters for signature. Then I again took up Gen. Meagher's private work, the copying of his poem. The following five days were spent by me in pretty much the same routine of business.

On the night of Thursday, December 4th, 1862, the poem was completed and ready for presentation to its author and owner. I did not present it, however, until late next morning as I wished the general to first see it in daylight. I have been complimented for good penmanship, deservedly or not. The truth behind the praise for my skill is not for me to say. But in this case, I must admit that my effort to please was one of the strongest that I ever put forth. To my own eye, the result of that effort appeared superior to any other before or since—this, however, may be mere imagination.

On the night of the 4th, soon after finishing this poem, General Meagher informed me that my work on the official documents had, in every instance, passed inspection without a fault. My penmanship always gave universal satisfaction. Meagher further stated that my written reports were much admired for clearness and ease of being read by all. "And now, Mac, I take the pleasure in informing you that your name is on the list for promotion to `adjutant,'" he said. Of course I thanked him. I could not avoid feeling a little proud for the honor thus conferred.

Friday, December 5th, 1862

As none of the regiments of the brigade were ordered on the picket line, brigade inspection and regimental drill were made the order of the morning for two hours. All the officers of the command were present and in place, including the head inspector, General Hancock. As usual,

Hancock indulged in a little tall swearing, especially when some dirty musket was presented or neatness and cleanliness in the dress of any member of the Irish Brigade did not come up to his required Regular Army standard. I had commenced writing at eight a.m. When inspection began, I went to the door of the tent to see it. But when the "Lion's growl" reached my ears and when Hancock's hasty, quick temper in a few instances seemed to be getting the better of him, I retired inside again to my pen. I had seen Hancock before in similar circumstances and did not now care about witnessing another of his fiery ordeals when I was not actually compelled to do so.

At about 11:30 a.m. after inspection, I saw a fit opportunity to hand the poem and scrapbook to General Meagher. He was standing carelessly at an outside fire conversing with the colonel of the 69th New York [Col. Robert Nugent] at the time. I opened the desk, taking the book and hurried to where Meagher stood. I handed it to him saying, "General, here it is, finished at last." Then turning right around, I hastened back to work at my desk again.

Five minutes later, being anxious to see if he was reading it, I arose and advanced to the tent door and peeped out. Meagher still occupied the same position. But instead of conversing with one officer, as he was doing a few moments before, he was talking to some ten or eleven others surrounding him, all of whom were intently looking at the open book in his hands. I soon discovered by their talk that the copied poem was the object of attraction. I then withdrew inside again, not wishing to be seen by them, resumed my duties and awaited the general's return to his tent with a verdict, favorable or not, to my effort. But in this I was disappointed for he did not come.

In a few minutes, however, the orderly appeared at the tent door saying to me in a very polite manner that General Meagher wished to see me outside. Of course, I quickly responded. In two minutes I was at his side. Then, addressing me in the presence and hearing of his brother officers, he said, "McCarter, I am really proud of this. I am still prouder that the man who executed it is a member of my command. I shall forward it to Ireland for exhibit in a short time."

He then introduced me to all the officers present and invited the entire party into his tent to take, as he termed it, a smile.[4] Ten minutes later, they separated. General Meagher, with the book under his arm, went towards Hancock's headquarters. The officers headed to their various commands. I re-seated myself at the desk for another hour's work which would finish my duties for the day. It was now about 12:30 p.m.

At one p.m., Joseph appeared and commenced setting the little table for dinner. "Jo," I said, "I guess the general is dining with General Hancock today. He went over there a while ago."

"Oh, yes," he replied, "he told me so, but bade me get dinner here for you."

I thanked him. Then I thought to myself how different the fare and treatment received now from that which I experienced in the ranks only a day or two before. Joseph soon turned up again, bringing with him for me a big apple dumpling, two potatoes and a corncake. "Now, my boy," he said in his broad Irish dialect, "ate yer fill."

Old Joe's order was promptly obeyed to the letter.

General Meagher returned to his headquarters at three p.m. Upon his arrival, I was engaged talking with some members of my regiment at a campfire close by. He called me over, and I followed him into his tent. There, he put his hand into his pocket and drew out an old fashioned long steel-bead purse, such as was used in England and Ireland several years ago. Meagher opened it and drew from it a folded up greenback. It seemed to me to be of the denomination of five dollars. He handed it to me saying, "Mac, here's a slight acknowledgement for your beautiful work. Perhaps you need some things from the sutlers. This will be useful to you."

I thanked him as I took the note. I said that it would certainly be of much service to me at the present time, but that I expected nothing of the kind for copying the poem as I had done. My only object in doing the job had been to express my profound respect and admiration of the commander of the Irish Brigade. He smiled and modestly said, "Thank you, Mac."

I then withdrew to have another chat with the boys outside. My writing duties for the day had ended. I left the general all alone in his tent.

As darkness was now approaching, the thought struck me that instead of mixing in again with my old comrades, it would be better to pay a visit to the brigade sutler who was about 200 yards distant. I would purchase from him the articles which I had determined upon. To use an old Irish saying, I was in black need of these items. Accordingly, there I went and selected from the sutler's stock the following articles priced as listed:

1 pair common suspenders $1.75
1 pair wool socks .75

2 red pocket handkerchiefs .60
(very thin)
1 muffler (cotton) 1.00
Total $4.10

I drew out my little memorandum book in which I had deposited the greenback without opening it. Handing the bill to the sutler, thinking still that it was a $5 note, I said, "Take the amount out of that."

He opened it quickly and hurried to his money drawer in the back part of the store to bring the change. I watched him closely. He counted out 19 one dollar bills, very surprising to me. Then stopping short, he held the note that I had given him up in his hand saying, "My friend, I can't make your change. Have you nothing smaller?"

What can this mean I thought? Now somewhat bewildered, but hiding my confusion, I quietly replied, "No, nothing less. Just hand the bill this way again and I will get it changed." He did so. To my amazement, there was the identical greenback received from General Meagher with the same figure 5 on the corner, but with an 0 after it. Then, and not till then, did I find out that my effort had been rewarded with $50. Nor was this all.

Thinking that the general had certainly made a mistake in the amount given me, I at once determined to ascertain the truth. I started for his quarters to see him about it. I found him alone, smoking a cigar, seated on a low bench near his tent fire. Addressing him, I suppose somewhat nervously as I held the bill before him, I asked, "General, isn't this a mistake?"

He looked at the money in my hand, then at me. With a good natured smile on his countenance, he replied, "How, in the amount? Why, no, man, I knew exactly what I gave you and you are welcome to it."

What to say now I positively did not know for a moment. At length I said, "Well, General, the amount is entirely too large for the work performed and I cannot conscientiously accept more than $10."

All was in vain, however. The more I insisted, the stronger he protested. At last he actually compelled me to put the money in my pocket and to say nothing more about it. "To be in the army is to obey your superiors there," said Meagher.

This finished the job so far as my choice in the matter was concerned. I then told him about my visit to the sutler, what I had purchased thanks to him and how I first found out the denomination of the note that he had given me. He laughed. I continued, "It's such a handsome present, general, that I will not break it. I will send it home to my wife and family in Philadelphia. They will make better use of it than I could. I can do without the articles at the sutler's for a while longer."

"Happy thought, my boy," he replied. "Old Ireland again, Mac. I think more of you now than ever. Just take an envelope and enclose the money in it. Write your wife's full address upon it and I will guarantee its safe delivery to her next Monday (Dec. 8th). Lieutenant Starr is going to New York tomorrow morning for a day on official business. I will get him to take it and deliver it. He is a reliable man and will stop for a few hours in Philadelphia on his way to New York."

I thanked my good and large-hearted benefactor. Of course I embraced the opportunity of sending to the dear, far off and deserving ones the result of my effort and the magnanimous token of General Meagher. After enclosing the money in the envelope and addressing it, I handed it to the General for its destination. "Now, Mac," he said again, drawing out the long purse. "Here is $10. Go right over to the sutler and pay him for the things you bought and keep the balance for pocket money. Don't send it home."

I had just commenced to remonstrate when, jumping up, he forced the money into my hand, saying, "Not another word, now." Meagher then hustled me out of the tent.

On the following Wednesday, I received a note from my wife. It acknowledged receipt of fifty dollars on Sunday evening, December 7th. She wrote that my envelope was delivered into her hand by an officer who reported that he had been requested to do so by General Meagher of the Irish Brigade. The officer also said that he was in a great hurry and had but a few moments to talk to her. He had come all the way from the Baltimore Depot at Broad and Pine Streets, especially to deliver the note to her at our residence on Howard Street.

Do I say too much in terming General Thomas Francis Meagher, a soldier and a gentleman, my benefactor and my friend? Certainly not. He possessed traits of character rarely combined in any one man at the present day. As a soldier, he was second to none in the American army. Meagher was cool, collected and brave in the most trying and dangerous military duties. As a gentleman, he was not excelled by any. The general was polite, obliging and kind to all, especially to the common private soldier in the ranks. As a benefactor and a friend, the men of the Irish Brigade who fought their way by his side up to the mouths of whole batteries of Rebel cannons at Fredericksburg will never forget him. They and I prayed, "God reward General Meagher."[5]

Saturday, December 6th, 1862

My duties consisted entirely of writing orders and communications as acting adjutant. I performed these penmanship tasks every day with apparent satisfaction to my superior officers of the Adjutant's department and also to General Meagher. Nothing worthy of note transpired within our lines until Monday, December 8th. It became evident from quick movements of the officers to and fro, as well as regiments and brigades changing position, that some new and important movement was about to be made on our side of the river. The entire Army of the Potomac seemed to be massing in the vicinity. From every hilltop, as far as the eye could see, there was one consolidated camp of Federal soldiers. The host numbered at least 100,000 men of all arms, not including our artillerymen. These cannoneers, with 143 heavy guns[6], were already in position on Stafford Heights. The artillerymen were ready to open fire on the doomed city at the word "go."

I have omitted to state, however, that on December 1st, orders were issued for the men to erect winter quarters. Since winter had now set in in all its severity, no further hostilities were expected to take place before spring. But in this hope we were disappointed. To use the words of the poet of Scotland, "the best laid schemes o' mide and men, gang aft aglee."

Officers' Quarters

Winter quarters for officers were generally built by the men of the company or regiment over whom the officer was placed. They consisted of trees felled for the purpose and cut at a certain length according to the size that the officer wished his house to be. A level spot of ground for the site was chosen. It was always within the camp lines.

The cut trees were notched at either end and set or locked into each other. In this way, a little winter cabin was constructed from the foundation tree to the crowning one. The crevices in the sides and ends were filled or plastered up with moistened mud. A canvas tent leaf constituted the roof and little door. An old pork barrel, or cracker box, served as the chimney. A hole dug in the earth in the center of the structure became the fireplace. A few boards, if lucky enough to be found by hook or by crook, were laid down for a floor.

Our enlisted men usually built a rough bench for the officer's bedstead. About a foot high from the ground, this bed was formed of trees or branches. Although the air holes and crevices in these little shanties were to all outside appearance plugged up, the sharp, keen cutting winds invariably gained admittance through them. The wind held a high carnival within, especially at night, often making sleep fly away. These little structures were of different sizes and sometimes occupied by two or three officers. Generally, they were not over twelve feet square.

Enlisted Men's Quarters

Our shanties, although each one was occupied by three or four men, were smaller than those of the officers. In several instances, they were much more comfortable, some of them showing the results of much care and good taste in their construction. A few, however, bore the marks of having been erected without regard to care, neatness, or anything else conducive to the health and comfort of the soldier in the field. They were about eight feet square.[7]

Fredericksburg

But to return to the important movement. At about this time, another demand was made upon Mayor Slaughter of Fredericksburg for the unconditional surrender of the city to the Union forces. A reply was received, evidently dictated by the Confederate commander-in-chief, General Robert E. Lee. Mayor Slaughter, Lee's messenger, stated "that said demand would not be acceded to and that any attempt made to enforce it would be met by a determined resistance." This of course settled the matter. As the occupation of Fredericksburg by the Federal army was necessary for operations against the Rebel capital, it was evident that the only means by which the city could be gained was through stubborn, hard fighting. General Burnside no doubt had come to that conclusion. This accounted for the massing of troops near the river. Determined to occupy the city if possible during the remainder of the winter, Burnside was ready to move, even though his forces would have found more comfortable winter quarters on our side of the river.

The indications now pointed to an almost immediate attack on Fredericksburg. Few, if any of the private soldiers knew positively that this would happen until the day before the advance occurred. In my position, however, I was considerably posted on these matters far in advance of the rank and file. Secrecy bound me, not allowing me to divulge the Union army's plans.

The Confederate army on the other side of the Rappahannock, judging by its reinforced picket line along the riverfront, seemed to be aware of the preparations going on in our camps. They were ready for an immediate assault upon their works. The Rebel position had seemed very strong before, but now it seemed impregnable. Fredericksburg, Marye's Heights and all the surrounding hills were literally covered with cannons and dotted all over with earthworks of every conceivable shape and form. There were countless rows of rifle pits.

All along the riverfront could be seen long, high banks of freshly turned-up earth behind which hundreds of Rebel sharpshooters were concealed. They were ready to shower a rain of death upon any object moving out towards them from the opposite shore. From the windows of houses and corners of streets, iron hail awaited any living thing venturing out on the water from the Union side of the stream. Close to 80,000 Confederate soldiers were fortified on the heights behind Fredericksburg. To use Mayor Slaughter's words in reply to the demand for the surrender of the city, the Confederates "were ready to resist any attempt made by our forces to either cross the river or occupy Fredericksburg." Such then was the position of the Rebel Army of Northern Virginia on the 5th of December, 1862.[8]

The position of the Union Army was good. It included about 100,000 men.[*] Twenty-five batteries (150 guns) were posted, ready for immediate action, on the tops of Stafford Heights directly opposite the city. Although numerically considered the Union forces had the advantage, General Lee is said to have remarked, "My position is worth 100,000 men." So it was—thus placing the balance of power in the hands of the Confederates, after all.

Sunday, December 7th, was a most exciting day. Wagonloads of ammunition poured into each brigade camp. All the remaining artillery in the rear was ordered to the front, there to await further orders. Long lines of ambulances could be seen winding their way over distant hills and through valleys with their retinue of doctors, surgeons and nurses,

[*] Some say 125,000.

fully prepared to administer the drug, amputate the limb, and apply the lint and bandage. Cavalry, to the number of five or six regiments, awaited the signal to move forward. Every hour from morning to night witnessed the arrival of several four-horse teams with boats for pontoon bridges. These boats had been built for the purpose at Aquia Creek and transported to the front on large four-wheeled trucks, each truck being hauled by two or four horses—no easy matter over Virginia roads in the winter season. These were some of the indications of an important movement. This very soon convinced every man in the ranks that another battle was at hand.

Monday, December 8th, 1862

No part of the Irish Brigade being on picket today, a general inspection of the regiments took place in the afternoon, each man appearing fully equipped and ready for service. This over, the men were ordered back to their quarters again with instructions to hold themselves in readiness to march at any hour. This was the first official intimation to the rank and file of the impending conflict.

Tuesday, December 9th, 1862

These 24 hours were to me the busiest day during my life in the army. General Meagher found it necessary to have detailed from division headquarters an assistant. We needed him to write up the piles of orders, requisitions, instructions to officers and other papers incident to a forward movement of the army. These papers revealed to me that the assault on the Rebel works at Fredericksburg was all planned, laid out and engineered by some of the best generals in the Army of the Potomac. Moreover, they disclosed to me the very day and hour that the ball was to open and the part to be played in it by my own division, especially by my own Irish Brigade.

Wednesday, December 10th, 1862

At noon, marching orders for the next day were issued to the troops. They well knew their destination. Each man was to be furnished with three days cooked rations and 80 rounds of ammunition—40 rounds to fill his cartridge box and 40 rounds for his pockets. Now comes the tug of war, I thought.[9]

*"A terrific hissing noise came through the air. Looking up, I saw
a huge round shell which fell among a clump of trees, tearing off several
of the largest limbs. . . .the thing exploded, killing three horses and two of our
own men. . . .Our cold and chilly quarters here for the night might become hot
enough for us before morning."*

Chapter 8

Crossing the Rappahannock River

Among the saddest of all evils sad,
That Heaven's judgment ever sent on earth,
Or hating man inflicts on hated man,
Is War—relentless, ruthless, bloody War.
War, thou art a cruel monstrous fiend,
Wholesome murderer—thy name is Legion.
War —'tis writ in sighs and tears and blood,
`Tis stamped on fields made desolate—
On hamlets burned—on towns destroyed —
On populous cities sucked.
`Tis heard amid the cannon's roar—the tramp
Of furious, frighted horse— the clash of arms—
The maddened charge of hostile ranks glowing
With fell revenge, and burning hot with wrath.
My soul is sick of War —its carnage, crime,
Distress and stern, severe necessities.
Oh, war is sad.

The marching orders for Thursday were issued to the troops. Each man was to carry with him three days cooked rations and 80 rounds of ammunition. This indicated that hot, bloody work was anticipated. Forty rounds of cartridges (consisting of powder, ball and three buck shot to each cartridge) was the normal allotment on other occasions for what might be termed an ordinary battle or engagement.[1]

During the entire day, the greatest activity prevailed in every camp. Orderlies on horseback dashed to and fro, delivering dispatches to commanding officers. Infantry regiments and brigades marched from one point to another, visible for a short time and then disappearing from view behind some distant hill or down in some dark valley skirted by dense woods. Heavy siege guns rumbled along, drawn by four or six splendid horses to each gun. Cavalry regiments took up the various positions assigned them on this side of the river, ready for an advance of any manner in the passage of the Rappahannock if ordered to do so. Many of the boys were also engaged in cleaning their firearms and puting them in extra trim for expected use on the morrow.[2]

During the afternoon, hundreds of bullocks stopped many well-directed rifle balls and fell to the ground, dead and bleeding. The regimental butcher then operated, turning the cut-up carcasses over to the commissary of each regiment. These commissaries in turn distributed to each company its portion for the three days rations ordered. In the evening, a thousand blazing campfires behind the Stafford Hills burned all over a large tract of country north of that range of little mountains. They lit up the skies as well as the thick, dark and gloomy woods in which most of our camps were situated.

The scene was a lively one—every man seemed to be busy at something for the coming storm of battle. Here you could see a group of the boys seated around a fire, talking, laughing and joking as they attended to the boiling of huge chunks of "salt horse" and fresh beef in the large iron pots suspended over nearly every fire. In the best of spirits and good humor nearby sat several others, cooking pork by sticking lumps of it on long tree branches and holding the meat over the blaze until done. In another place could be seen men sitting or standing, waiting for their little tin cups of boiling coffee to be ready. Hosts of others, covered over with canteens, were constantly arriving with fresh water from some neighboring spring or brook while others departed in search of the precious liquid. Here and there you could watch men patching their coats or pants, sewing on buttons or cobbling shoes. Other soldiers occupied themselves by removing red Virginia mud from their uniforms. In every direction you could observe fellows brightening up button breastplates, muskets, bayonets and sabers. Officers congregated in groups here and there near campfires, under trees, or on piles of boxes and barrels. They discussed the chief topic of the day _ the anticipated struggle of tomorrow. Everybody seemed to enjoy the situation and the near prospect of having, as some termed it, "another heavy brush with the Johnnies."

My own desk duties on that day were constant and very laborious. I did not have a moment to myself except at mealtimes from early morn until eight p.m. when I finally finished up all the writing in my department. The night was clear and very cold. But being anxious to see what was going on outside and to mingle again, perhaps for the last time, with my old regimental comrades, I put on my overcoat. After drinking a glass of brandy handed to me by General Meagher and lighting a cigar which he also gave me, I sallied forth and soon found myself seated among my old companions from Company A in front of their roaring, blazing fire, in an unusually thick part of the woods.

No roll of the drum or sound of the bugle told that the hour to retire for the night had arrived. Oh, no. The work of the morrow seemed to have taken full possession of the minds and thoughts of every man wearing the blue, from the highest officer down to the little drummer boy. The desire for sleep had fled as well as everything else not connected with the coming struggle. The frosty night favored the preparations going on by keeping everyone awake. The morning would be well suited for the march of troops. The ground, which for a few days had been soft and damp, would become comparatively hard and dry by freezing.

After spending an hour with my old comrades and visiting a few other camps close by, I returned to the tent of General Meagher at about midnight. I found him overseeing the packing of some books and papers in a large metal case and getting things in general ready for the march in the morning. I asked him if I could assist in any way.

He replied, "No." The general added, "I will give you instructions in a little while what I want you to do in the morning."

I saluted him and retired to an outside fire, seating myself among several of the boys still there, awaiting the general's call to receive his instructions. At about one a.m., he called me into his tent. On entering, I found no one present but himself and old Joe, the cook. The general then in a low tone proceeded in substance as follows: "Now, Mac, everything here is packed and ready to be put on board one of the wagons in the morning. I leave in half an hour for Falmouth and expect to return here at three a.m. Our batteries are to open on the city at daybreak and the troops here will move forward at 7:30 a.m. I want you to remain in the rear, near my personal property, and on no account to go into the action or to the front. Here is a duplicate key of my tin case. Keep it safe for me until the fight is over. If my fate is to fall, hand it over to General Hancock. Here is also a paper which authorizes you to do as I say and to prevent your arrest by the provost or any other guard bringing up the rear."

I made no reply to the general except simply nodding. Queer instructions, I thought. Am I to be shut out from participating in this battle? The general now put on his overcoat and darted out of the tent, mounting his white horse held by an orderly. Accompanied by several other officers likewise on horseback, Meagher was soon on the double-quick towards Falmouth. Five minutes later, boom, boom, boom went three of our heaviest guns from Roundtop Mountain. This coming so unexpectedly and from a place so nearby, it gave my nerves a considerable shock. Instantly recovering, I rushed to the outside, there to find many of my comrades just as much startled as I was. Approaching a group of my own regimental companions at a fire under a tree, I said to them, "Well, boys, the ball's opened at last."[3]

And so it was. These three shots at half past one a.m. on the morning of the 11th of December, 1862, signalled and announced that the bombardment of Rebel Fredericksburg had commenced. Upon the return of General Meagher soonafter, he informed us that this firing, which afterwards continued at intervals of about 20 minutes until near daylight, was for the purpose of covering the troops then engaged in the construction of the pontoon bridges over the river at Fredericksburg.

Thursday, December 11th, 1862

During the greater part of the night, large numbers of Union sharpshooters engaged those of the enemy, the former vainly endeavoring to prevent the latter from shooting down our troops constructing the pontoon bridges. The work for the time being was abandoned.[4] It was now nearly daybreak. After partaking of a hastily prepared camp breakfast, every man responded to the clear, shrill notes of the bugle to "Fall in." At seven a.m., every regiment of the Irish Brigade and the rest of Hancock's Division stood ready to move forward to the river and the terrible conflict.

The sun had risen. Everything was complete save the laying of the pontoons. This must be done. Our boys patiently awaited for the word "March." A few of our guns had been playing on the city front during the night to dislodge the Rebel sharpshooters, but with no success. Something more powerful was needed. Our guns on Stafford Hills remained silent. Were they not going to speak to help our brave men to bridge the stream and let 100,000 men cross over? Yes, they would. Boys, patience a little longer. At precisely eight a.m., our batteries opened fire. From the iron mouths of 150 cannons on Stafford Hills, nearly two miles distant from our position at that hour, flew out a constant rain of shot and shell into Fredericksburg for fully 18 hours. The noise, although at such a distance, was fearful, shaking the ground under our feet. It was deafening to those unused to the thundering of artillery. Not a shot came from the Rebel works over the river.[5]

General Meagher was now at the head of his brigade, with the 69th New York as the advance. At last, he gave the order, "Attention, shoulder arms, right face, forward, march." The whole command, headed by the fifers and drummers of each regiment playing the martial tune of "Upon the Heights of Alma" (of Crimean War notoriety), marched off the ground towards Falmouth and that part of the Stafford Hills near which the passage of the river was to be attempted.

But to return to myself and the directions of General Meagher to remain behind and not to go near the front during the action, I now have something to say perhaps not to my credit. To be in the army, as I have before stated, is to obey. On this occasion, I was deficient. As I stood near the general's tent door in the company of old Joe and two or three teamsters looking at the boys on the march to the battlefield, the thought of remaining behind was too bitter a pill to swallow. I reasoned awhile with myself. Will I obey the general's instructions or not? Will I leave it possible for my comrades in the Irish Brigade to say that I, being one of their number, remained under cover in the rear without filling my place in my regiment on that terrible, bloody 13th day of December 1862, the darkest day in the annals of the Army of the Potomac? No, I shall not, I concluded. I will not be kept back. I must share in the perils of this fight with the boys, be the result life or death, defeat or victory.

Darting past old Joe into the tent, for my comrades were now fast disappearing in the distance, I put on my overcoat, belts and blanket. Seizing a new musket and bayonet standing in a corner, I rushed to the outside again where the old cook was still standing. He was not a little surprised to see me fully equipped and in marching order. Joe accosted me, saying, "What da ye mean? Whar the devil are ye gayn?"

I had little time to explain. Drawing out of my pocket the key given me by General Meagher for safekeeping, I held it toward him, saying, "Joe, give this key to the General when you see him again. Tell him to excuse me for disobeying his orders. I could not help it." I then shook him by the hand, saying, "Joe, I'm going with the boys."

He seemed much affected and said, "Well, ye'll never come out o'that place alive."

I had just turned away from him when, thrusting the key back again into my hand, he said, "Here, Mr., give it to the general yerself. Ye'll see him most likely first. I'll have nothing to do with it."

There was nothing then left for me but to take the key. I did so. After returning it again to my inside blouse pocket and bidding faithful old Joe another and last farewell, for I never saw or heard of him afterwards, I started on the double-quick after my comrades. I cannot help saying that "I legged it." Had I not done so, the chances were that my regiment and brigade would have been lost to my view and assigned to a position in the long line of battle, fully eight miles in length, where it might have been very difficult if not impossible to have found them. Another difficulty also presented itself to me. I knew not the moment when General Meagher might discover me in the ranks again, contrary to the orders so recently given me by him not to do so. But I risked this.

The morning was clear and beautiful. Although sharp and cold before sunrise, it became moderately warm and pleasant soon after. The ground was in splendid condition for marching, being frozen, hard and dry. This greatly facilitated me in my movements to overtake the boys. About thirty minutes after starting, I came up to my regiment, the last in the line of the Irish Brigade. Falling in alongside one of the men in the rear, I marched along with the command. Fortunately for me, the general was fully a mile ahead, in front of the 69th New York.

I was, however, without ammunition. Knowing that each man in the regiment had been furnished with 80 rounds before starting, I felt sure that I would experience no difficulty in obtaining from some of my comrades a share of the needed article. Accordingly, I said to my neighbor, who was a perfect stranger to me and a weak, sickly looking young man, "Have you any ammunition to spare? I have none."

"Certainly," he replied. "I would like to be relieved of some of it. It's like a 56 pound weight in my pocket. I expect to get my `bounty' (meaning that he would be shot) before one quarter of it is used."

He then handed me 40 rounds which I deposited in my cartridge box as we moved along. We had now passed along the base of Round Top Mountain. Some of our heaviest artillery rained from its summit a most unpleasant shower of solid shot over our heads into Fredericksburg. When ascending to the top of a hill over which laid our course, we came in full view of our entire line of batteries on Stafford Heights pounding away at the doomed Rebel stronghold with a continuous storm of shot and shell—a sight which I would not attempt to describe.*

We then descended the opposite side of the hill into a valley. Then we proceeded to a point opposite the center of the city and about 200 yards in the rear of our center batteries. Here we were ordered to stack arms and rest but not to leave the ground. This order was given so that the crossing of the river might be effected with as little delay as possible when the time to do so arrived. But the work of laying the pontoons was yet incomplete, notwithstanding the terrible fire from our artillery designed to dislodge the Rebel sharpshooters from their concealed positions in houses skirting the river. From behind walls, lumber piles and corners of streets, the Johnnies directed such a destructive musket fire on our men detailed to lay the bridges that the attempt was again temporarily abandoned. It was now about eleven a.m. and no indication of a further forward movement was visible.[6]

The men of the brigade sat or laid down on grass which was yet fresh and green in this immediate place. At noon, while seated on a stump of an old tree beside several members of my company, I discovered General Meagher accompanied by two or three other officers in the distance advancing towards my position. He walked slowly and carelessly, stopping here and there and conversing with the troops as if to kill time. Here's trouble, I thought. Gradually they came nearer. What was I to do to escape recognition by his keen, quick eye? I had no place to hide and to run would have been cowardice. I at once made my case known to three of my companions, who advised me to turn my face away when Meagher was passing. Should he stop to speak, they would rise up and reply to him. The general was now within ten yards of me. Suddenly, I thought that by leaning forward with my head and face downward, as if tying or fixing my shoes, Meagher might not recognize

---

* As yet, not a shot had been fired from the Rebel works.

me. I was right and lucky again. Although he passed within five feet of where I sat stooping, I was not discovered nor did he stop to speak.[7]

A few minutes afterwards, an incident occured which I could not help but to record. It showed the bitter feelings which some of the Confederate soldiers held towards "damned Yankees," as they termed Union troops. When evacuating Warrenton, by some means unknown to me, some 17 or 18 Rebel soldiers including an officer were captured. These prisoners were placed under guard and brought here with our army. For what disposition, I never knew. They were generally fine-looking and intelligent men, but miserably clothed. Although prisoners of war in our hands, they were in no way backward expressing their Secesh principles and their determination to stand by the Southern flag if they ever again had any opportunity to do so.

At this time they were located, still under guard, among a clump of trees some 150 yards to our right in a little ravine. In my company was a man who was known as both a good soldier and a "perfect devil." As time was hanging heavily on our hands just then, this individual proposed a short walk over to see how the Johnnies were getting along. Some eight or nine men of my own company, including me, and three of Company G agreed to go. Away we strode towards the captives.

We soon found them quietly conversing among themselves, seated on the ground around a few burning tree branches. Addressing the captive officer, our comrade who first proposed the visit said, "Cap, what in the devil are your fellows doing over the river there? They don't reply to our guns. I'll be damned, but I believe they have skedaddled."

I was standing close by the Rebel officer at the time. His face, which a moment before was of an ashy paleness, now seemed to turn crimson with rage as he indignantly and contemptuously replied, "Ah, you'll hear from them at the right time. When gunpowder and shot will tell. You thick-headed Yankees won't know what hell and damnation is till you meet them over that river."

That's a sickening thought, I mused. We had better leave the Reb prisoners alone since they seemed to know in advance what the results of the impending conflict over the water were to be. I expected bad results before I ever saw the Rebel officer or heard him speak. I could not help but think that his predictions were nearly about right, although discouraging. In five minutes we left for our position again in the valley. But before proceeding far, I turned back. Walking up to the Rebel officer whose gentlemanly bearing and appearance struck me very much, but whose countenance indicated want and hunger, I inquired, "How are you off for coffee?"

He replied with a sickly smile, "Coffee, coffee, I did not see it for six weeks before being taken prisoner. Since then, my men and I have been furnished with only four small rations each."

"Hard enough, old boy," I said. Being pretty liberally supplied with the article just then, for my little bag contained nearly a pound of it, I emptied fully three-quarters of the quantity into his cap. It was the only thing he had to hold it. He seemed very grateful and thanked me politely in genuine Southern style. Bidding him goodbye, I hurried after my companions.

It was now about one p.m. Soon after, we reached our regimental position again. We found the boys lounging around just as we had left them. Our batteries on the hills 200 yards in front were still pouring a steady, although not rapid, fire into Fredericksburg. Strange to say, no response was made by the Confederate artillery on the opposite heights. In the meantime, another attempt had been made to bridge the river. It was again frustrated by the enemy's sharpshooters, who seemed to laugh at any and every effort made to drive them from their cover. Our men grew impatient, desiring to cross the river and attack the enemy in his stronghold. Anything was preferable to remaining idle. The troops did not want to spend another afternoon and night doing nothing. From all indications, this seemed quite probable.

Suspense and inactivity in the very face of the foe are the most trying ordeals through which a soldier has to pass. On this occasion particularly, it was almost unendurable. But under the unavoidable circumstances, the emotion and inaction had to be borne.

While carelessly walking around at this time taking observations, my attention was directed to numbers of men from my regiment and brigade. In groups of six or eight, they were climbing up the hills to the batteries. To witness, I supposed, the effect of the artilleryfire upon the city. In our regimental position, hills completely obstructed the view of the town; it was only from the high ground occupied by our artillery that the city, the opposite shore and Rebel works could be fully surveyed.

My curiosity now being considerably excited, I followed my comrades to the dangerous heights above. Nearly every member of my company climbed behind me. We wished to see how matters looked over the water and down along the banks of the river, our own side of it particularly. Thousands of willing hands and loyal hearts already awaited the opportunity to again attempt the hazardous work of launching the pontoon boats. We were not long in reaching the desired place, a few yards behind a German battery of six heavy guns whose thunder shook the hills at their base. As I watched these brave men working these guns, I could not but admire the ease and regularity with which they performed the work. With clocklike precision, they loaded and discharged their huge instruments of war and death, all the time gabbling Dutch among themselves.

We stood a few yards in the rear of the battery. Just then we could not see farther than a few feet in front of the guns, owing to the dense clouds of white smoke produced by their discharge. At about two p.m., however, all the artillery suddenly ceased firing, the guns being red hot. Half an hour later, the smoke having pretty well cleared away, the object of our visit was attained—a view of the beautiful Rappahannock below our feet with thousands of Union soldiers scouting and picketing along its banks, awaiting the opportunity to cross.

Sappers and miners were ready to rush to their boats and cross the river as soon as their opponents on the opposite shore were dislodged. Suddenly, there was the quick, sharp snap of about 500 Rebel rifles from the other side of the river. The sharpshooters were still there. The once beautiful city of Fredericksburg was now on fire. Dense volumes of flame and thick, black smoke pierced the clouds above. Burning, tottering, cracking and falling buildings evidenced the efficiency of the Federal bombardment. The assembled host of armed men in blue covered the surrounding country like a carpet. There was the occasional bugle call or tap of a distant drum, as well as military commands from officers. A huge, ascending army balloon reconnoiterred the enemy's position.

The slanting afternoon rays of a December sun created a clear, blue summer-like sky. The air was mild and pleasing. Waving Confederate ensigns on the heights of Fredericksburg contrasted with the Stars and Stripes on Stafford Hills. All ears heard the deafening cheers and hurrahs of our men when the slightest prospect of crossing the river presented itself. The scene was a picture worthy of the artist's golden pencil. The terrible sublimness and awful grandeur of the moment can never be effaced from my mind and memory:

> "Forever through the soldiers thoughts,
> The soldier's life returns—
> Or where the trampled fields are fought,
> Or where the campfire burns."

We remained there for about 20 minutes. Then we decided to leave, not wanting to be absent from our regimental post too long. When scarce halfway down the brow of the hill, our ears were again greeted with tremendous long rounds of cheers coming up from the troops at the river. We halted and retraced our steps again to the hilltop with a thousand others, feeling confident that something there or down along the river had occurred or was about to occur.

We were now again on the heights, but to our disappointment nothing new was to be seen. The cheering ceased. The gunners stood silently by their guns awaiting the signal to again open fire. A report came up from the riverfront. The sappers and miners [engineers] positively refused to obey their officers and enter the pontoon boats. They said that they would be exposed to a murderous fire should they try it again. What then was to be done? Could those Rebel sharpshooters not be driven off?

Five minutes passed and the gunners went back to work. The muzzles of 150 Union guns were lowered to bear on the extreme front of the city along the water's edge. Confederate riflemen were concealed in houses there, picking off our soldiers. A long line of fire, shot and shell was soon poured into this dangerous place. It was our last hope to clear the waterfront of its desperate inhabitants. Would it succeed?

The expected signal was soon given. The guns, as if hell was let loose and with voices like thunder, reopened a rapid and furious fire. The houses crumbled to dust before the terrible onslaught. Fresh flames with fiery, hissing, forked tongues shot heavenward. Thousands of Union soldiers, side by side, stood silently witnessing the awful scene with nervous anxiety. The volley was repeated, fast filling the air with the smoke of battle. The opposite shore was once more hidden from view.

Twenty minutes later the firing ceased. The smoke soon lifted and the opposite shore stood out before our eyes. But what a change. Had our hopes been realized? Yes, to a great degree, they had. The prostrate remains of many recent hiding places for the Rebel sharpshooters laid in the dust. Not a graycoat could be seen. No living object was visible on the Confederate banks of the river.*

Now or never for the pontoons. The sappers and miners refused again to lay the pontoons. A call was at once made for volunteers to row

---

* Strange as it may appear, not a shot of any description up to this time had been fired at our troops by the enemy. The only exception had been fire on our troops who tried to lay the pontoon bridges.

across the river. They would take possession of the opposite banks and drive the enemy's sharpshooters, if still concealed there, up into the town. Our men then would have a chance to commence the construction of the bridges from the north side of the stream. The colonel of the 7th Michigan Infantry was the first to respond and offered his regiment for the enterprise.[8]

His men, numbering between five and six hundred, stood ready to enter the boats with loaded muskets. They were ready, if necessary, to fight their way across the water. The sappers and miners were asked to row these brave men across but they refused. The men of the gallant Michigan regiment themselves rushed to the boats. Some of them picked up oars while others hefted muskets, ready to blaze away at any of the foe making an appearance on the opposite side of the stream. This brave little navy pushed out from the shore amid the deafening cheers of at least 5,000 men. Every eye was focused upon them and every heart wished them success in their courageous and self-sacrificing mission.

The boats with their brave and daring crews dashed onward. Scarce had they reached the middle of the river when at least 50 rifles were levelled and fired at them from the opposite shore. Concealed below low banks of earthworks skirting the stream, these Rebs had escaped the destructive fire of our artillery. It was a terrible moment both for the actors and the lookers-on. But the heroic Western men were not to be foiled. On they pushed, against a furious rain of Rebel bullets beating square in their faces. The Johnny fire was fatal to quite a few.

Several squads of the enemy's infantry were seen from our observation point as the boats neared the other side. These Johnnies were hurrying down the streets of the town to the river to assist their comrades. They opened a galling fire on our men, who, without the slightest indication of wavering, plied their oars the quicker. Our boys returned volley after volley of musketry with telling effect on their opponents. A few minutes later, the shore was touched. A furious hand-to-hand fight ensued. Sabers, butt-ends of muskets and bayonets were freely and desperately used, together with powder and ball on both sides, tinting the beautiful Rappahannock with the blood of the Confederate and Federal slain alike. Success at length crowned our arms. The foe was beaten back from the river's front.

The surviving Western troops quickly formed on the opposite bank. With bayonets fixed and wild demoniac yells, they charged the now demoralized enemy on the streets of the ill-fated town. Our boys drove the Rebs back into their works in the rear. For the third time, the old city was in the hands of Union soldiers. But the great Battle of Fredericksburg had yet to be fought.*

The valor and daring of this brave regiment, the 7th Michigan, elicited the praise and admiration of every man in the Army of the Potomac who either witnessed or heard of its conduct on this particular occasion. At one time, the work which it accomplished was not only considered a terrible risk but pronounced to be impossible. The crew of each boat numbered ten or twelve men, four of whom manned the oars while the others, some standing erect and some crouching down, kept up a constant musketry fire on their opponents as they advanced on their position and the opposite shore. It was truly a pitiful and heart-sickening sight to watch.

Hundreds of my comrades and I on the hilltops looked down on the brave fellows on the river, tugging and fighting with death itself. An oarsman would be seen relinquishing his oar and falling down dead or wounded in the bottom of his boat or overboard into the river. Then another would drop while not a few of their partners with rifles in hand were suffering a similar fate by their side. I think this was sad. It may have been the saddest sight during my life in the army. The scene forced tears from many of my comrades and me who were eyewitnesses to it.[9]

The enemy now having been driven out of the city, the laying of the pontoon bridges was again commenced with double vigor. In a short time, the middle bridge immediately opposite the center of the city was completed. At about 3:30 p.m., the Federal troops without further opposition began to cross. Two other bridges, one a short distance below the city and the other a short distance above it, were thrown across the river during the evening. The former was constructed for the passage of General Franklin's and a part of General Hooker's Divisions. The latter was built for the remaining troops of Hooker's command and the Pennsylvania Reserves. The middle bridge was reserved exclusively for the use of General Sumner's Division. In this way then, the Federal line of battle was to be as follows: Franklin's Division and part of Hooker's on

---

* Owing to the close proximity of the Western troops to the opposite shore during this fight, our artillery on the hills could render them no assistance whatever. Had the artillery opened fire on the position of the enemy then contesting the landing of our troops, our own boys would have been just as much exposed to shot and shell as the Confederates.

the left; Sumner's Division in the center (or right opposite the city), and the remainder of Hooker's Division and the Pennsylvania Reserves on the right. Some difficulty existed between the commanders of the above divisions in the disposition of their forces for the assault on the Rebel works, but the matter was finally and satisfactorily arranged among them. The positions I have named were occupied by the troops.[10]

It was fast growing dark. As the way was now open to cross the river and, not knowing how soon our brigade might receive orders to follow those who had already crossed and were still crossing, I and my companions bade goodbye to the heights. We hastened back to our regimental position. Here we were soon greeted with the call "Fall in." After standing for fully an hour "in place" and resting on our arms, a second call was given to "Break ranks and stack arms." Soon after, our officers communicated to the men that an order had just been received from headquarters. It countermanded the one given about an hour and a half before for the entire division of General Hancock to cross the river that night and occupy the opposite banks. We were to wait for further orders on next morning. In addition to this, we were strictly prohibited from kindling any fires whereby our position would be disclosed to the enemy. Our officers remarked, "Boys, you'll have to make yourselves as comfortable as possible here for the night, without fire."

This was "cold comfort" indeed, when taking into consideration that a light, drizzling rain had commenced to fall, wetting all our clothing. The drizzle created a chilling, damp atmosphere, as well as causing the ground to become slippery, wet and muddy. Yet here we were to bunk for the night—a cold December night. We were to camp in total darkness.

After remaining in this exposed situation for an hour or more, word was brought to us by our officers that, owing to the state of the weather, General Meagher took the responsbility of permitting his own troops to kindle small fires. The general's directive was in violation of an order issued from division headquarters the same afternoon. It was already decided that we were not to cross the river until next morning. Our officers, suffering alike with ourselves, also reminded us of the risk we might have to run after our fires were started. Rebel shells could fall among us. But this risk we took to make ourselves more comfortable during the night.

Each man now went to work, groping and fumbling about in the darkness over the ground and in the adjoining woods for fuel in the shape of leaves, fence rails and branches of trees. Found with much difficulty, the fuel was lit and our fires kindled. These fires, although small and burning dimly, illuminated the sky and revealed to the enemy on the opposite heights the whereabouts of this part of the Union army. About ten minutes after, h-i-s-s came a shell over our heads. Falling among troops of another brigade 100 yards in our rear, it burst. But the missile only wounded one man and demolished a commissary's wagon.* Two or three others of a similar kind were sent over soon after, but falling a considerable distance from our post, I did not learn the nature of the damage done, if any. No further trouble from such unwelcome visitors was experienced for probably an hour after.

Suddenly, a loud report was heard and a terrific hissing noise came through the air. Looking up, I saw a huge round shell which fell among a clump of trees, tearing off several of the largest limbs. Rolling over the ground towards the Rebel prisoners some 150 yards to our right, the thing exploded, killing three horses and two of our own men. The missile wounded three more Union soldiers and also killed one of the Confederate captives. Before it spent itself, the round wounded four more Reb prisoners. This brought many of us to conclude that our cold and chilly quarters here for the night might become hot enough for us before morning.

But happily we were disappointed in such expectations. After spending two or three hours in moving around, momentarily looking for another Rebel shell and none appearing, many of our boys sought rest and sleep on old mother earth within their respective regimental lines. Two of my comrades from my company and I bunked together on a bed composed of small branches of trees laid on the cold, muddy and wet ground. We spread our India rubber blankets. Laying ourselves down upon them with our woolen blankets covering us, close together to keep warm, we were soon lost in sleep to all consciousness of our very dangerous and most uncomfortable quarters. Thus ended Thursday, December 11, 1862, in the Army of the Potomac in front of Fredericksburg, Virginia.*

---

* This was the first fire from the Rebel works.

** The tired and weary soldier far away from home seeking sleep, even on the battlefield covered with the dead and dying, thinks but little of his position and surround-

Friday, December 12th, 1862
Opposite Fredericksburg, Virginia

Notwithstanding the chilling, damp night, our slumber was only broken this morning by the roll of the drum at five a.m. We arose from our couch, wet through to the skin, to find our fires nearly extinguished by the light rain which continued to fall all night. Orders were now given to hold ourselves in readiness to cross the river at daylight and join the troops on the other side. They had crossed the previous evening and night, numbering probably 20 or 25 thousand men. Fires were at once renewed and a hastily cooked breakfast partaken of. After this, the regiment awaited the command to "Fall in line."

It was yet quite dark. Being suddenly obliged to obey a call of nature, I retired to a lonely spot in the woods, supposing that I would have sufficient time to obey the call and be back at my regiment before the command to "Fall in" had been given. This brings me now to state the fate of the Bible found in the slaves' hut near Falmouth on the night of November 27th while on the picket line. For safekeeping, I kept this Bible always in my bosom between my woolen overshirt and blouse, supported by my waistbelt. On this particular occasion, having to un-buckle the belt, I laid the book down on the ground for a moment. I had scarce done so when the bugle sounded the "Fall in" much sooner than I expected. In the excitement of the moment and my haste to get back to my place in the regiment, as well owing to the darkness which surrounded me at the time, I was most reluctantly compelled to leave this valuable and interesting relic of the war behind, although not with-out one or two unsuccessful efforts to find it. I have ever since sincerely regretted its loss.

Daylight at length appeared. But for some reason or other, our Irish Brigade was not moved forward as soon as was expected. The rain had ceased, stopping long before morning's dawn. A little after seven a.m., the bright, warm and welcome sun, peeping up from behind the eastern hills, indicated the opening of another clear, bright December day. At eight a.m., the brigade of General Burns, some 1500 strong, was or-dered forward. Crossing the river, the men deployed to the right, taking up a position near the extreme eastern end of the city close by the stream.[11]

ings. To him, the cold, wet or frozen sod, is as the softest, feathery bed. To him, the sleep and rest and dreams thereon enjoyed are luxuries indescribable.

The Irish Brigade
Crosses Into Fredericksburg

December 12, 1862

Federal
Confederate

Falmouth

Rappahannock

Fredericksburg

IRISH BRIGADE

Lacy
House

WATER
CAROLINE
PRINCESS
ANNE
CHARLES

Canal

Kenmore

UPPER
BRIDGE

River

STONE

GEORGE
HANOVER
CHARLOTTE
WOLFE

Plank Rd.

WALL

MIDDLE
BRIDGE

Irish
Brigade
Bivouac

Marye's

Cobb

Heights

R. F., & P. RR

Run

Telegraph Rd.

Hazel

N

LEE'S
HILL

Approx. 1/2 MILE

Mark A Moore

Other brigades followed in order, all of them suffering more or less from Rebel shells thrown among them as their ranks emerged from behind the Stafford Hills. The roads running down the face of the hills facing the Confederate works were dangerous places, being open and exposed to three crossfires from Reb artillery on Fredericksburg Heights. The Johnnies took every advantage in this way of shelling Union troops as they descended the hills to the river, causing not a few casualties among them.

From daybreak, a constant stream of men four abreast had been crossing on the center pontoon. At half past ten a.m., our brigade was ordered to take its place in the throng. The command "Attention, shoulder arms, right-face, forward, march," was received amid the deafening cheers of the troops. They moved forward at the regular marching gait. Upon reaching the open face of the hill down which we had to go to the pontoons, we received the additional order, "Double quick." The troops descended the decline, facing the Rebel works on the run. This was done so as our men would be exposed as little as possible to the enemy's fire.

My regiment on this occasion was the advance of the brigade, fortunately for me. I was perhaps in the front rank. In descending the hill, three men in the rear were severely wounded and had to be removed to a field hospital far away in the distance. At the same time, the casualties in the four remaining regiments of my brigade immediately following were three men killed and 13 wounded. The low ground at the river, however, was soon reached. Together with the city on the opposite shore, this position hid us from the enemy's view and to a great degree shielded us from his fire.

The regiment now crossed the river. Unfortunately, one of our drummer boys with his drum slung upon his back, walking too near the edge of the planks of the crowded bridge, toppled over and fell down into the water between two of the pontoon boats. I think that he was drowned for I never heard of him afterwards. The regiment then marched to a long wharf on the river at the extreme western end of the city where it was massed and ordered to stack arms and await further orders. The remaining regiments of our brigade were assigned temporary positions close by and along the streets of the town.

It was now pretty generally understood that the assault on the enemy's works would not be made until the following morning. Consequently, our men spent the interval in an endless variety of ways. Our rations being exhausted except for fat pork, our officers gave us permission to appropriate for the use of ourselves and our regiment any and everything in the shape of food found in the now uninhabited dwellings or stores near our position. A raid therefore was soon made upon these places, but for a time without success. Nearly every building entered appeared to have undergone a complete gutting out by the Rebels before they evacuated the town. Our bombardment also had destroyed many of the best stores along the riverfront by knocking them down or setting them on fire.

A small bakery, partially destroyed, was at length discovered and entered. In its cellar we found barrels of flour under a lot of rubbish and fallen walls. These barrels were speedily extricated from their unnatural abode, hoisted to the pavement and rolled along the street. Far up in the air over our heads, Rebel and Union shells were hissing and screaming on their errands of death to the artillerists of both armies on their respective heights. On reaching the top of a slight decline leading to our regimental quarters on the edge of the stream, the barrels of flour were released. Rolling down the hill into the regimental lines, the barrels and their finders were received with rounds of cheering on all sides. The heads of the barrels were soon knocked in. Each man of the regiment was immediately supplied with a haversack of good flour. One distinguished officer in the command remarked after all had been supplied, including himself, "Boys, we are surely the flour (flower) of the Army of the Potomac now."

Next came the cooking process. A tin cup was three parts filled with flour, to which was added a little water scooped up out of the river and a quantity of the melted pork fat. All was then stirred up together with a spoon or a piece of stick until it became a dough. Then it was spread out into a cake between the hands and cooked on tin plates or pieces of iron hoops over a fire. In this way we were furnished with a good supply of what I may term "army shortcake." The food was relished and enjoyed in a way only known to hungry soldiers in the field like ourselves.

The next part of the program was a short walk to a place within 100 yards of our regimental position. We headed towards what had been an exceedingly neat, cozy little cottage home in the middle of a garden of fruit trees and rosebushes, surrounded by a low, green wooden fence. Our artillery fire, however, had almost destroyed everything about the place. Nothing remained in its original position except about ten feet of the fence at the west side and end of the enclosure. Seeing something lying there which looked like a Rebel uniform, my two companions and I slowly approached the spot. What a sight met our eyes.

Three dead Rebel soldiers laid close together, stretched out at their full length on the cold ground. The upper parts of their bodies and heads were covered and hidden from view by an old army blanket. A friend or some kind of sympathizing comrade may have thrown this cover over them. We could only observe the lower parts of their legs, which the blanket did not cover. "We must see more of this," I said to one of my companions.

Taking hold of one corner of the blanket, I gently and softly raised it. One of my other companions lifted another corner of the blanket, revealing the faces of the sleeping dead. Poor fellows, I thought, shot down like dogs in defending what perhaps they conscientiously believed their rights as citizens of this mighty Republic. Here was another sight, another ghastly spectacle, connected with my life in the army which cannot be eradicated from my memory. One of the bodies was that of a young man with a beardless face, probably not over 25 years of age. On his shoulders were straps, indicating the rank of an officer. His uniform, which seemed to have come through some rough and hard service, was of the regular Confederate army gray. By his side laid a broken sword. The only trace visible of the cause of his death was a small bullet-hole in the neck about two inches below the ear. From this wound had flowed a stream of blood, saturating his upper clothing. With this exception, one would have thought that he laid there in a quiet, peaceful slumber.

Another of these victims was the body of a man apparently much senior to the former. He was probably the late owner of a musket that laid upon the ground only two or three yards distant. One of his arms had been shot off close into the body. This very possibly caused instantaneous death, judging from the quantity of blood with which the remains were literally covered.

The third victim was a man whose age we had no means of guessing. The upper part of the body, head, shoulders and part of the breast had been blown off. It was a spectacle painful and sickening in the extreme for my comrades and me. Yet who could have forseen that

---

* The first casualty named, that of the Confederate officer, probably resulted from the musketry fire of the 7th Michigan Infantry fighting their way across the river in their boats the previous day. The latter two were undoubtedly caused by one and perhaps the same solid shot or cannonball from our artillery on Stafford Heights.

before tomorrow's sun would set that our own fate would just be a similar one?

After gazing a few moments longer on this horrible scene, we carefully replaced the covering over the remains of the three dead soldiers, leaving them to sleep their last sleep after having fought their last battle. These were the first dead Confederate soldiers that I saw south of the Rappahannock.* We returned to our regimental quarters certainly with sadder hearts than when we had left them. But we said nothing to our comrades about our painful experience of the last half hour.

There was still another incident that afternoon. It was truly a sad one. Yet it was the cause of considerable merriment and laughter among all the troops on the south side of the river who witnessed it. Reckless bravery or presumption in the face of a powerful enemy with little or no regard for life is closely allied to foolishness. The man or men who practice or risk it are, in my opinion, worse than fools. Sooner or later they come to grief. I will now give an instance of this folly.

While encamped behind Falmouth, a New York State regiment of cavalry, some eight or nine hundred strong, all green troops never having been under fire, laid about a mile in our rear. The colonel of this regiment, quite a young and flashy officer with more head and money than brains, unceasingly fond of his bottle, made himself not only conspicuous but ridiculous by the almost constant drilling of his men. He did so regardless of wind or weather. Contrary to the laws of health, reason and army requirements, he tortured men and beasts. I saw the poor horses of his command drilling in a cold, pelting rain when all other troops were under cover of some kind. The animals stuck fast in the mud up to their knees, but it made no impression on the colonel who persisted in the exercise. He was no doubt stimulated to it by a brain fired with strong drink and perhaps a desire to show himself and his regiment superior to any others in the vicinity.

Owing to such conduct and habit on the part of this distinguished cavalry officer, our boys nicknamed him "Whiskey-head." It stuck to him during my time with my regiment. But the conceit was soon to be taken out of him. He was soon to realize that with all his drilling, pomp and show, Rebel shells would pay no more respect to him and his men than they had done to those less pretending and to many who had before experienced hard military service.

This regiment had not yet crossed the river, but we knew it was to do so sometime during the afternoon. It was now nearly three p.m. But the cavalrymen had not put in an appearance on the top of the Stafford

Hills. They would come down the slope to the pontoons, the only route available, which had already been taken by my own regiment and the rest of the Irish Brigade. From our position on the wharf, we had a full view of the route and could plainly see every regiment coming down the declivity. The route was fully exposed to three Rebel crossfires. Judging from our past experience that "Whiskey-head" would put on some of his "fancy airs" in coming down the hill with his regiment, thereby attracting a double share of the enemy's attention and a heavy fire from his batteries, we anxiously awaited the head of his regiment to emerge from behind the hills to the road.

A fine band was attached to this cavalry regiment. About half an hour afterwards, its music in the distance sounded faintly in our ears, indicating the approach of the command to the dangerous locality. The troops that had already descended had done so on a "quick run" to get out of the range of the enemy's fire as soon as possible. Every eye now was strained upon the approach to the pontoons. Various were the surmises as to how the colonel would descend with his horses and troops.

At length he appeared, elegantly mounted on his beautiful prancing, chestnut brown charger, advancing on a "slow walk." Immediately behind him was the band, likewise mounted and playing a military march. They were closely followed by the regiment. Down the hill they came at the same slow speed under a bright shining sun, with their new uniforms and glittering drawn sabers. It presented to us at our point of observation the grandest and most imposing military appearance that I ever witnessed. "Just something like what I thought he would do, the damned fool," said an officer of my regiment, seated among a number of our boys on a long prostrate telegraph pole, intently eying the view. "Watch now," said he, "wait till the whole regiment is fairly on the face of the hill where it can be raked by the enemy's fire. Then see how quick the Rebs will make them scatter and stir their stumps."

A moment later, the rear of the regiment came in view and the whole unbroken line was steadily but fatally slowly descending the hill. What a target! A painful silence ensued among our number. "What then, look out there," cried one, then another. Seven h-i-s-s-i-n-g Rebel shells now in rapid succession came flying overhead from the Confederate works behind the town. They burst all along the line of cavalrymen, killing seven of them and wounding 27. So much for probably the effect of whiskey, conceit and stubborn pride of one man.

These casualties were indeed sad, but the colonel's conduct and actions on the occasion, even amid such gloom, provoked a most hearty laugh from all of our men who saw him. He seemed to lose all self-possession when the shells commenced to come. Instead of hastening on down the hill to the low ground where he would have reached safety and been out of reach of the falling missiles, the colonel put spurs to his animal. He darted up the hill again as if ten thousand devils were after him. His hat fell off. His whole appearance, as well as his actions, was cowardly and ridiculous in the extreme. It plainly indicated a state of complete demoralization. I suppose the Rebels saw this too, for they sent another shell after him. But fortunately (or unfortunately, I know not which), it did not hit him. When near the top of the hill, the horse either stumbled or was shot, for it fell. The last we saw of this gallant officer was him quickly scrambling away from his now prostrate steed into a ditch on the wayside out of further danger. He left his wounded men to do the best they could with themselves and their dead comrades. The remainder of the regiment beat a hasty retreat from the dangerous place.[12]

But another incident of the afternoon. We were all hard up for tobacco. Hearing that our bombardment the day before had sunk a schooner laden with the weed in the river near our position on the wharf, we soon discovered her whereabouts. By means of ropes and hooks made out of pieces of iron, we succeeded in fishing up from her deck low down in the water fifteen boxes of good plug tobacco, sufficient to satisfy the wants of every member of our regiment and two others of the Irish Brigade. Verily, tobacco smoke that night filled the air.[13]

Now, to finish up the day, the 12th of December, 1862. At eight p.m., some of my comrades and I strolled into the first street near the river to kill time. Here we found the houses yet standing. Their former occupants had fled, and the residences were all taken possession of by our soldiery as quarters for the night. Those of them who could not get into houses quartered on the street where they had kindled numerous fires fed by such fuel as they could lay their hands upon. Here we saw elegant and costly furniture chopped up for firewood. In one instance, a magnificent rosewood piano. Yet the officers made no effort to prevent it. I thought this was wrong.[14]

We returned to our quarters, there to spend the night knowing what was before us next morning, namely our participation in the assault on the Rebel works. The ever memorable Battle of Fredericksburg, Virginia, December 13, 1862, followed.

"My own turn came next. Bullets had been singing their little songs around my head and ears since arriving on the battleground, piercing my uniform from head to foot and cutting open the cartridge box by my side."

Chapter 9

Up the Hill: The Irish Brigade
Assaults Marye's Heights, December 13, 1862

The full description of a great battle as observed by a single individual is, to my mind, an utter impossibility. It reminds me of what the Duke of Wellington once said to an individual who asked him for the correct information concerning the great Battle of Waterloo. "No man," he said, "is more incapable of giving you that than I am, because I did not see the whole battle but only that portion of it that came within the limited range of my own vision." This exactly suits my own case in my feeble effort to describe the Battle of Fredericksburg. Therefore, what I write concerning this terrible fight will be confined to what I actually saw and experienced myself on that part of the battlefield upon which Sumner's Grand Division and especially my own regiment and Irish Brigade were engaged. Bear in mind that the entire line of battle of the Federal Army was fully eight miles in length and the Confederate line about the same.

Sleep was unknown to the majority of my regiment during the night. A few others and I, however, enjoyed about two hours rest and repose alongside the mast of a ship, lying on the wharf.[1] This was not prohibited by our officers. On the contrary, they advised the men to take whatever rest they could within certain bounds. But few did so. I suppose for the reason that the approaching struggle counteracted all such inclination, except in a few cases, such as my own. Although not over probably over 1000 yards from the enemy's front, we felt pretty secure from being taken by surprise by any part of the Rebel army for the reason that between our position and the enemy stood the houses of the city and a picket line of Union troops numbering 4,500 men on the other side of the town. Consequently, had the enemy advanced out of his works upon the city, then filled with our soldiers during the night, he would first have to drive in our picket line which certainly would have awaked any slumberers like a few of my companions and myself. Under such a feeling of security from at least sudden danger, a few of the boys had a short nap on the cold ground.

At a little after four a.m., I was awakened by the loud talk of some of our men close by, standing near the edge of the wharf watching Rebel shells bursting and falling in the river. I quickly jumped up, rubbed my eyes and joined the boys. These shells with their fiery tails came whizzing over our heads, evidently intended to take effect upon that part of our artillerymen yet on Stafford Heights. Falling far short of their intended destination, they burst over the middle of the river or fell into the water. The Rebel gunners had either lost our range or were firing too high, for the shells thrown took no effect anywhere among our troops. In about half an hour, their fire ceased until long after morning's dawn. This, however, was only "the calm before the storm."

At about six a.m., several officers of our regiment visited their men busily engaged cooking breakfast at the various fires here and there on the ground. To the question asked these officers, "When do you think that the regiment will go into action?" the reply was, "Don't know," adding, "Hold yourselves ready any moment after daybreak."

Breakfast over, the intervening time was spent in smoking and talking over the situation and prospects of the day. A few minutes later, volley after volley of musketry broke upon our ears, as if proceeding from the Confederate works on Marye's Heights behind the town. The very place, as we were soon given to understand, which was to be assaulted by Hancock's entire division. Hancock's command numbered between five and six thousand men.[2] We soon learned that the firing now going on was between the Confederates on the heights just named and General French's whole division of our army. French's boys had the honor of first assaulting this distinguished Rebel stronghold. In the event of the attack not proving successful, another was to be immediately made by the veteran troops of Hancock.

French's division was now engaged in real earnest.[3] Thousands of muskets rattled on the morning air in one long unceasing roll and roar of death and destruction. The smell of burning powder almost suffocated to us in our position, probably not less than half a mile of the scene of the actual conflict. The city and a broad tract of ground laid between us and the battle-field. The ball was now fairly opened by French and his men. Their music of death floated upon every breath of air. Countless little minie balls were singing unpleasant songs in passing the ear of many a Rebel soldier, causing not a few to bite the dust. Their fire ceased—why was this? Had our boys taken the coveted heights? Driven out the enemy out of his works or made them prisoners of war? A few minutes more told the tale of the terrible defeat and retreat of the gallant French with scarce half of his men, leaving the other half dead, wounded and dying on the battle ground immediately in front of Marye's Heights. Sad, bitter, crushing defeat to Union arms. But the fearful task must be tried again—by the invincible, desperate and unyielding Hancock and his old and well tried veterans.

By this time, the distant musketry firing had almost ceased, except a few scattering Rebel shots fired after some poor, unfortunate Union soldier fleeing for dear life from the immediate battleground. Our officers now commenced to assemble within their respective regimental lines, indicative of a forward movement by my regiment, brigade and division. One of our lieutenants, approaching a squad of men conversing upon the situation and prospects of the day, was asked, "What news from the battlefield, Lieutenant?"

To which he replied exactly, "Well, boys, French is licked to beat hell," and added in substance, "We are soon to go over the same ground and try the same job that he failed to accomplish. We expect the order momentarily to move out to the assault. Be ready, be firm. Keep cool and do your duty when brought face to face with the enemy."

This news, although discouraging, was by no means unexpected so far as the defeat of this part of our army was concerned. We had good reason to believe not only that French's division had met with a terrible repulse, but also that the Confederates had gained a great victory over them. In our then low position near the river, we could not see the contending forces. But we distinctly heard the wild, taunting cheers and yells of the foe in his works as he poured his deadly rain of bullets, grape and canister into the faces of the devoted body of Union soldiers. They had advanced into the very jaws of certain, unavoidable death, falling down by tens, by scores, by hundreds, leaving the fortunate survivors to be driven back in the utmost disorder, a confused, demoralized mob.

Up to this time, the only troops that had engaged the enemy in his works on Marye's Heights was the division named, numbering about 6,000 men. Our Commander-in-Chief probably thought this force sufficiently strong to defeat the Confederates and drive them out of their entrenched position on Marye's Heights, the chief point aimed at by the Union troops. But how must Burnside have felt when he saw, and that too in a very brief space of time after making the attack, the brave men of French's division blown as chaff before the wind, beaten, crushed, demoralized? Half of their number dead, bleeding and dying in front of the enemy's lines, and the remainder scarce knowing which way to flee out of the terrible tempest of fire and death.

In a very short time, we saw for ourselves the fearful havoc made in the division of General French, which scarce an hour before presented a front which few would have thought could be broken except by overpowering numbers of the enemy. But such was not now the case. It was now about nine a.m. and the weather which had been clear and sunny an hour before suddenly became dark and cloudy as if mourning over the recent catastrophe to one portion of the Union army. A few minutes later, the sound of a horse's hoofs was heard galloping at the top of his speed down the first street running parallel with the river towards our brigade position. In another moment, the horse and his rider appeared at the end of a row of houses which had hidden both from our view until reaching that place. The rider we soon recognized to be Hancock, clad in his usual battlefield uniform, that of a private soldier ready for the fray. In a voice like thunder, he gave the order to the brigade commanders, "Fall in." Then putting spurs to his fiery charger, Hancock dashed away with lightning speed and was again lost to our view.

In another moment, likewise mounted and similarly clad, appeared our own beloved and no less brave brigade commander, General Meagher, reiterating Hancock's order to "Fall in." The command was at once taken up by each officer. In turn, the order was telegraphed throughout the Irish Brigade in a moment of time. It was the long looked for and wished for summons. Ah, that "Fall in" was the "deathknell" to many a brave and loyal heart in the Irish Brigade of the Army of the Potomac on that ever memorable dark 13th of December, 1862. But the order was quickly and willingly responded to, with an alacrity never equalled by the same troops on any previous or similar occasion, each man seeming to thoroughly realize his own individual responsibility as a soldier in retrieving the terrible defeat and repulse of French not quite an hour before.

The troops were soon in line with loaded muskets, anxiously awaiting further orders. Just then, Gen. Meagher again appeared on horseback at the end of the row of houses already mentioned. Two orderlies were with him, bearing in their arms large bunches of green boxwood. The general then did not come nearer the regiment. But he sent to our officers the bunches of boxwood, requesting them to present in his name a green sprig to each man in the ranks.[4] They were to stick these bits of green in their caps before advancing against the enemy. This was something that I did not at first understand but soon found out what it meant. General Meagher had always been in the habit of leading his brigade into battle with at least two emblems of Erin's nationality—the "green sprig" and the "green flag" which the Rebels had frequently admitted was a terror to them because they well knew the dogged, stubborn fighting qualities of the men who bore them.* In ten minutes, the order to advance was given by our lieutenant colonel [St. Clair A. Mulholland] who gave the commands, "Shoulder arms. Left face. Forward, march." The regiment was soon moving towards the field of battle.[5]

The streets of Fredericksburg ran north and south and east and west. The Rebel artillery was located on Marye's and Fredericksburg Heights, the former about half a mile and the latter three-quarters of a mile distant from the city on its southern side. Consequently the enemy's guns commanded all the streets running north and south and could rake them from end to end.

The streets running east and west, although greatly exposed to falling and bursting shells, were much safer than the others because troops passing along them could do so with comparatively little loss of life by hugging close to the sides of the houses. For the time being the residences intercepted the enemy's fire. The crossings of those streets running north and south were, however, fearfully dangerous and fatal places to many of our men. Although they invariably crossed them on a run and in single file, many were killed in doing so by the steady well-directed fire of the enemy from his batteries.

---

* The piece or sprig of green that was presented to myself on the above occasion, or rather the remains of it, I can show today (March 20, 1878) preserved in a bottle.

My Regiment leaves the Wharf

My regiment now filed off of the wharf at the extreme of the town into the first street south of it running east and west. There we joined the other regiments of the Irish Brigade, namely the 69th New York, 28th Massachusetts, 88th New York, and 63rd New York, all infantry. Together with my own regiment, the force of the brigade numbered on this occasion nearly 1,700 men.[6] We found the regiments just named drawn up in line in the middle of the street and resting on their arms, awaiting orders to advance. These regiments were separated from each other by the streets running north and south. To stand in these streets for a moment was almost certain death, owing to the enemy's fire having full sweep up them.

My regiment at this time was the rear of the brigade and the 69th New York the advance or head. This arrangement or disposition of the troops, I soon learned, was made so that the position of the 116th regiment would be the extreme right and the 69th New York the extreme left of our brigade line of battle in attacking the enemy.[7] My regiment after reaching a certain point in this street was ordered to halt and, like the others, to rest in place on their arms. Then followed another season of that terrible suspense and anxiety. Oh, what fearful suspense —I fancy I experience it yet.

A large woolen or cotton factory stood upon one side of the street in our front. It had been set on fire by our artillery early in the morning and its contents continued to burn amid fallen walls and broken, crushed machinery. Our position, therefore, was anything but comfortable or safe here, owing to the smoke from the burning ruins and a high wall yet standing. This wall threatened every moment to tumble down on the top of us—but we dare not without orders change our position.

The Irish Brigade remained there for perhaps half an hour or a little longer. I had no means of ascertaining the exact time of day nor indeed did any of the men seem to think of it. This halt or delay in our advance, when Rebel shells were flying in all directions and falling and bursting in every street in the town, was most trying and painful to all. I thought it worse, in every respect, than confronting the enemy face to face on the field of battle.

While in position here, I witnessed many horrid sights. Here and there Negro women were seen rushing out of half demolished houses, frequently with young children in their arms or crying and clinging to their skirts, perfectly frantic with fright. They evidently wished to escape to some place of safety outside of the town and out of the range of the falling, bursting Rebel shells. Yet at the same time they did not seem to know which way to run in their confusion. All were to be pitied. Although our troops could render them no assistance, the fleeing Negroes had our sympathy, the little children especially, who were being dragged along shoeless and barefooted over the rough street and in front of a line of soldiers. One aged Negro woman in particular attracted our attention and pity. She was coming along in a terrible hurry with a large basket in her arms and three crying youngsters holding onto her old and torn dress. Upon reaching the intersection of two of the streets, not fifteen yards from where I stood, a solid Rebel shot struck her, cutting her body literally in two and killing her instantly. Two of the children were also killed by the same missile and the third fatally injured.

Next came along a tall and elderly man and a lady dressed in deep mourning, the only white people in citizens' dress that I ever saw in Fredericksburg. All the other white residents had either left the city previous to its bombardment by our forces or hidden themselves away in the cellars of houses out of view of our men. This man approached the colonel of my regiment and, in a rather rough and abrupt manner, addressed him thus, "Say, are you the colonel of this regiment?"

"I am," replied Col. Heenan.

"Well," continued the stranger, "I am a minister of the gospel and stationed for the last three years in this city. You damned hot-headed Yankees have burned me and my wife here out of house and home. I can't stay here any longer. The people in the North must now give me at least a living, for what they have deprived me of here. Damn them, the fools."

Our colonel smiled and said, "Well, what do you want me to do in the matter?"

"I want you," returned his reverence, "to get me and my wife safely over the river and within Union lines."

Col. Heenan again smiled and then said, "My friend, it is not in my power to grant your request."

The "parson" raged, swore and actually sent, at least in word, the whole Union army to the bottomless pit. Our soldiers laughed and hissed at him. A shell passing overhead reminded him that for his own and his wife's safety, he had better be jogging along. The colonel, however, taking no notice of his profanity and threats, so unbecoming to his alleged profession, advised the reverend to report to the provost guard in charge of the pontoon bridge at this end. Under the circumstances, our

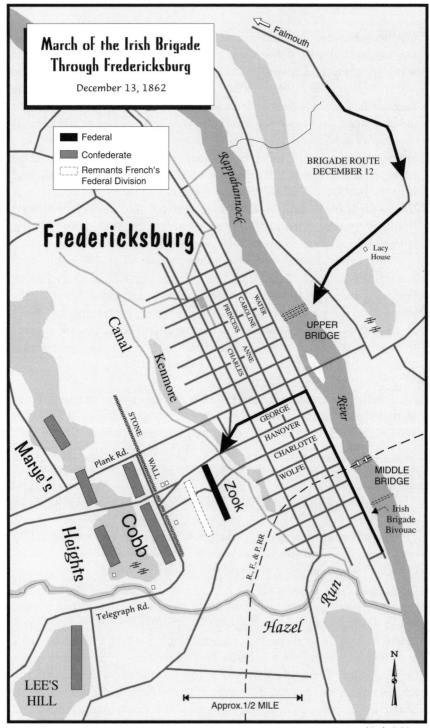

March of the Irish Brigade
Through Fredericksburg

December 13, 1862

Federal
Confederate
Remnants French's
Federal Division

BRIGADE ROUTE
DECEMBER 12

Rappahannock

Fredericksburg

Lacy
House

WATER
CAROLINE
PRINCESS

UPPER
BRIDGE

Canal

Kenmore

ANNE
CHARLES

River

STONE

GEORGE

HANOVER

CHARLOTTE

Plank Rd.

WALL

Zook

WOLFE

MIDDLE
BRIDGE

Marye's

Irish
Brigade
Bivouac

Cobb

R. F. & P. RR

Heights

Run

Telegraph Rd.

Hazel

N

LEE'S
HILL

Approx.1/2 MILE

Mark A Moore

men would likely allow the parson and his wife to pass over to the other side. He left us. In ten minutes, I saw him leading his fair companion by the hand over the bridge of boats with a hat on the back of his head. Owing to the music of the shells passing to and fro over his reverend head, he was to all appearance not quite so happy and composed as he perhaps had been when quietly reclining in his velvet-bottom pulpit chair amid the pealing notes of a splendid church organ and choir.

Many of the wounded of French's division were now being carried into the town from the battlefield. They presented to us who were just about to go into it fearful pictures of the horrors of war.[8] Very shortly, every house in the city considered comparatively out of the way of Rebel shot and shell was a hospital. Yet even in these, cannonballs frequently crashed through the roofs and windows, instantly killing some of those who were then fast dying of their wounds within them. While still in position here, one poor fellow was carried past us on a window shutter by two soldiers. His uniform indicated the rank of captain. His face was young and deathly white. He had been hit in the leg above the knee by a cannonball which had almost torn the limb from the body, a small thready sinew only apparently holding both together. As his comrades carried him along, the lower part of the leg, nearly severed from the body, hung over the edge of the board, dangling backwards and forward at every step taken by the bearers, an extremely sickening sight to those witnessing it. Some of our boys seeing this shouted to the men carrying the poor, unfortunate officer, "Lay him down and cut the leg off at once—that will ease him."

No attention, however, was given to this. But as the men with their wounded commander reached the center of my regiment in passing down along our line, one of the boys there seeing the situation of the sufferer sprang out of the ranks. With pen-knife in hand and quick as thought, he cut the thread-like sinew that seemed to be the only thing then that held the two parts of the leg together. This done, the limb from the knee down dropped to the ground, evidently much to the satisfaction and relief of its late owner. Very faint and weak from loss of blood, the officer could only smile and nod his head as a mark or token of thankfulness and gratitude to his thoughtful and kind benefactor.

General Meagher now came galloping down the line in front of the men. He soon reached the end of it, turned quickly around, passed up again at railroad speed in the rear of the troops and was soon lost to the view of my regiment. In five minutes, he appeared again in the distance at the head of the column, waving his glittering sword overhead. A moment longer and the order to advance with fixed bayonets was tele-graphed from regiment to regiment, from officer to officer, and the Irish Brigade was in motion once more. We headed up the street to the other end of the town, our route to the point to be assaulted on Marye's Heights.

The enemy evidently saw the movement, although our troops were well hidden from his view by the houses except when crossing the streets running north and south. No sooner were the soldiers in motion than the Rebs opened a furious fire of artillery, killing and wounding several of our troops, especially at the intersections of streets. The brigade, however, by regiments about ten yards apart marched steadily onward amid this terrible rain of fire and death until arriving at the other end of the town. Here we were again ordered to halt under cover of the houses and close to a high brick chimney in the rear of a mill.

Cannonballs and shells were now flying faster than ever, dropping thick in every part of Fredericksburg, crashing through roofs, windows and walls. In many instances, these missiles set the houses shielding our men on fire, killing or wounding several soldiers in each regiment of the Irish Brigade. But here we were halted and dared scarcely move except when a Rebel shell came rushing along close overhead. I must confess that many of our boys, including me, paid due respect in the way of a low bow or curtsy, having no desire whatever to make a closer acquaintance with the flying messenger or to interrupt him in his course. Our position and surroundings were certainly well calculated to stagger the bravest of troops and cause a general stampede. But such did not occur.

Meagher stood firm as a rock at the head of the column. The only uneasiness visible among the rank and file was when men bowed their heads to keep them out of the way of the flying enemy cannonballs. Yet notwithstanding this, some of them were instantly killed. At one time on this occasion, our lieutenant colonel [St. Clair A. Mulholland], thinking it perhaps necessary, shouted out, "Steady, men, steady. You'll soon get forward." Not a moment after, he himself made obeisance to a solid shot in close proximity to his head. Looking along the line of soldiers with a rather nervous smile on his countenance, he shook his head as if to say "Steady," which under such circumstances is easier to say than to do.

Almost at the same moment, a large, round shell, evidently from the lighter Rebel batteries on Marye's Heights was seen "coming for us." But falling short of our line, or about twenty yards south of it, it rolled quickly down the street without bursting through the interval between two of our regiments. The shell very probably found a grave in the waters of the Rappahannock. This missile had scarce disappeared when another of much larger dimensions neared us at lightning speed, probably from the heavy batteries of the enemy on the upper or Fredericksburg Heights. It soon proved to be a shell, the largest one too that I ever saw in circumference. It apparently was as large as a flour barrel. It struck the brick chimney in its center, very near which I stood at the head of my regiment. The projectile knocked the chimney down on the top of a row of low frame houses with a terrible crash, crushing all the structures to the ground. This stopped the progress of the shell, which then fell on the earth and burst not a dozen yards away. It wounded Colonel Heenan very severely in the hand. A piece of it hit me in the calf of the left leg, drawing blood quite freely. Seven of my comrades were wounded, some of them slightly and others seriously. Sergeant Marley of Company B of my regiment was killed instantly by the explosion.[9]

I paid but little attention to my own wound although it left the ground crimson at my feet. Colonel Heenan had his hand bandaged up and remained at his post. The other severely wounded men were sent back to the rear, then over the river, while three of my other slightly injured comrades and I kept our places in the line. We were more anxious than ever for the word "Forward" to try our powder face to face with our strongly entrenched opponents.

I have before stated that, to my mind and observation, attacking the enemy here with even double our numbers, say 200,000 men, in his almost impregnable position would be simply foolishness and would undoubtedly prove disastrous. I was right, although claiming only very limited military experience, as the close of that terrible day proved in the annals of the Army of the Potomac. No doubt General Burnside (Commander-in-Chief) was only carrying out the instructions of his government in assaulting the place. Yet at the same time I think he was to blame for doing so, or in other words, for rushing his men into the jaws of death. But for the providence of God, we would have been utterly annihilated. Burnside soon afterwards discovered his sad mistake. Although a good man in loyalty to his government and the Union, second to none, he was relieved from the command of the army after this Fredericksburg defeat and General Joseph Hooker (Fighting Joe) assigned to it. Ever after, all confidence in General Burnside as a military leader capable of successfully handling a "large" army was completely lost.[10]

Shouts were soon heard away up at the head of the line—it was the order to advance, come at last. Nearer and nearer, from regiment to regiment, until it reached my own. Every man and officer was in his place, notwithstanding the continued rain of Rebel shot and shell. "Attention," shouted our wounded colonel, "Shoulder arms, forward, double-quick. Now, men, steady, and do your duty. March."

My regiment followed close upon the heels of the other regiments of the Irish Brigade, also advancing on the double-quick towards the Rebel works on Marye's Heights. Our artillery, which for several hours previous had been silent on Stafford Hills, now opened a furious fire over our heads on the enemy's works to cover our advance. This fire, however, seemed to make as little impression as if directed against the rocks of Gibraltar. The Confederate artillery fire increased and their deadly messengers were hurled against our ranks in a manner never before experienced by the oldest regiments of the brigade. From the time that the Irish Brigade was drawn up in line on the streets of the town before advancing on the Rebel works and before even seeing a Rebel soldier, its loss was reported to be 17 men killed and 26 wounded. Hot quarters, indeed.

My regiment was now on a double-quick. Turning round a corner at the end of the town, we proceeded at the same speed until we reached the base of a hill. On the top of which stood a long, white wooden fence now prostrated by the fire of the enemy. Immediately below this fence, probably 25 feet down, was the Fredericksburg and Richmond Railroad. Arriving at the foot of this hill, the regiment halted for a few moments to rest the now almost breathless men. Here, although much nearer the enemy than before, we were well sheltered from his fire by the hill in front.

Our colonel now informed us, through orderlies, that our further route lay along the top of the ground above the railroad and close to the fence I have named. There was a very narrow path and it was a most dangerous place, open and exposed to all the Rebel batteries. But there could be no back-out. For what reason this route was selected for the passage of the Irish Brigade to the assault I never knew. Certainly it was a fatal road to many a Union soldier upon this occasion. At the same time, Colonel Heenan notified the regiment that as the summit of the bank of earth was so narrow, not admitting of two men abreast, the troops would have to break ranks in crossing and get over singly or as best and as rapidly as they could. This was accordingly done, but with a loss of two men killed and three wounded—a very small loss considering all the circumstances.

After crossing, we reached a canal, probably four or five yards wide, running through a small valley. It also had to be passed. Fortunately, it contained little water at the time, for many of the troops waded across while the rest passed over on a narrow corduroy bridge of five or six small trees stretched over the water. Earlier on the same day, its construction cost four men their lives. Over this bridge I passed myself.

The regiment, now over the canal, was quickly reformed and dressed along the base of another hill which also covered it from the Confederate fire. To our left, about 20 paces apart, stood the other regiments of the Irish Brigade ready to spring forward with my own to the top of the hill. The enemy in his works stood awaiting our approach and ready to give us a warm reception. To the left of the brigade and running along the same valley stood the brigades of Zook and Caldwell, also ready for the charge. The hill in front now only intervened between Hancock's division and the enemy. It was an exciting moment—the long lines of armed men waiting with breathless anxiety for the word "Forward." It was a scene never to be forgotten.

Silence reigned among the rank and file while generals, followed by orderlies, dashed up and down the lines giving their final orders to regimental commanders. All was ready. Then came that most terrible military command, "Fix Bayonets." This was done amid the yells and cheers of the men, resounding from one end of the valley to the other. The enemy undoubtedly must have heard. And as the clink, clink, clink of the cold, glittering steel being placed in position sounded down the long rows of soldiers, many of them soon to lay down their lives on the altar of their country, one could not help thinking that war, indeed, is sad. Well did the Irish Brigade know what this meant and what the nature of the work was which now laid before them. Well did the men realize that in preparing to use their favorite weapons of war, so dreaded by the enemy, especially when accompanied by the green flag, that a fearful, bloody struggle laid before them. One poor fellow at my side, who soon afterwards was killed, remarked in his good natured, broad Irish dialect as he placed his bayonet on the muzzle of his musket, "Damn them. That's the `thing' to fetch the sons of bitches."

I find that I have omitted to mention in their proper place a few observations. While passing along the high ground close to the white fence, the terrible effects of the Rebel fire in that particular place were sadly and painfully visible. The ground on the top of the embankment was literally covered with dead Union soldiers of French's division, shot down in their attempt to cross it. Wounded men also laid thick on the face of the bank and along its base, close to the railroad, whither they had crawled out of the Rebel range. While my regiment and I were passing over the same ground, my companion, Sergeant John Strechabock, who afterwards lifted me off the battlefield, suddenly attracted my attention by shouting out as he pointed down to the railroad, "Oh, look there, Bill. Look at the watermelon."

We were then on a run to clear the dangerous ground. I had not a second of time to lose for the enemy was hammering away at us from his heights. I merely glanced at the object he pointed at. It was the body of a dead soldier, face downwards, lying on the railroad in the center of the track. He had evidently been struck on the head by a cannonball which cut it in two as clean as if cut with a knife. Then I fully understood what my companion and friend meant by the "watermelon." The poor, unfortunate, dead soldier's head or rather the part of it still attached to the body presented at our distance from it the exact appearance of a large, ripe watermelon cut through the center, "red."

Sometime after this, I learned that but one Rebel gun had operated against this place and had caused a terrible loss of life. It was on the enemy's extreme right, a twelve-pounder Napoleon under command of Major Pelham, Chief of Stuart's Rebel artillery. With such deadly precision was this gun worked that for three hours it was impossible to silence. Thirty Federal cannons tried. General Stonewall Jackson was reported to have said, "That with two such guns on either flank commanded by Major Pelham, I could vanquish the combined armies of the world."[11]

The three brigades I have named, Meagher's, Zook's and Caldwell's, numbering in all about 5,800 or 6,000 men in double line of battle, were ordered to advance.[12] With a bound and a yell characteristic of perhaps Irish soldiers only, the men of the Irish Brigade did so, determined to force their passage at all hazards with the point of the bayonet. They saw what had befallen the men of French's noble division only a short time before. With lips closely pressed together, they were bent on revenging it if at all possible to do so.[13] On they went until they reached the top of the hill and the level ground within 200 yards of the first line of Rebel rifle pits and a long stone wall running close along their front.

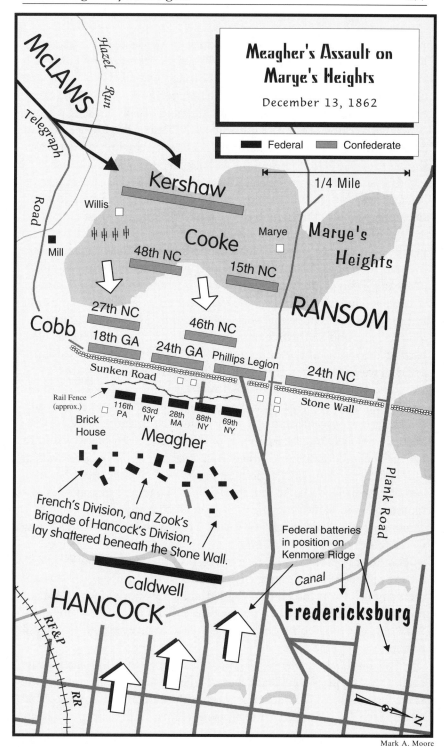

Meagher's Assault on Marye's Heights

December 13, 1862

Federal Confederate

1/4 Mile

McLAWS

Hazel Run

Telegraph Road

Kershaw

Willis

Mill

48th NC

Cooke

Marye

15th NC

Marye's Heights

27th NC

46th NC

RANSOM

Cobb

18th GA

24th GA

Phillips Legion

24th NC

Sunken Road

Rail Fence (approx.)

Brick House

116th PA

63rd NY

28th MA

88th NY

69th NY

Stone Wall

Meagher

French's Division, and Zook's Brigade of Hancock's Division, lay shattered beneath the Stone Wall.

Federal batteries in position on Kenmore Ridge

Plank Road

Caldwell

Canal

HANCOCK

RF&P

RR

Fredericksburg

N

Mark A. Moore

A blinding fire of musketry met them in the face. It staggered the line for a few seconds. But the Irish Brigade soon recovered, although after the loss of several men killed and many wounded, including one officer killed and three wounded.[14] Thanks to the first Rebel musketry fire upon us here, I came very near "stopping a ball" myself. We had scarce reached the top of the hill when a bullet cut the leather front or peak of my cap from its fastenings, leaving it dangling by a solitary thread at my ear.[15] But onward pushed our line, firing as it advanced.

The storm of battle increased its fury and the crash of musketry, mingled with the roar of cannon from the peaks, was terrific. To reach the stone wall was the first object in view. We certainly tried hard to do it. When a large part of the distance had been gained and we were within 50 paces of this wall, Cobb's solid brigade of Rebel infantry, said to have been then 2,400 strong, suddenly sprang up from behind it. They had been entirely concealed from our view until that moment. The Rebs poured volley after volley into our faces, at once stopping our further progress.[16] In connection with this fire, other Rebel infantry, in long lines behind earthworks and in rifle pits on Marye's Heights, were blazing away at us at the same time. It was simply madness to advance as far as we did and an utter impossibility to go further.

General Meagher, who at this time was on the extreme left of his command, saw the very critical position of his men and the terrible slaughter that was being made among them with no prospect of success. He ordered the five regiments of his brigade, then pretty well torn up, to be closely massed together in double line of battle. This was at once done, taking up only a moment or two of their time. Meagher then gave the command, "Load and fire at will." Away we went at it. A few moments after, he was very severely wounded himself in the thigh by a cannonball and carried off the field. That was the last time I saw General Meagher.[17]

Up to this moment, I had received no very painful wound myself, having only been struck on the left shoulder by a spent ball. It was not then painful. I was also hit on the left ankle by another, which caused me some uneasiness but did not prevent the full discharge of my duty. But I was not to get off so miraculously easy, as five minutes afterward proved.

The rattle of musketry was now deafening. Our fire against the enemy was rapid and constant, but its effect could not be seen for the stone wall in front. The Rebel fire, although perhaps not quite so rapid as our own, was decidedly much more regular and steadier, probably owing to the men being so well protected by earthworks. It was now beginning to tell fearfully among the men of my regiment, ploughing great gaps in the ranks. Every third man had fallen and, along some parts of the line, every second soldier had been killed or wounded.[18] To make matters still worse, we had lost nearly all our officers. Colonel Heenan was again severely wounded and taken off the field, also Major Bardwell, Lieutenants Willauer and Montgomery, the latter mortally, and Lieutenant Nowlen seriously wounded. Lieutenant Colonel Mulholland fell next. In quick succession, Lieutenant Maguire dropped, shot through the shoulder and leg, followed by Captains Smith and O'Neill and Lieutenants Rielly and Miles. But still my regiment held its ground.

My own turn came next. Bullets had been singing their little songs* around my head and ears since arriving on the battleground, piercing my uniform from head to foot and cutting open the cartridge box by my side. Yet, strange to say, none of them inflicted any wound worth naming except the two already mentioned—one on the left shoulder and the other on the left ankle, neither of them at the time causing inconvenience or much pain.

But now something much more serious occurred. I had discharged six or seven shots, I don't know which, up to this time into the ranks of Cobb's brigade right in our front behind the stone wall. I was getting ready to fire again, had taken the cartridge out of my cartridge box, bitten the end off it, inserted it into the muzzle of my musket, drew the ramrod from its place, and had just raised my right arm over my head to send the cartridge home, or down into the musket, when a bullet struck me in the uplifted arm, close up to the shoulder. The limb dropped powerless at my side. I knew something serious had happened to me. But at the moment did not realize that a Rebel bullet had hit me, inflicting a very serious wound. At first, I thought that the man in the rear immediately behind me in the second line or one of the men in the front or first line by my side had accidently struck my elbow with the butt end of a musket. For my feelings then were exactly like those produced by being suddenly hit in that way or by knocking my elbow a hard blow against a brick or stone wall. But in a very few more seconds, I discovered what was the matter. I actually was shot but in what

---

* The sound or song of the bullet, as it is often called, in passing close to the head and ear is exactly the same as that produced by a person pronouncing the word "Whist" very quickly in a sharp, low whisper.

particular spot, I was yet in ignorance. I felt it to be somewhere in the neighborhood of the shoulder. A stream of warm blood now came rushing down the inside and outside sleeve of my uniform, then down the side of my pants into my right foot shoe until it overflowed. Next, a dizziness in the head and partial loss of sight came over me, accompanied by violent pain in the wounded part. Then growing very faint and weak from loss of blood, I fell down flat on my face on the ground with my musket, which I clutched with my left hand by my side. My comrades now stood over me and near me, still in line, although few indeed continued to blaze away at the foe.

My consciousness speedily returned, I suppose due to the fall. I attempted to rise and make my way to the rear or to somewhere out of the range of the enemy's fire. But I had scarce raised my head when a shower of bullets came around it. I at once concluded that to move was dangerous and to rise up would be fatal. Accordingly, I lowered my head again, stretching my body out upon the earth and lying as close to the ground as I possibly could. I hoped to let the enemy's bullets pass over me. No sooner had I done this than one of my comrades, the third man from the head or right of the regiment and almost my next neighbor there, was shot dead and fell about two yards in front of me. Poor fellow, he was afterwards riddled with bullets. Owing to the position of his body, it stopped many a ball that otherwise would certainly have entered my own. At it was, bullets kept constantly whizzing over me, around me, and burying themselves in the ground not a foot from my head. These rounds threw mud and dust all over my person.

My situation was truly an awful one. I was not more than 50 paces from a powerful, victorious foe—exposed to his three fires, left, center and right, and also in danger of the fire of all the other Union troops coming to the attack behind me as well as bursting shells from our own artillery on Stafford Hills thrown over here at the enemy. In the enemy's clutches, I may almost say, I laid disabled, disheartened, hope a mere shadow. I might be torn to pieces by a cannonball or shell at any moment or sent into eternity by the lesser, but just as fatal rifle ball or musket bullet of the now tantalizing Confederates. I then offered up the simple but earnest prayer, "Into thy hands, oh my God, I commit my soul and body." After which, thank "Him," I felt more composed in mind and perfectly reconciled to my fate—death or life. In another instant, another of my comrades fell almost at my feet, mortally wounded in the stomach, exclaiming as he went down, "Oh, my mother." He tossed about in agony and blood for a few seconds longer, then all was over. His spirit had fled.

The regiment by this time had lost close to half of its rank and file and nearly all of its officers, yet the men who were still unhurt continued to blaze away at the Rebel troops behind the stone wall. The other regiments of the brigade had suffered in like proportion to my own. It was now, I suppose, about two p.m. No success whatever at any point within my own view had crowned the Federal arms. Death, havoc and carnage was visible at every step on the ground fronting Marye's Heights. I could not see now, owing to my low position, who had command of the regiment, but distinctly heard the order given by someone in authority, "Fall back, men, and every man for himself."

This was immediately done and not a moment too soon. Ten minutes more of such work would have resulted in the total butchery of the regiment, leaving no man in it to tell the tale. The men turned their backs on the foe and fled in the greatest confusion towards the base of the hill which they so recently ascended to the assault. The Rebel fire followed them in their retreat until the low ground was reached. All that now remained of the regiment was once more comparatively out of the reach of Confederate bullets.[19]

But where was I? Left all alone in my glory if such it really was. Lying among heaps of my wounded, dying and dead companions. Cannon to my right, cannon to my left, cannon in front and cannon behind volleyed and thundered to the music of thousands of minie balls flying about in all directions. To rise up and run was impossible. First, because the nature of my wound would not admit of it then. Second, because had I done so, I would undoubtedly have been shot down again and perhaps instantly killed. It became evident that the enemy was picking off our wounded men on the battlefield, firing at them and killing them outright. To get aid or even to expect it from any of our own men was out of the question. No one could get near me except at the risk of his own life. Was not my position a terrible one? I must confess that at that time I never expected to get off or to be taken off that bloody field alive. But it was otherwise ordered and I was spared to tell my tale.

I have spoken of the brotherly affection and attachment to each other that existed between two members of my regimental company and me. To show how strong these feelings were towards me in the hour of battle, I must relate the following incident concerning the conduct of Lieutenant Foltz. He was shot through the head and instantly killed trying to avenge my misfortune.

The incident was as follows. The survivors of the regiment had just commenced to retreat when Lt. Foltz, almost at whose feet I laid on the ground, stooped down and said to me, "Bill, we've got to get. Are you badly hurt? I wish to God I could get you out of here." Before I had time to reply, some new thought or idea must have struck his mind. For he seized my loaded musket by my side and, in an unusually excited manner and voice, moved a few yards forward, saying, "Bill, I see the bastard that laid you there. I'll fetch him." Foolish man, I thought, how can you designate the man that shot me among such a multitude of Rebel soldiers? But be this as it may, he knelt down on the ground with his left knee, placed the butt end of the musket upon his shoulder, and took deliberate aim at something in the direction of the stone wall. I watched him closely. Before he pulled his trigger the musket fell out of his grasp. He nervously raised his hand to his brow and then fell to the earth a bleeding corpse, pierced through the head by a Rebel bullet. His face was towards me, revealing the fatal wound immediately above the left eye. The profound sorrow that I then experienced no tongue or pen could describe. There laid my late beloved friend and companion in his blood, almost at my side, stiff and cold and dead. All to avenge only a wound received by me. He was of middle age, had a fair education, and was quiet and kind in his disposition. Foltz was a native of either Pottsville or Reading, Pennsylvania.[20]

On this occasion, my regiment and brigade went into battle, to use the military term, in light or winter marching order. Each man previous to crossing the river delivered up to a guard there such articles of his equipment as would in any way retard his movements or encumber his person on the march or on the battlefield. Orders, however, were issued to carry blankets. As was the custom, these wool and gum blankets were rolled up lengthwise in rope form, probably six or eight ply thick, tied with a cord at the ends and slung over the left shoulder like a sash. In this manner, the troops went into action. Immediately after my comrade Foltz fell, bullets were flying so thick around me that the thought struck me to pull or work my blankets off my shoulder and to place them in front of my head. They would serve as at least a slight protection from the deadly missiles.

Fortunate, indeed, that I thought of this. Double fortunate that I succeeded in doing it. The prospect of death now seemed to increase. My clothing was being literally torn from my back by the constant and furious musketry fire of the enemy from three points. A ball struck me on the left wrist inflicting another painful but not serious wound. Another one which would undoubtedly have proved instantly fatal but for my blankets pierced through six plies of the blankets. It left me the possessor of a very sore head for six weeks after. With such force did this bullet come that for some time I really thought it had embedded itself in the skull. My blankets were the receptacles of 32 other bullets which dropped out when I opened them up the next morning in Fredericksburg.

In this assault, lasting probably not over 20 minutes, certainly not more than half an hour, our division lost in killed and wounded over 2,000 men. It was an unprecedented severity of loss—nearly 35 percent of the entire number. Here I may state, in contradiction to statements that I have seen in print to the effect, that in making this assault the division of Hancock did not succeed in advancing on the enemy's works to within 25 paces of the stone wall. That clearly was not the case. My own regiment and brigade actually advanced, if anything, farther than the other troops of the division. To my own personal knowledge and observation, the point reached was not short of 50 paces—to go farther was simply an impossibility. As regards me, I was as near the wall as any man in the line, except my comrade Foltz who was killed two or three steps in front of me.[21]

A few minutes after the repulse and retreat of my division, a Federal battery of six guns was hurriedly brought up to the brow of the hill behind where I still laid to operate on the enemy in my front. The Rebels on the heights, however, at once opened a furious fire upon our gunners, killing several and forcing the others to abandon the guns and beat a hasty retreat without having fired a shot. These guns were now at the mercy and almost within the grasp of the enemy. Had the Rebs wished to have these cannons, they could have advanced out of their works to capture them. There simply would have been no opposition. Fortunately, however, for me and my poor wounded and dead companions lying all over the field, the Johnnies did not advance. For had the Confederates done so, their route would have been over our bodies. An advance would have resulted in instant death to the men already wounded and dying or their capture as prisoners of war. A squad of men with ropes soon approached the deserted battery. With great difficulty and dogged perseverance, amid the grape and canister fire of the enemy upon them, they succeeded in hauling the cannons off the ground.[22]

General Howard's division was now brought forward to the attack, supported on its left by two other divisions of the 9th Corps. It was now probably three p.m.. Evidently, a general engagement along our entire line had commenced, or very soon would do so.

A General Engagement and Defeat of the Federal Army

Shakes the ground beneath the onset,
Quakes the sky with answering dread,
And the iron waltz of battle
Whirls along with crushing tread.
Flash the flaming tongues of muskets,
Peals the cannon's angry roar,
And the shell's loud, awful hissing,
Swells the fearful din of war.
Iron hoofs are on men's bosoms,
Hearts are crushed by cannon wheels,
And no drum beat gaily soundeth,
Nor the cheering bugle peals.

To my right and to my left, as far either way as I could see, solid rows of Union soldiers were advancing up the slope to attack the enemy. Brigade after brigade and division after division were hurled against him time and again, but like my own, were blown back as if by the breath of hell's door suddenly opened. Shattered, disordered, they ran pell-mell back down the declivities amid the shouts and yells of a victorious foe which made the horrid din demonic. Howard's division which came up behind me advanced to within about 20 yards of the place where I was lying, but were quickly stopped by the enemy's artillery on the heights and his infantry in my front. After delivering several volleys into the Rebel lines, this division also retreated in great disorder, leaving hundreds of its numbers dead and wounded on the field. While all this was going on on the lower ground, the enemy's artillery on the heights of Fredericksburg and the Federal on Stafford Heights were vigorously firing at each other. With the constant rattle of at least 100,000 muskets, the noise was deafening and caused the ground under and around me to shake to such a degree that at times I actually thought it was sliding away. The dead and wounded now lay very thick all around. The cries of some of the latter were heart-rending in the extreme.

Immediately after the retreat of Howard's troops, my attention was directed to a fine, large chestnut-brown horse. It dashed out from behind the stone wall, dragging along a dead rider whose foot was caught fast in the stirrup. The poor animal presented an appearance wild, beautifully wild if I may term it so. Snorting so loud that I distinctly heard the noise with nostrils extended and like to burst, the horse darted to and fro, its mane standing stiff on end. Round and round rode the horse on the open ground between the two fires of the combatants, finally falling to the earth on the body of its lifeless rider, riddled with bullets. My attention was particularly directed to this horse because at one time it made a bee line in its fright for my position. I was afraid that the horse would run over me. But before he got near me, he was shot down, by Rebel bullets too.

I turned my attention to a house with a small red flag flying from the roof. This building was located near the center of the battlefield, only a short distance, probably not over 20 yards from the place where I fell. It fronted the city and its opposite side faced the Rebel works, thus fully exposed to their fire. When French's division was repulsed in the morning, many of the wounded crawled into it for protection and hoisted the little red flag as a signal to the enemy that the house was being temporarily occupied as a hospital. The small red banner notified the Rebs that the building was then filled with helpless, wounded men. Our boys hoped that the enemy would not fire upon it. The signal was at once understood by the Confederates and, to their honor and credit, the request made was granted. The only injury afterwards done to the house was from musket balls fired at our advancing troops. Some either fell short or missed their mark, striking the gable wall and glancing off. I afterwards learned that this end of the house had actually been reduced to a thin shell by the great number of Rebel bullets that struck it in the way I have described, grinding it away. Had the enemy been so disposed, he could have levelled this house to the ground in five minutes and blown its poor, mangled and bleeding inmates to fragments.

A burning thirst was now coming fast upon me—that most terrible of all thirsts known to and experienced only by the wounded on a battlefield where water was not to be had. Oh, how I craved a cup of cold water. I would have given $1000 for it had I had it. I could not rise from the earth and dare not do so. Had I been able to duck the flying bullets and look for water, I knew not where to find any closer than than the Rappahannock River.

A crowd of soldiers stood behind the brick house which shielded them from the enemy's fire. They dared not put their heads past the corner except at the risk of their lives. I laid within 20 yards of them. I called to them, "For God's sake, throw me a canteen of water."

A brave, sympathetic, fellow edged out from among the crowd with canteen in hand. He crawled on hands and knees, evidently intending to get near enough to throw the water to me. This soldier was struck by a bullet, causing him to beat a hasty retreat back to safer quarters, leaving me minus the relief he so nobly tried to render at the risk of his own life.

Darkness was now coming on, yet the conflict raged. But before eleven p.m. that night, the Army of the Potomac was a defeated, dejected and demoralized mob.

*"While burying their dead, I was particularly struck with the good feeling
that seemed to prevail among the troops of both armies. . .
as if they never had been enemies."*

Chapter 10

**Forlorn Hope:
The Wounded of Fredericksburg**

It was now probably half past four p.m. on that ever memorable
Saturday afternoon, December 13th, 1862. The sun had set. Twilight
had stolen out of the west and spread her veil of dusk. The town, the
flat, the hill, and the ridge were covered with our dead, dying and
wounded braves, all laying under the canopy of night's extending shade.
Blackness and gloom had settled down upon the battlefield. A division
of Federal troops, truly a forlorn hope covered by the darkness, advanced
up the hill behind me, intending to charge the enemy by surprise. They
reached a point within a few yards of where I still laid. A tremendous
volley of musketry was poured into the Rebel lines in the direction of
the stone wall. The Johnnies immediately replied with a storm of fire
from their works, driving the division back under cover of the hill, again
with enormous loss.[1]

The attack now ended. The Battle of Fredericksburg was over and
the Army of the Potomac was sadly and crushingly defeated, with a loss
of 1,725 men killed, 7,010 wounded, 300 prisoners and 211 missing—
total 9,246 men. General Lee of the Confederate Army reported his loss
in killed and wounded to be only 1,800 men—a striking difference,

showing at once the advantage of "position" to any army such as that occupied by the Confederate forces at Fredericksburg.[2] The loss of my own regiment was 27 killed, 84 wounded and 31 missing—total 142 men out of about 300 that went into action.[3] The casualties were nearly 50 per cent of the whole command. The Confederate force was said to have numbered 80,000 and the Federal a little over 100,000 men at this place and time.*

The fire of the enemy after repulsing the last Union attack commenced to slacken and soon afterwards ceased altogether, except at intervals of about ten minutes each when volleys were directed at the ground and place over which Federal troops might advance to surprise him in the darkness. I know of no other reason for such discharges of Rebel musketry as took place then. The enemy undoubtedly thought that by occasional volleys from his front he would deter the advance of any other bodies of Union troops at night. The Confederates, however, might have saved all the powder so wasted. For no further attack was intended to be made by any of the Federal commanders, nor were their men in condition and force to make it.

Here I must say a word in regard to the appearance of the Rebels and the interval firing at night. I still laid on the ground directly in their front, awaiting a safe opportunity to rise up and get out of the range of their fire. Such an opportunity, however, had not yet arrived. About every ten minutes, a storm of bullets came from Cobb's brigade behind the stone wall, only 50 paces to my front. The sudden flashing fire of their muskets in the darkness for a second of time so illuminated the faces and uniforms of this part of the Confederate army that the men looked strangely red and savage—more like devils than human beings. Then the blackness and darkness of night covered them. The only sounds heard were the shrieks and groans of our wounded and dying, strewn on every side like scattered seed. Truly, war is sad.

Soon after dark, rain commenced to fall and continued until morning, making the battlefield still more horrible than before, aggravating the sufferings and condition of the wounded. Fortunately, however, the night was mild for the season, one of those murky, warm winter nights.

---

* The venerable and lamented General Sumner, Commander-in-Chief of one of the three grand divisions of the Army of the Potomac, of which Hancock's sub-division of the Second Corps was a portion, was reported to have said, with tears running down his cheeks, "The troops of my division gained imperishable honor, but melted away like snow— they did all that men could do."

Otherwise, hundreds would have died from cold and exposure, especially those who were unable to get up from the field and remained there until next morning.

I decided that my only chance to escape safely from my dangerous position would be during the intervals between the Rebel fire. I resolved to attempt it. Just as the sounds of another volley of the enemy died away at about eight p.m., I regained my feet with much difficulty and excruciating pain. I started for safer quarters on the low ground immediately in the rear of the battlefield. To move along now, situated as I was, was no very easy matter. It was pitch dark and raining. There was no friendly light to guide me. I crept slowly back from the dangerous Rebel front, frequently stumbling over the dead body of some unfortunate comrade laying in the restful arms of death under the solemn pall of that dark and terrible December night on the plains of Fredericksburg. My clothing was saturated with the rain and my body was covered with blood and dirt. My friendly blankets, although then mysteriously and unaccountably heavy, I did not relinquish. I dragged them along.

My right and seriously disabled arm had to be supported by my left, also slightly hurt. The motion of my body in walking caused almost unbearable pain in the right arm when not propped up or kept from shaking. To add to these, as soon as I got up from the ground, my wounds re-commenced bleeding. But I pushed on as well as I could in the direction of the valley where we had started our charge.

According to my calculations, it was now nearly time for another volley of Rebel musketry over the ground. I laid down again, flat on the earth to let it pass over me. I intended afterwards, if fortunate enough to escape from being struck again, to get up and continue my journey. As yet, I was a considerable distance from a place of safety. The expected rattle of firearms, sure enough, did come, but not quite so soon as I anticipated. A bullet struck the heel of my shoe, tearing the half of it away, but doing no injury to the foot. It was now evident that the Rebel fire was gradually slacking off, the intervals between the volleys becoming much longer.[4]

I now got up on my feet again and, as before, groped my way onward in the darkness, finally reaching the top of the hill running down into the valley. Two minutes later, I was on low ground and, thank Heaven, once more out of the reach of Confederate bullets. I was still within range of their exploding shells, had any been thrown then, which fortunately was not the case. I crawled over beside a ditch or gully in the ground. I hoped to find some quiet spot to again lay down and await assistance from any of our men then in the city or close to it. There was a chance that some might venture out to or near the battlefield in the night for the relief or removal of the wounded.

With my left hand, I succeeded in untying the cords that fastened my gum blanket around the woolen one, then laying the former out flat on the wet, muddy ground beside the ditch. I laid down upon it in the hope of the assistance named. My strength by this time was completely exhausted from a great loss of blood. Had I been able, which I really was not, to have walked to the city, in all probability I would have failed in the attempt. Fredericksburg was yet at a considerable distance. There were no guides to it except a few small flickering lights borne by some members of the ambulance corps here and there.

A burning, raging fever now attacked me. I felt as though I was being consumed. The pains of my wounds increased. My thirst grew to such an agonizing degree that my tongue literally stuck fast to the roof of my mouth, almost preventing articulation. My sufferings now from the pains of my wounds were indeed light compared with my suffering from thirst. I really prayed to God with all my soul to end my life then and there or send me water. Oh, that terrible, consuming thirst. I shall never, never forget.

I had been laying there for probably an hour when suddenly the sound of voices in the distance broke in upon my ear. By this time, I was in what might be termed a half-dead condition, caring but little whether I died or lived. But the sounds I heard revived my hopes for assistance. I raised my head to hear more distinctly. I also tried to catch a glimpse of any approaching light, close or distant. I discerned a very small ball of fire not then much larger than a spark. It would sometimes suddenly disappear and then reappear, moving round and round, backwards and forwards, sometimes almost touching the ground, and at others raised up above it. I watched it intently with nervous anxiety. Gradually, to my joy, it came nearer and nearer to me, soon convincing me that it was a dark lantern in the hands of some of our own men looking up their wounded comrades along the edges of the battlefield. The sounds of mens' voices also became more distinct, causing me to make an effort to call out for assistance. In this, however, I failed. Owing to the great thirst that was then consuming me as well, as my strength being almost prostrate, I was scarce able to utter a sound much louder than a whisper. All then that was left for me to do under the circumstances was to watch and hope.

Every minute now seemed like an hour to me. I prayed that the men whose voices I distinctly heard would come near enough so that by some means or another I might attract their attention. My prayer was heard and answered. In a short time, the light was within twenty yards of me, occasionally showing the dark forms of two men. They were all that constituted that little party.

I soon recognized the voice of one of them as being that of Sergeant John Stretchabock, a Philadelphian and a member of my own company and regiment. Now or never, I thought, was my chance for help. Such an opportunity was not to be disregarded. Not knowing the moment that the attention of these men might suddenly be drawn away to some other part of the field, leaving me perhaps to perish during the wet, dark night, it was time to do something. By a great effort in a thick, muttering voice or sound for the former was gone, I called out as loud as my strength permitted, "Stretch, is that you?"

It was heard. The light at once stood still, the men evidently stopping to listen from what direction the sound proceeded. I then repeated my question. My friend seemed to recognize it for he quickly shouted out, "My God, is that you Bill? Where are you?"

In the same voice, I replied, "Yes. A little more to your right and you'll find me."

My directions were at once followed. The two men as they approached carried the light close to the ground as if to avoid stumbling over any dead bodies that might lay in their course to the place where I was lying. I soon discovered that the lantern was in the hand of my friend. As he arrived at my side, he held it down to my face, exclaiming, "Heavens, Bill, it is you. We have been hunting for you and Foltz for the last two hours. Where are you wounded, in the head? Your face is covered with blood."

I did not answer his question just then, but asked him immediately for water. Water to quench my burning thirst. At that moment, his partner, who had been a few yards behind him, also came up to my side with several canteens slung from his shoulder. Oh, what a refreshing sight to me, and how my heart was cheered in the hope that the canteens contained what to me then was worth more than all earth's riches—a draught of cold water. Without saying anything, my friend took one of the canteens from his partner's side, drew out the cork and stooped down, putting the canteen into my hand. On, what relief, relief, which neither my tongue nor my pen can give my reader anything like a real description of. The canteen was full, holding as did all our regular army canteens just a quart. At one draught, without taking it away from my lips, I drained it of every drop of water that it contained, then asked for another one. It was at once given to me. The water shared the same fate as the first canteen. I now felt greatly revived and thanked God and my kind, thoughtful and self-sacrificing comrades and benefactors.[5]

After drinking freely of this God sent water, I felt like another man. My natural voice returned. Dear friend Stretchabok then inquired again where I was wounded. I told him, "Very severely in the right shoulder and slightly in other parts of the body."

"Well," said he, "how under heaven did you get out alive? I saw you when you fell up near the stone wall. But it was too hot there to get you away when the regiment fell back. But come, we must help you up and get you out of here. The Johnnies are expected to advance during the night. But where to take you for shelter and to have your wounds dressed, I don't know."

"A few ambulances came out of the city but returned immediately laden with wounded," Stretchabok said. "In your condition, you could not walk to the city. It's rammed, packed, jammed anyhow, with our wounded. We'll stay by you, however, for awhile and see if some other ambulances come along."

I then had the chance to give him the particulars about my wounds and escape from the Rebel front. He then said, "Bill, did you see them two regiments go down in the valley?"

I did not understand him and replied by asking him, "What valley and what regiments?"

"This valley that you are now lying in," said he, "Do you know that commencing some 40 or 50 yards east of you, it is full of dead men?"

"No," I said, "How is it Stretch? Tell me."

He then gave me the following account of the wholesale slaughter of the regiments alluded to: "You remember when we passed over this valley, going up to the attack, it was full of troops in line ready to advance. Why it was that our division was pushed by them, I don't know. I did not see them again until we were driven back across the same place—they were still there but all or nearly all dead lying on the ground in the same straight line as that in which they had stood. Looking just as though they lay there fast asleep. It was a frightful sight."

I then inquired how this occurred. He told me that he understood that these troops were western Ohio regiments placed in this valley. The Federal commander supposed that they were out of the enemy's view. These men were held there for the purpose of making a sudden dash upon the Rebs at some future moment and particular point during the day. The Rebels, however, discovered them and, bringing a battery into position on their right on the heights of Fredericksburg unobserved by our men, where the entire valley could be swept from end to end by its fire, suddenly opened upon our boys with grape and canister. It took the Union troops there by such surprise and with such deadly effect that only a few of them were left to tell the tale, the others being shot down where they stood. "Our boys now," said my friend, "and they are few and pretty well used up, have given this valley the name of `The Valley of Death.'"

My friend's partner, a stranger to me, now observed a light down in the bottom of the valley. Soon the sounds of an ambulance moving along were heard. In a short time, it suddenly stopped about 50 yards from me. "Now, Bill," said my friend, "here's a chance. We'll get you aboard of that coach if we can."

The two men put their arms gently under my back at my request. I could not bear being lifted up by my arms owing to my wounds. They raised me upon my feet to help me towards the ambulance, my friend remarking, "Bill, if you can't walk, we'll carry you. We have no time to lose. It may be driven away and God knows whether or not another may come this way again tonight."

I told them I thought I could walk with their aid and then requested one of them to bring my blankets along, as I might need them. My friend stooped down to pick up the woolen one which still remained rolled up. As he did so, he remarked somewhat astonished, "What in the devil have you in this blanket, Bill? It's as heavy as lead."

I did not then know what it contained and only said, "Nothing that I am aware of except water."

With the assistance of the two men, I proceeded towards the ambulance. Upon reaching it, we discovered that the wheels were stuck fast in the mud almost to the hubs. The driver beat his poor horses most unmercifully to urge them forward, but all to no effect. The vehicle then contained eleven wounded men, making my chances for room within of quite a doubtful character. My friend Stretchabock, however, leaving me at the end of the ambulance in care of his partner, went forward to the driver and said something to him that I did not hear. Whatever it was, it caused oaths and curses from the man with the whip. He stoutly protested against my admission, alleging that he then had an overboard of passengers. My friend, however, persisted and coaxed. Finally I received permission to enter, or rather to be helped aboard by my comrades. After they raised me up into the ambulance, I shook hands with them, wishing them God's blessing. Especially for my friend Stretchabock from the city of brotherly love.

It was now about eleven p.m. What a night—dark as death itself and raining in torrents. This is usually the case in the place where a great battle has been fought immediately after its termination. By the aid of the shoulders of my two friends at the wheels, the ambulance was again started. The driver mounted his seat and was soon on the double-quick for the city. My seat, the only spot that I could find, was on the floor with my legs hanging out over the end—a rather uncomfortable position for a wounded man. Yet I felt thankful for it. All those who occupied the conveyance were wounded, some of them seriously and others fatally, as two of them died before reaching the town. The ride was the roughest that I ever experienced. No road was sought nor followed. We rode over rocks and stumps of trees and probably over the dead bodies of some of our men. The ambulance drove out of one gully and into another, almost upsetting the vehicle. This shaking and jolting so increased the sufferings of its occupants that some of them repeatedly called out to the driver, "For God's sake, go slower, you're killing us." But he did not heed them.

After being tossed about in this way for fully half an hour, we entered the city at very near the place that my regiment marched out of in the morning to the assault. We had reached the place where the high brick chimney was located. A sight of the wildest confusion and demoralization presented itself to my view. Every house not demolished was either filled or was being filled with our wounded soldiers. The streets were filled with troops not knowing what to do or where to go, one part of a regiment being mixed up with that of another, while many men sought the whereabouts of their own regiments, but were unable to find them. Small arms and broken bayonets laid about in all directions. Disabled horses, dismounted guns and partly destroyed gun carriages blocked up the principal thoroughfares of the town. The officers exercised no control or authority. Had they attempted to do so, I think they would not have succeeded, so great was the excitement. In connection with this, some of the troops got hold of several barrels of whiskey which they freely distributed and drank, making the scene still more fearful and the defeat of our army look much more telling.[6]

In the meantime, the Rebel army laid quiet and close behind its works. Not a sound was heard from its place, nor a light visible. Yet it was known that their comparatively solid and unbroken ranks occupied the same position held in the morning, having suffered but slightly. Yet they inflicted upon the Army of the Potomac the most complete defeat in its whole history. The intentions of the Confederate generals were unknown to our own commanders. The prevailing opinion among many of our rank and file and some of our officers too was that the enemy would come out of his works during the night and advance upon the town. Indeed, there was nothing to prevent him. Had he done so, he might have annihilated the Army of the Potomac with the sword or driven every living man wearing a blue coat into the Rappahannock River. General Lee that night and all next day had the Federal army bagged and in a trap. Yet he did not know it until too late—then he saw his mistake. Providence perhaps cast a mist on his eyes so that he did not see the splendid chance of following up his victory.

I have said that the Army of the Potomac was in a trap this night. That trap was the City of Fredericksburg with the Rebel army on one side and the deep, dark waters of the Rappahannock on the other. Escape would have been impossible owing to the pontoon bridges being partly torn away. The darkness of the night made things worse. Resistance would have been in vain because of the terrible, demoralized and confused condition of the entire Federal force. In military skill and cunning, I always regarded the Rebel generals far superior to the Union during the war. In that respect, my opinion is unchanged. But I must say that I really cannot see why General Lee became so suddenly stupid or blind by not following up his victory and attacking the Federal army in the city that night. Perhaps the reason was that God cast a veil or mist over his eyes to prevent him.[7]

The ambulance, after being driven through crowds of soldiers in streets lit up by fires, finally halted in front of a fine looking four-story house. It did bear the marks of having been battered considerably with cannon shot. In a rude manner, the driver ordered his passengers out to seek quarters for themselves for the night. The two men who had died on the way were carried forth and placed on the cellar door of a house. A few dim lights burned in the building opposite which we stopped. The open, wide door was guarded by two soldiers with crossed muskets. I advanced towards these men, told them that I was pretty badly wounded and desired shelter within the house for the night. They said nothing but immediately drew the muskets aside to admit me. I passed in.

By this time, my fever had given place to chills and I shook from head to foot. I now found myself in a long, wide hall, on either side of which was a very large room. Entering the one on my right, I found seven wounded men lying upon the floor. The apartment contained a splendid and extensive library enclosed in glass cases, a long green covered bagatelle table, and a wood-burning stove. A blazing fire roared up the chimney of an old-fashioned fireplace inserted in the side wall. Its occupants were men not seriously wounded except one poor fellow of the 118th Pennsylvania (The Corn Exchange Regiment of Philadelphia, Colonel Provost). He was about breathing his last from a gunshot wound through his left lung. Being very cold, I laid down upon the board floor, resting my head on a pile of sawed wood close to the stove. I could have slept but for the intense pain of my wounds, my right shoulder in particular, which was then excruciating.

Other wounded men soon commenced to arrive. In less than an hour after my own admission, the room contained between 55 and 60 mangled victims. Every other apartment of the building was filled in like proportion. Among the arrivals in my department was a young man, apparently not over 20 years of age. My attention was particularly directed to him owing to his youthful, modest and handsome appearance. I did not know what the nature of his wound exactly was. A little blood stain on the breast of the white shirt that he wore was all the indication of injury that was visible. He was strangely, deathly pale. Upon entering the room, he walked quietly and slowly back to the end of it, sat noiselessly down on the floor in a corner, stretched his legs out in front, his back straight up against the wall, and, in a few minutes and in that position, he seemed to be enjoying a quiet, undisturbed and peaceful sleep. During the night, I kept my eye upon him, for I could not sleep, almost envying his apparent sweet rest and repose. But I will now leave the youthful soldier until next morning and continue my own story.

I tried to sleep but in vain. This was due not only to the pain of my wounds but also the continued noise and confusion outside as well as the groans and cries of the wounded lying upon the floor around me.[8] A poor fellow of my own regiment came in about one a.m., wounded in the back of the neck by a musket ball. The round, strange to say, after passing into the body in the place named, came out between the ribs on the left side. He could not lay down but sat by my side until morning in great agony. Here I may note some of the strange and unaccountable freaks of bullets entering a human body which came under my own observation. In my own case for instance, the bullet struck the front part of the arm, passed into it and around the bone, breaking 17 small pieces off of it and lodged in the arm-pit near the skin. In another case, a bullet passed into a man's thigh and came out near the heel. In another, it entered the breast and came out near the pit of the stomach. In still another, it entered the top of the right shoulder and came out close to the left hip. I could give other instances of a similar nature, but those stated will serve to show what curious courses these little messengers of death took after entering the body.

At about two a.m., we were surprised and startled by our artillery on Stafford Heights again opening fire on the Rebel position. The shots, however, were few and doubtless for the purpose only of ascertaining if the enemy retained his situation. Our men soon discovered that he did. No sooner was our first gun fired than the Confederate artillery on the heights of Fredericksburg returned it with at least 50 guns, hurling shot and shell high up in the air over the house now sheltering my wounded comrades and me into the Union lines on the northern side of the Rappahannock. This fire instantly either silenced our guns or caused our gunners to cease such an experiment on a victorious opponent. The cannonade on both sides soon ended and time rolled sluggishly on towards morning's dawn. Oh, how we longed to see it. The anticipated advance of the Rebel army on the city during the night fortunately and providentially did not take place.

At six a.m., while it was yet dark, three army surgeons came into our apartment. From the appearance of their uniforms and the instruments that they carried, I judged that they had seen hard service during the night in the line of their profession. One of them held a burning candle without a candlestick in his hand. With his two companions, he advanced to where our young, apparently sleeping soldier rested. When within a few feet of him they suddenly paused, gazed upon him and conversed among themselves in a whisper for a moment. One of them then went forward, placed his hand upon the young man's brow, then looked round at his two partners. The surgeon just shook his head. When moving away to another part of the room, one of the doctors said, "Poor young fellow, he's dead. Some mother will miss her son."

The scene I shall never forget. That calm, quiet, unruffled countenance even in the cold embrace of death. My young comrade had met with the King of Terrors bravely and without a sigh or struggle. He had passed away into the invisible world, having laid down his life in the service and upon the altar of his country. The visit made by these surgeons to our apartment at this time was merely one of inspection. They were hurriedly ascertaining the condition of the wounded prior to their removal to a field hospital. Large canvas tents were then being put up on the opposite side of the river, behind Stafford Hills and near to the Falmouth and Aquia Creek Railroad Freight Depot for treatment of our casualties.

One of the surgeons, a tall, fine looking man, approached me as I laid upon the floor. He inquired where I was wounded. I told him severely in the right shoulder by a musket ball. "Has the bullet been extracted?" he said.

I replied, "No, sir. I wish to God you would take it out for I am in agony."

"Well, I will see what I can do for you, my man. Get up and let me examine you on this bagatelle table."

"I can't rise," I said, "without help. My shoulder and arms are so stiff and painful."

He then helped me to my feet and upon the table. There another difficulty presented itself. My coat, vest and shirts had to come off to admit the examination of my injuries. How to accomplish this was the trouble, since I could not move my arms sufficiently to draw the clothing off in the usual way. My wounds and the upper parts of my body were covered with blood which now had become hard and clotted. Seeing this, the surgeon, with a long knife, soon cut open my clothing, commenced to examine my wounds, and tried to find the location of the bullet.

For five minutes his labor was in vain, every effort to find the ball proving unsuccessful. "I fear," he said, "it has gotten beyond my reach." As he was about giving it up for a "bad job," as he termed it, he put his hand in the socket of my right arm and then exclaimed, "I've got it at last. Here it sticks just beneath the skin, having passed around the bone which is considerably shattered and broken. Put round your left hand and feel it for yourself." I did so and there it was. "Now, my man," he said, "you will have to suffer a little extra pain, for I will have to cut the bullet out."

"Slash away," I replied, "I'll stand the pain, only get it out."

He smiled and then opened his instrument box, from which he brought out two or three curious looking tools, laid them down on the table by my side and rolled up his coat sleeves. The operation, which gave me no small relief, was soon performed, causing little pain. The surgeon, after cutting out the ball, washed it in a bucket of water, and then handed it to me, saying, "I suppose you would like to preserve this relic of the war."

I replied, "Yes," and dropped it into my pocket.[9]

I then asked him his name, with the object of sending him a note of thanks at some future time, if spared, for his kind attention and services. He replied that his name was Doctor Hart of the Eight Illinois Cavalry. The doctor also said, "I make no distinction in doing what I can for the relief of the wounded of any regiment, as well as my own."

He then took my name, company, regiment, brigade and division, down in a little book, shook me by the hand, wished me safe over the river and left the room.* With the aid of an old soldier, a Rebel prisoner of war placed in charge of the fire in the room during the night, I succeeded in gathering my cut-open clothing around my body again. I tied the pieces together with coarse strings. At eight a.m., another surgeon entered our apartment, giving notice that all of the wounded who could walk were required to remove to the fourth story of the building. Those who could not walk would be carried in order to make way for the hosts of other unfortunates then being brought in from the battlefield. Accordingly, some 16 or 18 men of the walking wounded, including me, soon made our way to the place designated on the fourth floor, which we found to be thickly covered with clean, dry straw. Each man sought his own place upon it and there laid down.

My own place was in a corner under a window, from which a splendid view of the city, the battlefield and surrounding heights was to be had. Hot coffee and hardtack was then given us, our first refreshment since going into battle the morning before. Blankets were furnished to those of our number who had none or who had lost or thrown them away before entering the conflict. I had held on to mine.

Feeling chilly at this time and taking advantage of the presence of an officer of the 63rd New York on a flying visit in search of a missing comrade, I asked him to remove the strings from my blanket which still remained rolled up. He willingly and cheerfully complied, remarking in doing so, "How many blankets are here?"

"Only one," I said.

---

* About three-quarters of the bullet was all that was extracted, the remaining part of it having been broken off in coming in contact with the bone. This latter portion, the surgeon stated, had lodged near the top of the arm where it would be hard to find and remove. The part of the ball that I put in my pocket for safekeeping I afterwards lost, it having probably rolled out due to my movements.

"It's damned heavy then," he said.

The strings off, the officer, in order to open it up and spread it over me, raised it from the floor. To his sudden astonishment, a shower of Rebel bullets, 47 in number, dropped out of it around his feet, with a rattling noise on the boards. "How's this?" he said, "do the men of the 116th carry ammunition in their blankets?"

I smiled and replied, "Oh, no, we carry it in a much more convenient place and get rid of it as soon as possible."

I then explained to him the circumstance of my having placed it in front of my head while lying on the ground as a protection against the enemy's fire. "Lucky boy," he said, "it just saved you from being riddled with Rebel lead."

I was as much surprised myself as was the officer. Not until then did I know and realize what a friend an army blanket had been to me. Surely the Almighty's hand was in this. The blanket was really a curiosity, being perforated with innumerable holes. Had any one of the bullets which it had contained struck me, the result might have proved fatal. With such force did some of the balls strike the blanket when tightly rolled up that five of them almost went through it, penetrating some ten or twelve folds or thicknesses. Such, then, is the history of a wonderful blanket which I left behind me in the city of Fredericksburg, Virginia.

We spent a most miserable day here in our new quarters, suffering much from our wounds. Owing to the constant stream of many dead and dying from the field of carnage, we received no further medical attention except at our own hands. The demand for surgeons far exceeded the supply. Many extra ones had arrived from Washington soon after the defeat of our army was telegraphed to the Capital, but still there were not enough.

As night again came on, I arose from my rude bed of straw on the floor and looked out of the window upon the battleground. It was a sorrowful, sickening sight. Far away up on the heights of Fredericksburg, particularly in the vicinity of the ever memorable stone wall, squads of the enemy were hard at work burying their dead. Their effort showed the results of the fire from the assaulting but defeated Union divisions at that point. I plainly saw them digging large holes in the ground into which they threw their dead comrades with little ceremony or respect, as if they had been dogs. In one place, I counted 27 bodies thrown into one hole or grave—how many more afterwards, I do not know. Sad as this was to look upon, work of a similar character was being performed by our own army on the level ground below the heights as far as the eye could reach in all directions. Large bodies of Union troops were scattered over that field of blood, digging holes and great long trenches which they literally filled and packed with our fallen braves. It proved how terrible and how fearfully destructive the Confederate fire had been upon our men. Darkness soon after shut out the scene from my view. Returning to my couch of straw, I thought again, how sad, indeed, was war.*

Sunday Evening, 5 p.m.
December 14th, 1862

Darkness and night generally were trying seasons to the sick or wounded soldier. It was now five p.m. and the shades of night again covered the battlefield and the city. A small, burning oil lamp was placed up on a mantlepiece in the room now occupied by my wounded comrades and me. Several pieces of wood were added to a fire in an open grate built in the wall, throwing out a bright, cheering light. The noise and disorder in the streets below still continued. A few cannon shots now fell upon our ears, but from which army on their respective heights, we could not discover. In half an hour, the footsteps of men were heard rushing up the stairs towards our apartment, voices shouting, "Put out the lights up there, put out the lights." Two men now hurriedly entered the room and dashed for the windows, the shutters of which stood wide open. Closing them, these soldiers said to the man in charge of the fire and lamp, "You damned old fool, are you going to let these men be blown to pieces?"

We did not realize our dangerous position until one of our number asked, "What is the matter?"

He was told that the enemy was opening up his batteries on the city. The light streaming out of the windows made the house a regular target for Reb gunners, who now had evidently gotten the range. They would, in all probability, direct part of their fire upon our house—terrible news for the inmates, especially those occupying the upper room with me, so exposed to the Rebel artillery.

---

* While burying their dead, I was particularly struck with the good feeling that seemed to prevail among the troops of both armies engaged in the work. They worked almost side by side with each other. The men acted apparently in perfect harmony, as if they never had been enemies.

The enemy's fire was not near as severe as expected. It lasted scarce three hours, a most providential circumstance for us. A great many shots, however, were fired, killing and wounding several of our men on the streets. The shelling was also slow and irregular, seeming not to be intended for a genuine bombardment. While it continued, we distinctly heard the hissing missiles and balls flying close to and over the roof of our quarters, causing no very agreeable sensations to those men who were under its shelter. The house had evidently been aimed at. Owing to the darkness of the night and the windows being shut, hiding the light within from the outside, the shots fired had little effect, except for one. A cannonball came very near to doing considerable mischief. At about seven p.m., while quietly lying upon my bed of straw in the corner of the room, I heard this missile hit in the upper corner of the building, not eight feet from where I laid. It left a large hole in the roof just above my head. Thanks to this unexpected guest, the blue sky was visible on the following morning and the sun poured his welcome and cheering rays. Had this ball struck the house squarely, many of our wounded men then within it would undoubtedly have been killed. Here again, God's hand was visible. My disabled comrades and I were protected from perhaps instant death. Soon after, the Confederate guns ceased firing, much to the relief of my companions and me in the room. The door had been locked so that our apartment would not be overcrowded with other wounded men who still continued to arrive in the city from the battlefield and its vicinity.[*]

I need hardly say that we spent another most miserable and uncomfortable night.

Monday Morning, December 15th, 1862
Evacuation of Fredericksburg by the Army of the Potomac
The army falls back to the northern side of the Rappahannock,
defeated and demoralized, and occupies its old position near
Falmouth.

I learned in the morning that during the preceding night large numbers of our wounded had crossed the Rappahannock for transportation north by railroad from near Falmouth. Many of these men, very severely injured, could not proceed further than the railroad depot.

---

[*] For some reason unknown to me, during this bombardment by the Rebels, the Federal guns did not respond, not a single shot having been fired in return by our men.

There they tried to shelter behind a miserable half-demolished low shed, open on both sides. The place afforded but little comfort from the inclement, cold, raw December night and morning. Field hospitals consisting of large canvas tents had been ordered forward to this place immediately after the battle for the temporary accommodation of the badly wounded. Through some mismanagement or accident, these tents did not arrive until nearly ten a.m. in the morning. Consequently, the suffering of our wounded was terrible in the extreme from exposure during the night and morning. Several soldiers died.

The Army of the Potomac had to evacuate Fredericksburg. It was defeated, crushed, demoralized and at the mercy of a powerful, victorious foe. If the Rebels thought it proper to advance, they could, with one well directed blow, wipe our army out of existence. But such God did not permit.

General Burnside, now taking in the situation, gave orders for the withdrawal of the entire army to the northern side of the Rappahannock.[10] This was to commence on the night of Monday, December 15th, under cover of darkness and hidden as far as possible from the observation and eye of the enemy. Many of our wounded had crossed the river on the preceding night, but there were many more to follow them, including me. All the sick and wounded were to be removed first. The artillery and cavalry were then to follow. Lastly, as usual, the infantry.

As night approached, this program commenced to be carried out. When the artillerymen with their horses, heavy guns and carriages were ready to move across the stream, great quantities of fir and pine tree branches were spread thickly upon the pontoon bridges to deaden the heavy, rumbling noise of the cannon wheels. Thanks to this strategem, the artillery passed over the water without the enemy hearing the movement then going on within our line. On the following night, the evacuation was continued. On Wednesday morning, all that remained of the noble Army of the Potomac, including every sick and wounded man, had reached the northern side of the Rappahannock in safety, encamping again in the old position around Falmouth north of the Stafford Hills. The movement was well planned and most successfully carried out, reflecting great credit upon General Burnside and his aides. Thus our army was saved from that total annihilation which probably would have overtaken it had it remained much longer in Fredericksburg. The evacuation did not seem to be discovered until Wednesday morning by the Confederates who still laid quiet behind their works. But as soon as they found that "the bird had flown," the city was again occupied by their infantry and the Rebel flag once more waved in triumph over its yet burning ruins.[11]

But, I must return to my own story. At about seven a.m. on the morning of the December 15th, an army surgeon entered the apartment and gave notice that all of the wounded men there who could walk were required to go across the river as soon as possible on foot. Those who from the nature of their wounds could not do so were to be carried over on stretchers or in ambulances. Fortunately for me, I belonged to the former class. I arose with much difficulty from my rude bed of straw upon the floor. Gathering around my person my bloody, almost destroyed and cut-up uniform, I descended to the street and started for the pontoon bridge only a short distance away. I succeeded in crossing it in safety, but not without great bodily pain, owing to the jostling among the wounded men passing over at the same time. The intense cold aggravated my almost uncovered wounds. Upon my arrival on the other side, I thanked God for bringing me off the battlefield and out of Fredericksburg with my life. It was now probably half past eight or nine a.m.

I proceeded up the Stafford Hills, behind which I expected to find the field hospital tents. Much to my surprise, nothing of the kind was to be seen. To my inquiry about them, I was told that they should have been on the ground and spread at six a.m. that morning. But no tidings of them had been received. It soon commenced to snow, rain and freeze, which together with northeasterly wind blowing made our situation a terrible one. At this time, there were between 2,500 and 3,000 wounded men awaiting the arrival of the tents and surgical aid. No shelter could be had from the storm except that offered by the friendly branches of large trees, under which the wounded men crouched and huddled together and where some of them died from the exposure.

Up to this hour, some four or five thousand wounded had been sent north by rail from the Falmouth Depot on trains composed of every description of car, passenger, cattle, freight and open. These trains were very long, some of them numbering 28 or 30 cars. They literally packed each trip with wounded soldiers and were generally drawn by four locomotives, two in front and two behind. The distance to travel by these trains was short, being only from Falmouth to Aquia Creek, where the men were transferred to steamboats on the Potomac. The ships took them up to Washington and Alexandria for hospital treatment.

As soon as a train backed into the depot to be filled with mangled humanity, it was both amusing and wonderful to see how quickly it received its load. The wounded soldiers crowded and jumped aboard by the hundreds in their eagerness to get away. It was not without risk. I saw three wounded killed by falling under the car wheels as a locomotive began to move. It was simply every man for himself to get on board any train as quick as a chance offered to do so. The sooner a soldier got away, the sooner he would get his wounds attended to.

Although the route from Falmouth to Aquia Creek was short, the journey (from three to four hours) taken by these trains was long and painfully jarring to the poor, suffering passengers. Why such slowness, no one appeared to know. At ten a.m., three hospital tents arrived, into which about 50 of the worst wounded men then nearby were consigned. I, being considered by two examining surgeons to be a fit subject for one of these tents, was assigned a place within. My bed, like those of my new companions, was simply a few branches and leaves of trees spread over mother earth with an old blanket to cover me. In the evening, a hole was dug in the ground at the center of the tent. Then a fire was kindled. But up to seven p.m., no refreshments were offered to or seen by the wounded. Although all severely hurt, we were then hungry as wolves.

A little later, while I laid in a half-sleeping condition, shivering and shaking with cold and my very painful wounds, a soldier from the outside of the tent pulled the fly-leaf or door open. He entered with a tin bucket full of strong, hot coffee and biscuit. Each man was supplied bountifully with the God sent luxuries. Oh, what relief. Hearing something blowing and puffing like a steam engine outside, I inquired what it was and was told that it was the caring machine of the "United States Christian Commission," an organization formed for the relief of the wounded soldiers of both armies, bodily and spiritually. These people had provided the hot coffee and victuals which I and my comrades were then enjoying.

This Commission, whose exact title was "The United States Christian Commission for the Army and Navy," I had not heard of. Nor had I seen any of its glorious workings, probably for the reasons that it was then in its infancy. It had not reached that degree of popularity and Christian usefulness which it soon afterwards attained. The organization was characterized in all its works for charity and kindness among soldiers and sailors, until the close of the war.[12]

Its revered president, however, George H. Stuart of Philadelphia, whose central office was located at No. 11 Bank Street, I knew by reputation. I had frequently heard him styled "the Soldier's Friend," and "a Christian Philanthropist." My own experiences afterwards as a volunteer in the central office of the Commission convinced me that he justly merited these titles. His loyalty and unselfish services to his adopted country in its dark days of war and bloodshed, as well as his arduous and unceasing labors to promote the comfort, welfare and happiness of the brave boys in blue, made the name of George H. Stuart of Philadelphia unforgettable to the American nation.

Tuesday Morning, December 16th, 1862

I spent a most uncomfortable night, owing to a cold rain and sleet which fell continuously in torrents. The chilling water made its way through the roof of the hospital tent to the ground, where it saturated the clothing of every man to the skin and extinguished our little fire. At seven a.m., another ration of hot coffee and biscuit was supplied us, after which I arose from my wet bed and left the tent. I was fully determined to board the first train starting north. Upon emerging from my quarters, the scene before me was horrible, far exceeding even the horrors of the battlefield. Up until dark the evening before, only two tents had arrived, but now upwards of 40 were erected, including eleven for surgical operations. It gave the place the appearance of a little slaughterhouse, or, as I then termed it, a "village of butcher shops." Wounded and mangled soldiers laid about in all directions, the hospital tents being all full. Others walked quietly and silently around awaiting transportation to their homes or Northern hospitals. Hundreds of those slightly wounded crowded the little railroad depot and its immediate vicinity with eagerness to board departing trains to Aquia Creek.

Seeing that my chances were but slim indeed, for getting off, unless I would run the risk of being fearfully crushed, I concluded to walk about and wait until the afternoon. Hopefully, the rush and excitement would subside by then. Accordingly, gathering my torn and bloody uniform around my body and lighting my old faithful pipe (a great source of comfort and consolation to me at all times and especially now), I started from my damp and dreary quarters on a tour of inspection among the various tents. My curiosity, notwithstanding my terrible bodily condition, was as great as ever before. I wanted to see and to know what was going on among the boys. During my journey, streams of wounded men continued to arrive from the battlefield. Many sad cases and sickening sights were brought along on stretchers, window shutters, and the like.

Walking slowly along the front of long lines of tents, I was particularly struck with those used for surgical operations. There were many amputations then going on, faint descriptions of which I will now give, although it may not be pleasant. These tents were each 20 feet square and ten feet high and entered through a canvas door in front. In the center stood a rough, wooden bench large enough for the patient to be operated upon. Lying around were cases of ugly looking surgical tools, including the saw and the knife. In the back end of each tent, a hole was made. Through it, amputated arms or legs were thrown out upon the ground outside.

The amputations were very numerous and, to my mind and eye, in many cases entirely uncalled for. This experience fully convinced me of what I had frequently before heard regarding the surgical arm of the service. Namely, that it was, to a large extent, comprised of young students who were inexperienced and who entered the army to "experiment." Be this, however, as it may, I saw several limbs sawed off that had been only slightly injured by a musket ball or saber cut. These appendages could have been saved by proper care and the exercise of a little patience.

In my own case, one of these surgeons, after asking me where I was wounded and then looking at the wound said in rather an authoritative manner, "Young man, you must have that arm taken off. It will never be of the least use to you and you'll better have it amputated here at once."

"Nix," said I, "I'll hold onto the old arm till it has to go, then I want to go with it."

He turned away in disappointment. I had refused to be a subject for his knife, saw and probably his inexperienced hands. Taking another stroll early in the afternoon, I found that so numerous had been the amputations that the bloody limbs were piled up in heaps four or five feet high. I peered at a young surgeon walking and smoking a cigar with sleeves rolled up to the elbow. He held in one hand a bloody knife or saw and in the other a newly amputated leg or arm dripping with human gore.

I saw the most frightful wound of my whole army experience here. A young man, a member of the 118th Pennsylvania Volunteers, was brought in on a stretcher. Apparently his entire stomach had been shot out or carried away by a cannonball, yet he was living. But oh, the cries of agony and pain. God keep me from ever witnessing the like again. He died soon afterwards.

At about three p.m., seeing a train coming into the depot for another load of wounded soldiers, I hurried towards it. I tried to get on board but the crowd was still too large. Again disappointed, I sat down on a pile of salt bags, intending to wait on another train. Being wet already, the cold rain chilled my skin. The rain continued to fall. Feeling quite frozen, I soon arose and sauntered about.

At 4:45 p.m., another train on the same errand as the last arrived. It hauled 28 cars of every description. Just as the locomotive was about to start for Aquia Creek, well loaded with our wounded, I reached it. Seeing an open door in the side of a freight car filled with soldiers, I sprang into it. Thus commenced my slow return from bloody Virginia to the peaceful North. The train being very long, it proceeded very tardily and cautiously. When the train arrived at Aquia Creek at ten p.m., we found that nine men who were severely wounded died on the way.

"And while one spark
of life is warm
Within this mould of clay,
My soul shall revel
in the storm
Of that tremendous day."

Chapter 11

God's Hand Was Visible:
Life in the Hospital

Upon the arrival of our train at 10 p.m., a company of soldiers, about 100 men, were in waiting to assist our wounded and to help them from the cars to steamboats which were to carry them to Alexandria and Washington. The steamboat wharf was closeby, where three large steamers awaited their cargo of sick and wounded soldiers from the battlefield of Fredericksburg. These unfortunates numbered 700 or 800 men, many of whom were very severely wounded and not a few of them fatally. Consequently their safe removal from the cars to the steamboats was difficult and several hours were taken up in doing it.

We proceeded at once on board the boats already pretty well packed with passengers like ourselves. Feeling tired, as well as suffering much pain from my wounds, I sought a quiet corner for rest and sleep. The cabins were full of wounded men, every bench and lounge being occupied as well as the floor. Seeing a vacant spot on the lower deck immediately under the shaft of the paddle wheels, I seated myself there, but did not long enjoy the treat. In less than an hour afterwards, as the boat started on her trip northward and the paddle wheels revolved, they threw a shower of water over me which caused me to beat a hasty retreat. I then made my way to the bow of the boat. Seeing a large coil of rope, hollow in the center, I crawled into the vacancy in the hope of gaining the coveted repose.

I was now somewhat isolated from my wounded comrades, but my whereabouts was soon discovered. On board were a large number of the "Sisters of Mercy" acting as nurses and doing everything in their power to alleviate the terrible sufferings of the cargo of our wounded, sick and dying soldiers. And here, I cannot proceed without paying my humble tribute of profound respect and praise to these women, ladies, well and truly named "Sisters of Mercy"—God bless them. Their noble, heroic and unceasing exertions, many of them self-sacrificing in the extreme, were certainly wonderful and beautiful to witness. They did everything to ease the pain of the wounded, comforting and satisfying the cravings of the men.

In my own case, I must relate the following incident. I had been reclining inside the coil of rope alluded to for about 20 minutes when I saw one of these good Sisters approaching as if looking up some other poor fellows needing care and attention. I made no effort whatever to make my position or circumstances known to her. She soon saw me, however, and then advancing almost to my side, she said in a most pleasing and feeling manner, "Are you wounded, Sir?"

"Yes, Madam," was my reply.

"Poor fellow, is it severely?" she asked.

"Pretty badly," said I.

"Well, you feel cold there, don't you? I will see if I can get room for you in the cabin. But as it is now so crowded with your unfortunate comrades wounded like yourself, I fear I shall not succeed, but I'll try," said dear sister, then darting away on her mission of mercy.

I was again alone listening to the groans of many of my suffering companions and the waves of the Potomac as they dashed against the sides and bows of our good and staunch steamboat now plowing her way through rough and dark waters to Washington. In ten minutes, the lady returned carrying over her arm a new, heavy army blanket which she spread upon me remarking that every spot in the cabin was occupied and that room for me there could not be made. "But," said she, "this blanket will be of use to you." Reaching for a tin cup half filled with some liquid, she continued, "Drink this down, it will heat your body."

I asked her what it was. "Good brandy," was her reply.

I at once drank it. "Now," she added, "I will bring or send you in a few minutes, some hot coffee and bread. This will strengthen you on your passage up the river."

She then left me again. About ten minutes after, the sister returned with a brimming tin cup-full of the delicious hot beverage and two thick slices of buttered bread. I relished these gifts and soon hid their remnants from sight. The lady then left me, wishing me a comfortable night, adding that her presence in other parts of the boat among the wounded was needed.

When my good lady friend left me, it was half past eleven p.m., after which I soon fell asleep and did not awake till nearly three a.m. in the morning. It was the most refreshing slumber and rest that I had enjoyed since several days prior to the Battle of Fredericksburg. We were now nearing Alexandria. But upon coming opposite that city, our boat did not stop as we expected, keeping on in her course to Washington. There the ship arrived at about eight a.m. in the morning after a rather slow trip up the Potomac.

Washington, DC
Wednesday Morning
December 17th, 1862

The morning was clear and mild for the season. As we landed from the boat, the long lines of omnibuses and ambulances extending along the wharfs to convey our wounded soldiers to the various army hospitals in the city and suburbs were soon filled and started for their destination. Nine of my unfortunate comrades from various regiments and I were assigned to a large, old fashioned omnibus drawn by four horses. The coach started immediately. After a drive of about an hour along several streets of the Capital, and then into the country for a mile and a half, we arrived at the Eckington Army Hospital. It was situated near the line of the Baltimore and Ohio Railroad. The buildings comprising this hospital were two in number, each about 100 feet long, 20 feet wide and one story high. They were entirely made of wood. A doctor directed a nurse to commence poulticing my wound with flaxseed meal and to place me in a certain bed near a stove. The nurse said encouragingly to me, "We'll try and make a pretty good arm of it yet for you," leaving right afterwards.[1]

There were 50 beds in this building, 25 on either side, eleven of which were occupied on our arrival, but by eight p.m. the same night, all of them were filled with wounded soldiers from the Battle of Fredericksburg. At two p.m., I partook of the first good dinner since my departure from Philadelphia on the 1st of September. It consisted of plenty of boiled chicken, buttered bread, hot coffee and mince pie. The fare was served by three ladies of a corps of the Sisters of Mercy on duty at this place. Their temporary residence here was in a beautiful private mansion occupied and owned by a United States Army officer who, on the outbreak of the war, espoused the Southern Cause and joined the Confederate army. The property was then confiscated by our government who used the buildings as temporary residences for the doctors, surgeons and Sisters of Mercy. One large lower room was reserved for the accommodation and treatment of wounded or sick Union officers.

Nothing unusual transpired during the afternoon. But at eleven p.m. at night, one of our number who had been wounded by a musket ball in the throat died in great agony. At three a.m., another poor fellow, terribly crushed by a gun carriage which had run over him, also died in great pain. Next morning, snow had fallen to the depth of six inches and covered the windows of our new quarters like a blind. I then thought of my old companions in arms down on the cold banks of the Rappahannock. I compared my now comparatively comfortable situation to theirs, exposed to the cold winter storm as well as the deadly shots of an exulting and, for the time being, victorious foe. Surely this was another matter for thankfulness to God. At eight a.m., the patients were visited by the ward surgeon, Dr. Edling of New York, a gentleman in every sense of the term. He examined each man's wounds minutely, operating upon them if necessary, and left such directions with the nurses as the circumstances required. Visits were made by the ward surgeon, often accompanied by the head surgeon and young students, to the patients each morning at nine. We were also visited each evening at seven p.m. and sometimes during the day as cases demanded. These visits were often the occasion of considerable merriment, interest and curiosity among the wounded soldiers. Often the surgeons themselves made a good joke or enjoyed a hearty laugh.

For three weeks following this time, my wound in the right arm refused to heal and became more painful. It gradually grew worse, causing me constant uneasiness and suffering, almost depriving me of sleep. I rapidly lost my flesh and became as weak as a child. But strange to say, my appetite, except on a few occasions, continued good. Dr. Edling said during one of his professional visits to me that it was the only favorable symptom in my case. *

I had been in this condition for perhaps five weeks when Dr. Edling entered our ward one morning on his visiting rounds. He seemed to take more than his usual interest in my case. He came right up to my bed upon which I was lying half dressed. The doctor seated himself beside me and took close, silent observations. Then rising, and moving away in a rather thoughtful and saddened manner, he left the ward without stopping to see any of the other patients. I did not know what to make of this, but felt sure something was wrong. I passed an entirely sleepless night. My arm, which a few days before had commenced to swell near the shoulder, was now swollen to two times its natural size, assuming a most sickening and revolting appearance. I had not before thought the wound dangerous. But now, seeing my arm in such a condition and turning gradually black, I must acknowledge that I felt considerably scared—mortification and amputation to follow. Fear continually haunted my mind and racked me with pain, torturing my body. My physical appearance must have been wretched in the extreme.

In twenty minutes, the doctor returned, accompanied by the head surgeon, Dr. Storrow, and two students. They came up to my bed and seated themselves near one another on the unoccupied part of the bed. They asked me several questions concerning my feelings, appetite, and sleeping. Then after examining my wound very gently and passing a few private remarks among themselves in whispers (evidently not intended for my ears), they left me, as if not knowing what was best to be done in my case. I again laid down on my bed with no very agreeable thoughts. At one p.m., I partook of a hearty dinner brought me by Nurse Zouvy, consisting of rare roast beef, potatoes, bread, mince pie and a glass of bitter ale. Dr. Edling had ordered the latter for me. Nothing of note occurred till about four p.m. Nurse Zouvy, coming carelessly into my ward with the suit of a new uniform hanging upon his arm, walked up to my side and presented "Uncle Sam's" clothing to me. He said, "Dr.

---

* Not being able now to write to my family in Philadelphia who I felt sure were uneasy about my fate after the great battle, the particulars of which had been published by the press all over the country, I succeeded in getting one of my companions to do so for me. A few days after, I received a reply. With it a copy of the *Philadelphia Sunday Dispatch* (date forgotten), giving an account of the Fredericksburg slaughter and a list of the names of the Pennsylvania troops killed, wounded and missing. Much to my surprise and horror, I found my own name among the killed. I need hardly say that my letter to my home quickly dispelled the gloom and sadness which the announcement made by the Sunday newspaper had cast over it. All my friends in Philadelphia who knew of my being in the army and in the Fredericksburg engagement were relieved to know I was alive.

Edling has sent you these and wishes you to report yourself to him in the head surgeon's office as soon as possible this afternoon."*

The first thought that now struck me was amputation. The amputating room was either in this mansion or adjoining it. I never knew what fear in the army was until now. I could stand the fatigues of the long and weary march under a burning sun, the intense cold of a lonely picket post, and the pain and horror of a bloody battlefield. But the idea of having my arm cut off completely broke my courage down.

I asked the nurse what I was wanted for at the house, as the mansion was familiarly termed among our boys there. He replied slowly, with a smile. This increased my suspicion regarding amputation. "Well, I don't know," he said. "The doctors are there and want to see your arm. They have just taken a poor fellow's leg off."

"Well," I said, hiding my emotion as well as I could, "I suppose I must go."

The nurse then assisted me in changing my clothing. After I dressed, I started for the house and my imaginary surgical operation with the nurse. A few minutes later, I was ushered into Dr. Storrow's headquarters. Dr. Edling and three other surgeons were comfortably seated there. I was very nervous. But owing to the manner in which I was received, I soon regained composure. Dr. Edling then helped me to uncover my wound and explained to his brother surgeons what to his mind was the nature and extent of my injury. He also related how he had been treating me. Then, after a few minutes of consultation among the doctors, Dr. Edling asked me if I still suffered much pain. I replied, "Yes, sir." I then thought I would know the worst, or at least what they were going to do with me. I said, "Doctor, I hope my arm will not have to be taken off."

With a good natured smile, he replied, "Oh, no, I hope that will not be necessary, but you have a damned bad arm, Mac."

Dr. Edling always called me "Mac." Of course, this announcement at once removed all my fears and dread of amputation. I again breathed free.

"Now, Mac," said Dr. Edling, "we have brought you up here to place you in much more comfortable and quiet quarters. You shall receive our best attention. I had a letter from a particular friend of yours today, now

---

* It will be remembered that the head surgeon, Dr. Storrow, had his office in the confiscated mansion which I have spoken of, some 40 or 50 yards distant. There he also temporarily resided.

in Alexandria, who wants you to be well cared for. He is a friend of my own, too. But," continued the doctor, "I will tell you more about this again."

Who this friend was in Alexandria, Virginia, I could not imagine. Dr. Edling now left the room and in a few minutes returned with the nurse in charge of the patients at the mansion. He was an Englishman by birth, had served in the Federal army and was wounded at the battle of Ball's Bluff. Afterwards, he was detailed for hospital duty. The Englishman was well educated, intelligent and one whom I soon found congenial company. The man was most attentive to me. The doctor introduced me as his new patient and directed him to give me one of the two unoccupied beds in his ward for wounded officers, four of whom were now in it. This ward contained only six beds and I was about to occupy the fifth.

My new nurse escorted me to my new quarters, a large back room on the first floor of the building. From the windows, you could see a beautiful and most extensive view of the surrounding country. The room was clean and tidy almost to a fault. A bright, clear fire of coal burned in a large open grate in the wall, giving the apartment an exceedingly cheerful and homelike appearance. My nurse then introduced me to my four new roommates, one of whom was a captain, badly wounded in the leg. Two were first lieutenants, one of them quite severely injured in the wrist and the other one in the neck. There was a sergeant-major terribly and fatally wounded in an unknown part of the body.

At six p.m., supper was served, consisting of hot coffee, bread and butter, preserves and cold meat in abundance. In addition, a large glass-full of fine country milk was given to those of our own little family who desired it. The remainder of the evening was spent in smoking, seated on comfortable arm chairs around the bright, cheerful fire, or in reading newspapers.

We were liberally and daily supplied with the latest from the press in Washington, New York, and, occasionally, Philadelphia. We also played cards and chess. There was conversation sometimes of a useful and elevating character, and sometimes not.

Our quarters in fact were elegant and extremely cozy and comfortable. As for the food, in quality, quantity and variety, it far surpassed anything in the way of good living that I ever experienced in America before or after during my eight week stay there. In this ward, no restrictions whatever were put upon its inmates. They were free to go through every part of the large house not occupied by the female domestics, the Sisters of Mercy, and, if able, to roam through the adjoining woods well stocked with game. The latter was a favorite recreation of my own here, and I enjoyed it very much on several occasions.

Was it any wonder then that I often thought of my late comrades, down in their cold winter quarters on the Rappahannock? No. I often wished that they could have shared and enjoyed at least some of the comforts and blessings that had fallen to my lot, I would have been most willing to have divided these pleasures with them, but this opportunity was denied me.

Next morning at nine a.m., Dr. Edling paid us his usual professional visit. I was the last to be examined by him. When my turn came, he sat down on my bed by my side and drew a letter out of his pocket and opened it. Covering the writer's signature with his hand, he held the document before me saying, "Now, Mac, whose fist is that?"

I at once recognized it to be General Meagher's and said so to the doctor. He smiled as he replied, "Yes, you are right, Mac, he is a good friend of yours. This letter contains his special request to me to take the best of care of you here."

"Well, Doctor," said I, "How did he know that I was here?"

He again smiled and replied, "Oh, you know Thomas Francis is a pretty smart fellow. He seldom loses the track of any one that he takes a fancy to, and I can assure you that you are no exception."[2]

After examining my wounds and giving Edward, the nurse, some directions about them, he left the room. A few minutes after, the doctor returned and told me that he had forgotten to say that the general wished me to write to him just as soon as I felt able to do so and to give him all particulars of my condition, future movements and whereabouts. I have never found out how General Meagher knew that I was wounded and in the Eckington Army Hospital. Nor can I tell how any of the surviving members of my regiment knew of my fate. Maybe Sgt. Stretchabock told the group about my wounds on his return after finding me and helping me into the wagon. I thought that I probably had been entirely lost from sight by nearly all of my old companions.[*]

On the day following my introduction into my new quarters here,

---

[*] Owing to the very painful and unfavorable condition of my wound while here, I could not use my pen to produce the ordinary decent penmanship which General Meagher had seen from me. Consequently, I did not write to him from the Eckington Hospital.

President Lincoln visited the Eckington Hospital, passing hurriedly from one ward to another. Upon entering my own apartment, he halted near the door and said in a quiet, pleasing manner, "I can't stay, boys. I hope you are all comfortable and getting along nicely here. Goodbye."

He then left the room. During the remainder of my stay here, we received many visits from the good ladies of Washington and its vicinity. These women brought us tobacco, fruit and plenty of reading matter, as well as a word of sympathy and encouragement. I was the recipient of every possible act of kindness and care which the officers of the institution could extend to me. Here again, surely God's hand was visible in casting my lot in so pleasant a place. I shall never forget the motherly attention shown me personally by one of the good Sisters of Mercy who visited our ward two or three times every day to inquire about our health and comfort.

She never came empty-handed nor without words of cheer and consolation. God bless her and women's blessed influences. Every morning at 11 a.m., she brought me a glass of wine and a few small cakes. Every afternoon, she supplied me with a large orange or apple. The sister seemed strangely interested in me and my speedy recovery. Had she been my own sister, she could not have done more to promote my comfort and happiness. To my companions, the nun was equally attentive in many respects. Our sources of evening amusements here included chess, cards, and dominoes. We were frequently entertained with beautiful and thrilling music on the clarinet, violin and its bass companion. It was exceedingly cheering and sweet, often kept up until 11 to 11:30 at night.

I cannot omit here the description of a certain piece of our ward furniture, a novelty to me, something that I had never seen or heard of before. It was a "water bed," occupied by a very severely wounded second lieutenant from a New England regiment, I think the 5th Maine. His injuries were severely painful. Whenever a nurse tried to change him from one position to another or to even remove him from his feather bed, everyone in the room shared his suffering. The lieutenant cried out pitifully with pain when he was moved.

In order to obviate this difficulty, the surgeons provided him with a water bed. It was about six feet long, four feet wide and 18 inches deep. It was made entirely of gum or India rubber, perfectly airtight, except in one corner. There was a brass nozzle that could be opened or closed at will. Each morning, this bed or, as it might be termed, an India rubber mattress, was filled with 60 gallons of fresh, cold water through the little nozzle. A blanket and sheet were then spread upon it. This process made the waterbed exceedingly comfortable and warm. It was a comfortable couch for its occupant, who month after month had been confined to bed from severe wounds. The poor fellow's body, owing to such close confinement, was almost destitute of flesh. His bones actually cut the skin and caused many bed sores. On account of his great sufferings from these sores, he was furnished with this water bed, superior in every respect to the finest feathers. He died soon after I left the hospital and his body was taken home to Maine by his friends.

My own general health at this time had considerably improved. My wound, although still very troublesome and painful, showed, at least to me, symptoms of healing. But I saw plainly that my doctor thought not. However, soon afterwards, I asked him his opinion in the matter. He frankly gave it in something like the following, "Well, Mac, your wound is not better. I would much rather see it keep open till the broken bones inside had all worked out.* It never will heal permanently till then."

This was somewhat discouraging, but when I saw and felt that everything was being done for my recovery that could be done by medical and surgical skill, I tried to banish all fear and worriment as to the result. The doctor never afterwards said much to me on the same subject except in answer to another question by me. Then he said that he thought my arm would be saved, but that I never could use it as before in shouldering a musket.

My quarters here were very comfortable and home-like. But I was doomed to not enjoy them much longer. I must confess that I felt sorry. On the evening of the March 14th, 1863, Dr. Edling entered our ward and gave notice that, according to an order just received from Washington from the War Department, all wounded and sick soldiers who could bear transportation were to be sent next day to their own respective state hospitals. Consequently, three of my companions and I were obliged to get ready for the journey, none of us being so wounded as to prevent our removal.

March 15th, 1863

At ten a.m. in the morning, everything being in readiness to start, inmates numbering 147 from the Eckington Army Hospital, Washing-

---

* No bones as yet had come out or made their appearance.

ton, DC, were driven into the city to the Washington and Philadelphia Railroad Depot by large four-horsed omnibuses. Three special passenger cars of a train of nine were for the returning and wounded soldier boys, me one of the number. Three army surgeons had charge of us. A few minutes before 11 a.m., we entered the cars. At 11 precisely, the bell signal notified the engineer to move forward. Five minutes later, the iron horse was rushing us along towards old Philadelphia and our dear ones at home to the tune of 30 miles an hour. We arrived in Philadelphia a little after three p.m., pretty well used up by the journey.

We were formed in line in the depot, and then marched to the Cooper Shop Volunteer Refreshment Saloon near Broad and Pine Streets, where we partook of an excellent supper and were provided with good beds for the night.[3] We were met at the depot by a crowd of people who welcomed us with rounds of cheers. As we marched towards our quarters for the night with bandaged heads, arms, hands and legs, many hardly being able to walk, crowds of people followed us, pouring out all kinds of sympathetic expressions, and welcoming us home from the war. The scene was unusually touching and impressive.

March 16th, 1863

It was with feelings of joy, gratitude and thankfulness to God that I awoke that morning to find myself safe and comparatively well in Old Philadelphia once more. These feelings became intensified as my mind reverted to Fredericksburg's bloody field and its surroundings, as well as my providential and most merciful escape from death.

At ten a.m., breakfast being over and the wounds of our men dressed, we were again formed in line and marched to a large building between 9th and 10th Streets. The street itself was known as Christian Street, because it was the site of a United States Army Hospital. The surgeon in charge was Dr. John J. Reese, who I soon found to be a kind-hearted Christian gentleman.4 On the same day at noon and while seated with about 150 other wounded men in the large dining room at dinner, my wife visited me. It was a heartbreaking reunion.

During my stay here, my wound made no progress towards healing. The pain refused to abate. Patients received professional visits from the hospital surgeons every morning at ten a.m. In my own case, nothing whatever was done for my wound except to wash and dress it. This I was often obliged to do myself owing to either the scarcity of nurses or their bad management and neglect of duty. In regard to the medical and surgical treatment of patients, the quality and variety of the food which they received and the rough manner in which it was presented, the cleanliness of the wards and to the hospitality and sympathy extended to inmates, the Christian Street Army Hospital was no credit to the Quaker city of Philadelphia. Nor did it, in any respect, compare favorably with the Eckington Hospital in Washington.

On the 9th of May, 1863, a general and thorough surgical examination of the patients of this hospital took place. This was done, as I soon afterwards learned, to ascertain how many of the men were likely soon to become well again and capable of performing military duty with their regiments in the field. The review also occurred for the purpose of granting discharges from the service to those who desired them. If, in the opinion of the examining surgeon, a man could not again serve due to the character of his injuries, he could be sent home. It was, however, at the option of the men to accept their discharges or not, especially those who had enlisted for three years or the war, as was my own case.

When my turn to be examined arrived, the examining surgeon, Dr. Reese, scrutinized my wound very closely and then said, "Young man, you had better take your discharge. Your soldiering days are over."

I simply replied, "All right, doctor."

Accordingly, on the third day following, May 12th, 1863, Dr. Reese handed me the important document. I ceased to be a soldier of the United States Army, very much against my will and inclination. My life in the service, although short owing to the nature of my wound in the right arm, was very active and exceedingly interesting. I learned many useful and invaluable lessons. God grant, I shall never never forget these. May they redound to His praise, His honor and His glory.

Conclusion

I have written about my life in the United States Army solely at the solicitation of my family and some of my friends. They wished to know about my experience as a soldier in the war for the Union. Owing to my unfortunate impediment in speaking, I had been prevented in the past from verbally relating my experiences, at least as fully as I would have liked. Thus I have resorted to my pen in the hope that the effort made will not only give the desired information in all respects, but will also provide satisfactory, amusing and perhaps in some degree instructive lessons about the war.

I have been often asked why I entered the U.S. Army. I still have but one answer. I owed my life to my whole adopted country, not the North nor the South, nor the East nor the West, but the Union, one and inseparable, its form of government, its institutions, its Stars and Stripes, its noble, generous, intelligent and brave people, ever ready to welcome and to extend the hand of friendship to the down-trodden and oppressed of every clime and people. My full determination was to assist in any way that I could to prevent the Union's dissolution by the traitors of the North, as well as those of the South.

In reference to the fighting material of the South, as it is sometimes styled, I have frequently heard it said that the courage and endurance of the soldiers of the Confederate Army was far inferior to that of the Union. My own experience proved, at least to me, that such was not the case. In many respects the Confederates were superior to Federal troops. I am of the opinion that if the South had had the same number of fighting men as the North commanded, the former would certainly have gained that independence for which she was fighting. In my humble and candid opinion, so far as soldierly qualities were concerned, the North was in no respect superior.

There was another matter which my life in the army taught me about. In those parts of Maryland and Virginia occupied by our forces, slavery was not that "hideous monster" that I had previously heard it represented. Nor was it, as I so often heard it termed, the "darkest" spot on the pages of American history. I speak only of my own experience while in the Army, in those states, Maryland and Virginia, that I have named. Many of the Negro slaves that we met in our journeys, and they were hundreds, acknowledged when asked that they were well provided for and taken care of by their masters. Many also believed that they were better off and happier than they could be if freed from their bondage and compelled to search for employment among the free people of the North. One strong, hearty young Negro said in my own hearing that to take him away from "Good Massa" would be worse than "pulling his eye teeth." Many similar expressions on the same subject I heard from both male and female slaves in Virginia. This forced me to believe that their real position had not been understood by the majority of the Northern people, or else it had been grossly misrepresented.

But to conclude and bring to a close this narrative of my short life in the War for the Union, short only on account of the disabling character of my wound for further military duty. For nearly four years after my discharge from the service, the wound in my right arm did not heal. Seventeen pieces of broken bone and a piece of the bullet worked their way out of the wound at intervals of about one piece every three months.[5] The arm is, however, well now. But as Doctor Edling of the Eckington Hospital said, it is not and never will be a strong arm. It frequently causes my thoughts to revert to my life in the army and:

> "And while one spark of life is warm
> Within this mould of clay,
> My soul shall revel in the storm
> Of that tremendous day."

William McCarter   Philadelphia, Pa. March 3rd, 1879

Appendix A

Whose Assault Came Closest
to the Stone Wall at Fredericksburg?

Invariably in matters of this nature, the issue eventually arises as to which regiment made the deepest penetration against the enemy on a particularly hard-fought field. A similar and more prominent dispute concerns the competing claims of a contingent of North Carolina and Virginia regiments from Lee's Army of Northern Virginia, who have been arguing in the literature since the guns fell silent about which state's troops first breached the lines and then penetrated furthest on July 3, 1863 at Gettysburg. Several Union army units have claimed this distinction in the attack on Mayre's Heights at Fredericksburg. While most of the boasts are simply exaggerated recollections of aging veterans, there is a good piece of evidence that the Irish Brigade penetrated closest to the stone wall on December 13, 1862.

Colonel William R. Brooke, commander of the 53rd Pennsylvania in Brig. Gen. Samuel K. Zook's brigade, wrote a letter in 1881 supporting the Irish Brigade's assertion that its men actually held the honor of being the ones who died closest to the stone wall. This letter from William R. Brooke to St. Clair A. Mulholland, January 8, 1881, is reprinted below, and may be found in the Mulholland Collection, Box 2, Civil War Library and Museum, Philadelphia, Pennsylvania.

Fort Shaw, Md
January 8, 1881

Dear Colonel,

Yours of the 27th instant received. I've occasion to prove questions about the dead at Fredericksburg. The dead found nearest the enemy on that field belonged to the 1st Division, 2nd Corps. There was a question about this framed to me early in 1877 and I then settled the matter by the same answer I give you. The particular regiment they belonged to was the 69th New York and it occurred in this way. The regiments on the right of Hancock's three brigades were the 53rd Pennsylvania Volunteers [Brooke's], 5th New Hampshire, and 69th New York.

The three regiments marched the same point in their advance and after the 69th New York came up it was in the same line. The color sergeant guard of the 69th NY then moved forward about 20 feet to a low place in the ground for better protection, I presume, and there I found all or nearly all who went to that point dead. I do not know if any of the party escaped, it is possible that such is the case but I do not know.

These few men were, as nearly as I can remember, about 20 feet in advance of the point which the three regiments, 53rd Pennsylvania Volunteers, 5th New Hampshire, and 69th New York, marched. The regiments went into the fight in the order named. I know the 53rd PV led for I was in command of the regiment that day and had general charge of the right of the brigade, under the orders of the Brigade Commander General Zook who gave me verbal orders as we were moving to the attack to "take charge and look out for the right as it probably would be impossible to communicate during the battle owing to the character of the ground," or words to that effect.

Thanks for your kind wishes
I remain yours truly,

Wm. R. Brooke

Appendix B

"Our Men Were Mowed Down like Grass Before the Scythe of the Reaper."

Private William McClelland, 88th New York, wrote a facsinating and detailed letter to the *Irish-American*, a newspaper printed in New York City, on the fight for Marye's Heights. His letter appeared in that paper on January 10, 1863. McClelland, an exemplary soldier who rose from private to lieutenant and regimental adjutant on the basis of his merit and courage, was mortally wounded on July 2, 1863, while charging with the 88th New York in the Wheatfield at Gettysburg (*Irish-American*, July 25, 1863). McClelland's description of the fighting, never published before in a historical work, is important and deserves a wider audience. It should be especially welcomed by those readers who have only recently finished William McCarter's superb account of the same action.

To the *Irish American:*

. . .[on Dec. 13] a heavy fog hung like a pall over the ill-fated city. The rebels kept constantly throwing shells into the city and killing a number of men throughout the morning. About 12 o'clock we were drawn up in line, and the

General gave us each a sprig of evergreen to put in our caps. We all looked gay and felt in high spirits, little dreaming, though we expected a heavy battle, that in so short a time after so many of our poor fellows would have been sent to their final doom. After the evergreen had been inserted in our caps, the General came along the line and said a few words of cheer to each regiment. Our regiment was second in line; when the General reached the colors of our regiment, he uncovered his head; General Hancock stood behind. The General said: "Officers and Soldiers of the 88th Regiment—In a few moments you will engage the enemy in a most terrible battle, which will probably decide the fate of this glorious, great and grand country—the home of your adoption." The General hesitated a moment, and then with eyes full to overflowing, through which he could hardly speak, he said: "Soldiers—This is my wife's own regiment, `her own dear 88th,' she calls it, and I know, and have confidence, that with dear woman's smile upon you, and for woman's sake, this day you will strike a deadly blow to those wicked traitors who are now but a few hundred yards from you, and bring back to this distracted country its former prestige and glory. This may be my last speech to you, but I will be with you when the battle is the fiercest; and, if I fall, I can say I did my duty, and fell fighting in the most glorious of causes." The Regiment then gave three cheers, such as the 88th alone can give.

During the delivery of this speech shells burst in and amongst us, killing a number and cutting off legs right by our side. Also during this address we heard the musketry of French's Division engaging the enemy on the outskirts of the town. Silence in the Brigade was soon broken by the orders, `Shoulder arms—right face—forward—double quick—march!' Onward we pressed up through the city, and as we reached its outskirts, grape, shell, canister, and shrapnel met us, and made great gaps in our ranks, taking more than once the four ranks clear out and laying them on the roadside in death, but the 88th wavered not; onward we pushed until we reached the foot of a hill, where we lay for five minutes under cover.

The 69th first entered the field—then came our turn. `Forward!' cried the General; up hill and forward over an open plain a quarter of a mile wide, we rushed the enemy firing with their rifles deadly volleys, and our men dropping all the way up, though none of our company fell until we were within thirty or forty yards of the rifle pits, where we met dreadful showers of bullets from three lines of enemy, besides their enfilading fire. Our men were mowed down like grass before the scythe of the reaper. One hour on that bloody field did its work. The men lay piled up in all directions. We had done our work. . .We could do no more against an enemy entrenched on a high hill and in rifle pits at the foot of it.

The smoke of the battle is now over. Let us look at Co. G, so long the "lucky company." First of all drop a tear over the bravest of the brave—the noble, the heroic Sheridan. When we passed through the city on our way out to the battlefield, he was full of life. He took his blanket and canteen and threw them high up against the walls of a house, to be free from incumbrance, inspirits the men with a wild cheer, and tells them to push on. When our work was done he crawls out on his hands and feet, takes up the body of Tom Cox, brings him to the rear and puts him in a place of safety. Again he goes out to succor a fallen comrade in the face of a storm of bullets; this time it is Corporal Kelly, but. . .the gallant Sheridan himself falls, with poor Kelly on his back, mortally wounded. I with others carried him to the hospital, he suffering the most intense pain, we hoping and praying for him. After laying him down as comfortable as possible, I ask the doctor to look at him. The doctor feels his pulse and tells me to get the priest. The priest came and administered to him, and when he had gone Slattery asked him if he did not feel better now? He says, "Yes, John, I feel better now." I stayed with him and did all I could for him, and he appeared very strong. He would put his one arm around my neck and raise himself up in a sitting position, and would then lay himself down again. Captain Egan came in, and when he saw the brave fellow in the agony of death, he wept like a child—so did we all. At about eight o'clock that night the soul of the brave, the noble Sheridan took its upward flight, and our beloved sergeant was no more. God have mercy on his soul. The last scene of this sorrowful drama was enacted next day, when his body was taken and buried where the day before he stood in the full prime and pride of life. A small board marks his last resting place, with the simple inscription "John Sheridan, Co. G, 88th Regt., I.B."   . . .The battle of Fredericksburg should be written in letters of blood on the banners of the Irish Brigade.

We are back in our old camp again, and passing through our avenues you feel as if you were going through a graveyard alone; all is dark, and lonesome, and sorrow hangs as a shroud over us all.

Wm. H. McCleland

Appendix C

"We Are Slaughtered Like Sheep, and No Result But Defeat"

Captain William J. Nagle, of the 88th New York Infantry, wrote the following letter to his father on December 14, 1862, which was published in the *Irish American*, New York City, on December 27, 1862. Nagle's missive captures the mood of the Irish Brigade after their failed attack on Marye's Heights.

Dear Father,

Thank God for his great mercy; I came out of the most terrible battle-day of the war without a scratch. My brother Edmund is also unhurt. I can hardly realize the fact that I am so blessed. Oh! It was a terrible day. The destruction of life has been fearful, and nothing gained. The battle opened about ten o'clock yesterday morning with a terrific fire of artillery. As we were drawn up in line of battle on the front of the city, Gen. Meagher addressed us in words of inspiration and eloquence I never heard equaled, after which he ordered every one of the brigade to place a bunch of green boxwood at the side of his cap, showing the example himself. Every man appeared fired with determined zeal and a firm resolution, which the results prove to have been carried out in a manner scarcely paralleled in the annals of war. The 88th Regt. this morning numbers ten officers and forty-one men; the 69th, seven officers and fifty-nine men; the 63d, six officers and sixty-four men; the 116th , thirteen officers and fifty-seven men. The 28th Massachusetts also suffered heavily; but I have not the returns. Irish blood and Irish bones cover that terrible field to-day. . .The whole-souled enthusiasm with which General McClellan inspired his army is wanting—his great scientific engineering skill is missing—his humane care for the lives of his men is disregarded. We are slaughtered like sheep, and no result but defeat. . . .

Lieutenant O'Brien, of my company, is, I believe, mortally wounded. All I can find of my once fine company of brave men is two Sergeants and three men. That noble, grave man, Major Horgan, was one of the first to fall, shot through the head. Every field officer of the brigade in action was killed or wounded, except Colonel Kelly, and he had a very narrow escape. Lieutenant Granger was struck by a piece of shell, tearing through all his clothes and the flesh over his bowels—one inch closer and he would have been killed. A piece of shell struck my haversack, tearing it off me, and throwing me over. Today has been comparatively quiet, from a mutual desire on each side to attend to the wounded and bury the dead; but tomorrow morning it will, no doubt, be renewed with increased force and hotter fire on both sides.

I do not know what disposition will be made of us now in our shattered condition. Colonel Kelly is in command of the remnant of the brigade, which does not number half a regiment. We are under arms since six o'clock this morning. I have got cold in my limbs, and have felt very sick all morning; but it is nothing more than the results of exposure and want of regular food, which a couple day's rest will remedy. . . .

Your affectionate son,

W. J. Nagle

"The Death of
Lieutenant Christian Foltz"

William McCarter wrote this poem in honor of his fallen comrade. It appeared in *The North American* on March 29, 1880.

The Dead Volunteer

On the burial of a volunteer soldier (Sunday evening, December 14, 1862) of the Army of the Potomac, who was killed at the battle of Fredericksburg, Va., on Saturday, December 13, 1862.

`Tis eve; one brightly beaming star,
Shines from the eastern heavens afar,
To light the footsteps of the brave,
Slow marching to a comrade's grave.

The cold north wind has sunk to sleep,
The sweet south breathes so low and deep,
The martial clang is heard, the tread

Of those who bear the noble dead.

And whose the form all stark and cold,
Thus ready for the loosened mould,
That's stretched upon so rude a bier,
Thine, soldier; thine, the volunteer.

Poor volunteer! the shot, the blow,
Of rebel bullet laid thee low,
Few may thy early loss deplore,
Thy battle done, thy journey o'er.

Alas, no fond wife's arms carressed,
Thy cheek no tender mother pressed,
No living man was near thy side
"Save one," for whom thou bravely died.

Yes, volunteer, you died at noon,
Next evening came the small platoon,
And when they laid thee down to rest,
Placed sods upon thy manly breast.

Thy name and fate shall fade away,
Forgotten since thy dying day,
And never on the roll of fame,
May be inscribed thy humble name.

Alas! like thee, how many more
Lie cold on Rappahannock's shore,
How many green, forgotten graves
Are bordered by its turbid waves.

Sleep, soldier, sleep, from sorrow free,
And pain, and strife, `tis well with thee!
`Tis well, though not a single tear
Laments the buried volunteer.

"W. McC."
Meagher's Irish Brigade,
Army of the Potomac, 1862

Appendix E

"The Irish Dead on Fredericksburg Heights"

Reprinted from *Irish-American*, New York City, May 2, 1863

Sofly let thy footprints fall,
Upon this holy ground,
In reverence deep,
For those who sleep,
Beneath each lowly mound.

Here hath many a noble son,
Of trodden mother land,
Whose joy thro' life,
Was hope of strife.
For their love of native land.

They came from Carlow's fertile plains,
And Wexford's woody vales,
From Innisbowen,
And green Tyrone,
And Wicklow's hills and dales.

They came to seek amid the free,
Homes to reward their toil,
In which to see
That Liberty
Unknown on Erin's soil.

And well they loved the chosen land;
When menaced was her might,
Each grateful heart
A willing part
Took in her cause to fight.

And here they lie in unblessed earth,
No kindred eye to weep;
Far, far away,
From the abbey's grey.
Where their sires and grandsires sleep.

Oh! many a matron, many a maid,
Mourn in their native isle,
For the dear ones here,
Who no more shall cheer
Their hearts by their gladsome smile.

In many an ancient chapel there,
Nestled on the green hill side,
Will the good priest pray,
On the Sabbath day,
For his boys who in battle died.

Let us offer too, our orisons,
For each of the martyr band,
Who nobly gave
Their lives to save
The might of their adopted land.

Kate M. Boylan
Jersey City, New Jersey, March 17, 1863

St. Patrick's Day

Endnotes

Foreword

1. William F. Fox, *Regimental Losses in the American Civil War* (Albany: Albany Publishing Company, 1898), p. 118.

2. William Corby, *Memoirs of Chaplain Life* (Chicago: La Monte, O'Donnell, and Co., 1893; reprint edition, ed. Lawrence P. Kohl, New York: Fordham University Press, 1992), p. 69.

3. Ibid., p. 350.

4. Ibid., p. 350.

5. St. Clair A. Mulholland, *The Story of the 116th Pennsylvania Volunteers* (Philadelphia: F. McManus & Jr., Company Printers, 1903; reprint, ed. Lawrence P. Kohl, New York: Fordham University Press, 1996), p. iv. Mulholland, who won the Congressional Medal of Honor for valor at Chancellorsville, rose to the rank of brevet major general and became the chief of police in Philadelphia after the Civil War. He was the only soldier in the Irish Brigade to publish a postwar regimental history about the famed unit. Before the rebellion, he earned his living as an artist.

6. Corby, *Memoirs of Chaplain Life*, pp. 69-70.

7. Joseph G. Bilby, *Remember Fontenoy! The 69th New York and the Irish Brigade in the Civil War* (Hightstown: Longstreet House, 1995), p. x.

Editor's Preface

1. George E. Pickett, *The Heart of a Soldier* (New York: Seth Moyle, Inc., 1913), p. 66.

2. William McCarter, "Fredericksburg's Battle," *Philadelphia Weekly Times*, September 8, 1883; details on the Irish Brigade's attack on Marye's Heights from Kevin E. O'Brien, "Sprig of Green: the Union Army's Irish Brigade," *The Recorder: Journal of the American Irish Historical Society*, vol. 6, no. 2 (Fall 1993): 45-53.

3. Reprinted in the *Boston Pilot*, an Irish immigrant newspaper on February 7, 1863.

4. Kevin E. O'Brien, "`The Breath of Hell's Door': Private William McCarter and the Attack of the Irish Brigade on Marye's Heights—An Unpublished Memoir," *Civil War Regiments: A Journal of the American Civil War,* Vol. 4, No. 4 (1996), pp. 47, 48.

5. Information on McCarter's life comes from Military and Pension Records, Pvt. William McCarter, National Archives and Record Administration, Washington, D.C.

6. W. Springer Menge and J. August Shimrak, ed., *The Civil War Notebook of Daniel Chisholm: A Chronicle of Daily Life in the Union Army, 1864-1865* (New York: Orion Books, 1989). Diary of Samuel Clear and Letters of Daniel Chisholm, soldiers of the 116th Pennsylvania. Chisholm transcribed Clear's diary into his Civil War notebook after the war ended.

Chapter One

1. "Certificate of Disability for Discharge," May 12, 1863, Military Records of Pvt. William McCarter, National Archives and Record Administration, Washington, D.C.

2. The 116th Pennsylvania began recruitment on June 11, 1862. Dennis Heenan, a well-respected Philadelphia citizen and veteran of the militia, was appointed the regiment's colonel. Recruitment was slow from June-August since many other regiments were organizing at the same time. The regiment was ordered to Washington, D.C., on September 1, 1862. See St. Clair A. Mulholland, *116th Pennsylvania,* pp. 1-4.

3. The reception of the 116th Pennsylvania by the citizens of Baltimore in 1862 stands in sharp contrast to what happened a year before. In 1861, pro-Southern mobs hooted and stoned Federal volunteers as they passed through the city. See Margaret Leech, *Reveille in Washington: 1861-1865* (New York: Harper and Row, 1941; reprint, New York: Time-Life, 1962), pp. 71, 72.

4. The Union Army founded the Soldiers' Rest and the Soldiers' Retreat in some large buildings near Washington's major railroad depot. Both commissaries fed and lodged arriving volunteers. As troop trains neared the capital, the commissary department was notified, and gangs set to work cutting meat, cooking and laying down tables. Promptly upon arrival, the soldiers sat down to a hot meal. If their orders were cut for immediate field duty, the troops found a day's worth of cooked rations available for transport. See Margaret Leech, *Reveille in Washington,* p. 231.

5. Skirmishing took place at Point of Rocks, Maryland, on September 4, 1862. E. B. Long, *The Civil War Day by Day: An Almanac* (Garden City: Doubleday, 1971; reprint, New York: Da Capo Press, 1985), p. 261.

6. Mulholland noted that the Pennsylvanians made good use of their time in camp. He wrote that every minute was "well spent in drill and learning the various duties incidental to active warfare." Mulholland, *116th Pennsylvania*, p. 9.

7. Franz Sigel, born in Baden, Germany on November 18, 1824, was a graduate of the Karlsruhe Military Academy. He fled to America after the unsuccessful Revolution of 1848 against Prussia, in which he took a hand as minister of war. McCarter's opinions notwithstanding, Sigel proved to be a failure on the battlefield. For more information on Sigel, see Stephen D. Engle, *Yankee Dutchman: The Life of Franz Sigel* (Fayetteville, 1993).

8. No enlisted man named "Carson" is reported to have died while serving with the 116th Pennsylvania. The victim, however, may have been Lt. Patrick Casey, Co. K, who died of an accidental gunshot wound received during September 1862. See Mulholland, *116th Pennsylvania*, "Roll of Honor."

9. It is interesting to note that Robert E. Lee was in command of the Army of Northern Virginia at the Battle of Antietam. At this stage of the war, however, Maj. Gen. Thomas J. "Stonewall" Jackson, one of Lee's two chief subordinate commanders, was better known across the country and perhaps even more feared by those north of the Mason-Dixon Line.

10. When he could spare time, President Lincoln was fond of horseback riding, walking in the White House area, or visiting soldiers' camps late in the afternoon before dinner. David H. Donald, *Lincoln* (New York, Simon and Schuster: 1995), p. 392.

11. Rush's Lancers were also known as the 6th Pennsylvania Cavalry. Their name was derived from the fact that they carried European lances into battle. The 6th Pennsylvania Cavalry abandoned their lances, over nine feet long, when it was discovered how unsuitable they were to carry in wooded and broken country, not to mention that the opposition carried firearms. Frank H. Taylor, *Philadelphia in The Civil War: 1861-1865* (Philadelphia: By the City, 1913), p. 163. Rush's report of the encounter recounted by McCarter does not mention the loss of any prisoners. The U.S. War Department: *War of the Rebellion: The Official Records of the Union and Confederate Armies*, 128 vols. (Washington, D.C., 1890-1901), vol. 19, pt. 2, pp. 41-42, hereinafter cited as *OR*.

12. The 116th Pennsylvania became an official regiment of the Irish Brigade early in October. See Mulholland, *116th Pennsylvania*, p. 10. Brigadier General Thomas F. Meagher greeted the officers of the 116th on a splendid

mount, and passed around a canteen of "good Irish whiskey" to the new officers under his command. Mulholland, ibid., p. 12.

13. Thomas F. Meagher, the charismatic founder of the Irish Brigade, had a fondness for drink, although his friends tried to downplay his alcoholism. Father William Corby, chaplain of the 88th New York and president of Notre Dame University, wrote: "It is to be regretted that, at times, especially when there was no fighting going on, his convivial spirit [Meagher's] would lead him too far. But by no means must it be concluded from this that he was a drunkard. It was not for love of liquor, but for the love of sport and joviality that he thus gave way, and these occasions are few and far between." William Corby, *Memoirs of Chaplain Life*, p. 29. Meagher's enemies often attributed mistakes in battle to his heavy drinking. After Meagher resigned as commander of the Irish Brigade in May 1863, protesting the Army of the Potomac's refusal to pull his command out of line to recruit replacements, his dependence on hard liquor seems to have worsened. Restored to Federal service in 1864, he performed miserably in Union commands overseeing captured Southern territory. Even a biographer as sympathetic as Robert G. Athearn noted that Meagher was so drunk that he could not even understand his orders when delivering Union reinforcements to North Carolina early in 1865. The Irish patriot was sent home ignominiously in March 1865, at the orders of Lt. Gen. Ulysses S. Grant.

Meagher's professional career rebounded in the post-Civil War era, when he became Acting Governor of Montana—thanks in large part to his support of Abraham Lincoln's re-election effort in 1864. Meagher performed admirably in this arena, in which he helped organize settlers against Red Cloud's Sioux warriors, planned a territorial convention, and awed the local citizens with his golden Irish tongue. Although poised on the verge of carving out a successful political career, it was not to be. After a particularly heavy drinking spree, Meagher lost his balance and fell into the Missouri River from the deck of a steamboat, where he drowned. Robert G. Athearn, *Thomas Francis Meagher: An Irish Revolutionary in America* (Boulder, 1949), pp. 137, 138, 165, 166.

Chapter 2

1. McCarter's unusual writing ability made him a prized commodity in the Army of the Potomac. His penmanship was simply extraordinary. After the war, he earned a living as a scriviner, a clerk, retiring from the Pension Office of the Veterans' Administration. See William McCarter, Death Certificate, January 2, 1911, District of Columbia, National Archives and Records Administration, Washington, D.C. It is no wonder that Colonel Heenan and General Meagher

fought over the chance for McCarter's service at their respective headquarters. Men who could write crisp written orders were at a premium.

2. The Irish Brigade was ordered to march on Charlestown during the evening of October 15, 1862. Mulholland, *116th Pennsylvania*, pp. 14, 15.

3. St. Clair Mulholland agrees with McCarter on the beauty of the Indian Summer weather. "Summer lingered late that year. Stacks of hay not yet gathered into the barns were still in the field. The meadows were yellow with goldenrod, and the regimental line was formed in a field still green with rich clover. Ah, how beautiful that bright October morning when for the first time the command formed line to meet the enemy." Mulholland, ibid., p. 16.

4. The supporting artillery included Tomkin's Rhode Island battery (1st Rhode Island Light, Battery A), Mullholland, Ibid, p. 16. The artillerymen had just been heavily engaged at Antietam, where their battery fired close to 1,000 rounds. Stephen W. Sears, *Landscape Turned Red: The Battle of Antietam* (New York: Ticknor and Fields, 1983), p. 253.

5. St. Clair A. Mulholland, regimental historian of the 116th Pennsylvania, does not include this officer in the unit's roster. Perhaps the man transferred out of the Irish Brigade. Mulholland may have intentionally excluded the cowardly lieutenant from his roll of honor. Mulholland, *116th Pennsylvania*, p. 422.

6. McCarter's version of this affair against Confederate infantry does not agree with Mulholland's account of the Charlestown battle. St. Clair A. Mulholland reported that only cavalry and artillery defended the city. See Mulholland, ibid, p. 17.

7. The Irish Brigade did not fight at either First or Second Bull Run. The unit was first engaged at Fair Oaks on June 1, 1862, and was in the thick of the Seven Days' Battles, fighting at Gaines' Mill, Savage's Station, White Oak Swamp, and Malvern Hill. General Meagher lost 493 men killed, missing, wounded or captured during that campaign. At Antietam on September 17, 1862, the Irish Brigade suffered 540 casualties in a wild dash against the Bloody Lane position. *OR* 11, pt. 2, p. 24; 19, pt. 1, p. 192.

8. The three original regiments of the Irish Brigade—the 63rd, 69th, and 88th New York—mustered about 2,500 when they left New York City in 1861 to serve in the Army of the Potomac. D. P. Conyngham, *The Irish Brigade and Its Campaigns* (New York: McSorley and Co., 1867; reprint, ed., Lawrence P. Kohl, New York: Fordham University Press, 1994), p. 597. The author of this popular work on the Irish Brigade served in the unit through 1863. He became a newspaperman and novelist after the war.

9. The Confederate battery defending Charlestown was the Richmond Howitzers. The artillerymen only abandoned their position when Meagher and the 69th advanced. Captain B. H. Smith, Jr., the battery's commander, lost his

leg during the action and was captured by the Federals. Mulholland, *116th Pennsylvania*, p. 17.

10. In all, about 100 Confederate prisoners who had been wounded during the bombardment were taken prisoner. Mulholland, ibid.

Chapter 3

1. McCarter reports the war's cruel collateral damage on Confederate civilians and slaves throughout his memoirs. While a loyal Union man, he sympathized with the plight of innocent non-combatants.

2. Perhaps the Irish Brigade lived on better terms with the Confederates than any other unit in the Army of the Potomac. Rebel pickets, who would regularly fire on their counterparts, would often cease fire when the Irish Brigade came on the line. Conyngham, *The Irish Brigade*, p. 87. The Confederates knew that they could count on a lively barter with the Irishmen for coffee, sugar, whiskey and tobacco. Frequently, Union and Confederate Irish immigrants exchanged news on the fate of family and friends under the shadow of an unofficial picket truce. Corporal William A. Smith, a fellow member of McCarter's 116th Pennsylvania, remembered that both sides stuck muskets by the bayonet into the ground as a sign of cease-fire before exchanging goods and written notes. Smith noted that it was customary for Irish Brigade soldiers to yell out "Hardtacks" as they were being pulled off the picket line. This warning notified the Southerners that a fresh Union unit, more interested in killing Confederates than trading items, was relieving the Irishmen. Letter from William A. Smith to sister, April 3, 1863,William A. Smith Letters, Lewis Leigh Collection, U.S. Army Military History Institute, Carlisle Barracks, Pennsylvania.

3. The 3rd South Carolina, which fought in the West Woods near Dunker Church, did not fight the Irish Brigade at Bloody Lane during the Battle for Antietam. Mac Wycoff, *A History of the 2nd South Carolina Infantry: 1861-1865* (Fredericksburg: Sergeant Kirkland's Museum, 1994), pp. 39-52. The prisoner from the 3rd South Carolina may simply have wanted to win favor with his Irish Brigade captors by telling them what they wanted to hear.

4. John Brown was hanged for treason on December 2, 1859, at Charlestown. Stewart Sifkasis, *Who Was Who In the Civil War* (New York: Facts on File, 1988), p. 79.

5. The Irish Brigade left Charlestown, leaving behind a flock of sheep shot to death in the darkness by pickets, who mistook the charging animals for Confederates. Mulholland, *116th Pennsylvania*, p. 18.

6. Disease killed far more soldiers in the Civil War than combat. Some 250,100 Union soldiers died of sickness contracted during the war, compared to 110,100 battle deaths. The Confederates, whose records are less accurate, lost some 164,000 men to illness against 94,000 men lost in action.

7. Daniel Hauck, who enlisted on August 23, 1862, is not included in St. Clair A. Mulholland's Roll of Honor, which covered all men from the 116th who died of combat or disease. Somehow, his death from an illness was not reported and Hauck is listed as "not on muster out roll" in Mulholland's regimental history. McCarter corrects Mulholland and adds Hauck to the long list of Irish Brigade soldiers who died for their country. Mulholland, *116th Pennsylvania*, p. 423.

8. Private William McCarter was a Protestant, and despite his assertions to the contrary, the Irish Brigade was the spiritual center of Catholicism in the Army of the Potomac. The three original regiments of the Irish Brigade—the 63rd, 69th and 88th New York—were heavily Roman Catholic, including Irish immigrant officers who had served in Italy's Papal Brigade. The 28th Massachusetts, raised in Boston, was also predominantly Catholic. McCarter's 116th Pennsylvania, a strange mixture of Irish immigrants from Philadelphia and German farmers from the Pennsylvania countryside, had more Protestants than the other regiments. Despite these religious differences, there was a strange religious harmony.

Rev. William Corby, chaplain of the 88th New York and later president of Notre Dame University, noted in his memoirs that he served the spiritual needs of both catholic and crotestant. Corby, *Memoirs of Chaplain Life*, p. 74. Colonel Robert Nugent, commanding the 69th New York, a Protestant, saw nothing wrong in accepting absolution from a Catholic priest before going into battle. The hatred and animosity between Protestant and catholic in 20th century Irish politics had not developed at the time of America's Civil War. Both collaborated together in the effort to throw off British rule in the Irish Rebellion of 1798. Thomas Pakenham, *The Year of Liberty: The Great Irish Rebellion of 1798* (London: Granada Publishing, 1969). Wolfe Tone, the leader of the rebellion, was the son of a Protestant coachmaker.

9. Sadly, there is no written record of the Protestant ministers who served the Irish Brigade or the services which they provided to their flock, including McCarter.

10. The 116th Pennsylvania received its new colors from Samuel P. Bates on behalf of the State of Pennsylvania. Reverend Patrick D. O'Flaherty, *The History of the Sixty-Ninth Regiment in the Irish Brigade* (New York: privately printed, 1986), p. 168. The Irish-German 116th Pennsylvania—because of the mixed heritage of its men—carried the state colors of Pennsylvania as a second

flag, in contrast to the other Irish Brigade regiments who bore an Irish green flag.

   11. Psalm 121: 1-8.

Chapter 4

   1. Long, *The Civil War Day by Day*, pp. 280, 281 for a discussion of this expedition.

   2. On October 26, 1862, the Army of the Potomac struck its tents and the Federals left Harper's Ferry. Mulholland, *116th Pennsylvania*, pp. 118-119.

   3. Julie Ward Howe wrote the "Battle Hymn of the Republic," based on the melody from "John Brown's Body." Lois Hill, ed., *Poems and Songs of the Civil War* (New York: Fairfax Press, 1990), p. 192.

   4. McCarter is mistaken about the date of the arrival of the Irish Brigade at Snicker's Gap. The Irishmen reached Snicker's Gap on November 2, 1862, and immediately clashed with Confederate cavalry. Mulholland, *116th Pennsylvania*, p. 119.

   5. Caldwell's brigade, a hard-fighting unit and part of Hancock's veteran division, could hardly be called "Irish." The regiments—the 5th New Hampshire, 7th New York, 61st New York, 64th New York, and 81st Pennsylvania—did not carry green flags or publicize the ethnic origins of their men. Caldwell's brigade, however, fought bravely at the side of the Irish Brigade at Antietam. Sears, *Landscape Turned Red*, pp. 244-248.

   6. McCarter's account of the skirmishing at Snicker's Gap is not mentioned in any similar detail in any other published work about the Irish Brigade. According to Mulholland, Maj. Tom O'Neill and Maj. George Bardwell of the Irish Brigade rode over to meet cavalry observed at Snicker's Gap. O'Neill quickly found out that the horsemen were Confederates and was taken prisoner. Bardwell, discovering his mistake in time, wheeled around and galloped for his own column, the Southerners sending a shower of shots over his head. Luckily for Major O'Neill, a detachment from the 8th Pennsylvania Cavalry captured the Confederate patrol which had taken him prisoner later in the day. The fortunate O'Neill returned to cheering friends. Mulholland, *116th Pennsylvania*, p. 19.

   7. Only one other veteran of the Irish Brigade, Father William Corby, chaplain of the 88th New York, even commented on the struggle for Snicker's Gap. According to Corby, it was a "sharp fight." Corby, *Memoirs of Chaplain Life*, p. 128.

8. Like most of the officers and rank-in-file of the Irish Brigade, McCarter was an unabashed admirer of General McClellan. When McClellan resigned, several officers in the Irish Brigade tendered their resignations as well, none of which were accepted by Meagher. Conyngham, *The Irish Brigade*, p. 324. It was reported that the color bearers of the Irish Brigade cast their flags in the dirt for General McClellan to ride over them as he gave the Army of the Potomac his last farewell. Allen Nevins, *The War for the Union* (New York: Charles Scribner's Sons, 1960), p. 332. The story sounds, and probably is, apocryphal. As McCarter notes, never was a general loved in the Union Army by the troops better than George B. McClellan.

9. Mulholland, second in command of the 116th Pennsylvania, remembered the march of the Irish Brigade to Warrenton as "of the most delightful character. The weather, after the first night out, was charming—the air pure, clear and bracing—and as by slow marches the column moved along each day through a beautiful country, with the mountains of the Blue Ridge blazing with all the brilliancy of 'Indian Summer,' the fields aglow with the flowers of Autumn. The hearts of all were filled with joy. The evening campfires during this period were the most enjoyable." Mulholland, *116th Pennsylvania*, p. 20.

10. McCarter offers a touching, descriptive and heartfelt account of McClellan's departure from the Army of the Potomac. Among contemporary authors, only Bruce Catton can rival the depiction of the scene. Catton, *The Army of the Potomac: Mr. Lincoln's Army* (Garden City: Doubleday, 1951), pp. 329, 330.

11. McCarter's impression of Maj. Gen. Ambrose Burnside as a man is compelling. The Irish Brigade soldier captures Burnside's physical appearance, his demeanor towards the troops, and even his character. Burnside continues to be the most reviled commander of the Army of the Potomac. It took a modern biographer, William Marvel, to restore some measure of respectability to Burnside, earned primarily by his lengthy service in the Civil War. Marvel, *Burnside* (Chapel Hill: University of North Carolina Press, 1991).

12. General Meagher's parties, which always included copious amounts of liquor, were famous throughout the Army of the Potomac. D. P. Conyngham, historian of the Irish Brigade, includes several accounts of wild drinking under the roof of Meagher's tent, but, at least according to the author, the general himself never became intoxicated. Conyngham, *The Irish Brigade*, pp. 231-238. McCarter acquaints us with the truth about Meagher's conduct from one such heavy drinking bout. It is a touching and sad scene.

13. General Burnside reorganized the Army of the Potomac into three Grand Divisions. Marvel, *Burnside*, p. 165. Burnside believed that the new wings would be easier to maneuver.

14. President Lincoln called for "orderly observance of the Sabbath" by officers and men of the Army and Navy on November 15, 1862. Long, *The Civil War Day by Day*, p. 287.

15. St. Clair A. Mulholland concurs on the date of the move towards Fredericksburg. Mulholland, *116th Pennsylvania*, pp. 20, 21.

16. McCarter's claim that Meagher was offered a divisional command has no historical corroboration. See, e.g., Athearn, *Thomas Francis Meagher*, who found no documents offering the Irish general such a position at any time during the war.

17. Major's death deeply affected his friends. "The tears of his comrades," wrote Mulholland, "sanctified the soil where they laid him, and though buried far from his old home in Pennsylvania, hands as gentle and loving as brothers gave him the last sad rest." Mulholland, *116th Pennsylvania*, p. 21.

Chapter 5

1. McCarter is correct. The officers of the Irish Brigade seem never to have lacked for liquor in abundance. Meagher sponsored a St. Patrick's Day spectacular in 1863 that included a steeplechase and a plethora of food and drink. The fare consisted of 35 hams, the side of a roasted ox, an entire pig stuffed with boiled turkeys, and an unlimited number of chickens, ducks, and small game. The drinking material, shared by the Irish Brigade's officers with their guests, including Fighting Joe Hooker, commander of the Army of the Potomac, comprised eight baskets of champagne, ten gallons of rum, and 22 gallons of whiskey. Conyngham, *The Irish Brigade*, p. 373.

2. McCarter's version of this incident directly contradicts the Conyngham's account. Both men agree that General Sumner ordered the Irish Brigade to cross the Rappahannock and take the Rebel batteries. Conyngham wrote a stirring account of the event: "They plunged into the Rappahannock, dashed across it, flung themselves on a battery of the enemy, capturing two guns. As they dashed at it, they gave one Irish cheer, kicked over kettles, frying pans, coffee pots and everything else in the way. The enemy fled without firing a shot. Hancock cried out, `General Meagher, I have never seen anything so splendid.'" Conyngham, *The Irish Brigade*, p. 327. Unlike Conyngham, McCarter's account, where the Irish Brigade halted at the river's edge, rings true. Burnside had a fear of crossing the Rappahannock before all of his preparations were complete. If the Irish Brigade had waded the river and captured the Confederate guns, someone would have had to ordered them back. It is sad to debunk this fine legend of the Irish Brigade, but McCarter corrects the historical record.

3. See Edward J. Stackpole, *The Fredericksburg Campaign: Drama on the Rappahannock* (2nd ed; Harrisburg: Stackpole Books, 1991), pp. 48, 49 for a similar description of the topography around Falmouth.

4. Ibid., p. 94.

5. Who was to blame for the delay in shipping pontoons for a river crossing of the Rappahannock by the Federals? Stackpole attributes more fault to Maj. General Henry W. Halleck than Burnside. As General-in-Chief, Halleck should have ensured that the Army of the Potomac was equipped with proper bridging material at this crucial moment in the campaign. Stackpole, *The Fredericksburg Campaign*, pp. 89, 90, 91. On the other hand, Burnside denied Sumner permission to wade the Rappahannock at the cattle ford on November 17, when the Confederates at Fredericksburg were only strong enough to offer token resistance. Ibid, p. 85. See also, Marvel, *Burnside*, pp. 165-167, who defends Burnside's decision to keep Sumner on the north side of the river, arguing that the Federal troops would have been stranded and destroyed if they crossed into the town without support or a supply line.

6. St. Clair A. Mulholland, second in command of McCarter's regiment, gave a similar account of the Confederate defensive preparatons. "Every day gave new evidence of their industry. Every hour saw new earthworks rising in front, redoubts, lunettes and bastioned forts. Rifle-pits and epaulments for the protection of artillery arose in rapid succession until the terraced heights, which ran parallel to the city and two miles below and nearly a mile to the rear of it, were crowned with artillery, bristling with bayonets, and so formidable as to make an attempt to carry the place an act of insanity." Mulholland, *116th Pennsylvania*, at 29.

7. Father Corby reported a conversation with a private in the 88th New York where a similar conclusion was reached. "Father," said this soldier, "they are going to lead us over in front of those guns which we have seen them placing, unhindered, for the past three weeks." Father Corby replied, "Do not trouble yourself; your generals know better than that." Unfortunately, Corby was wrong. Corby, *Memoirs of Chaplain Life*, p. 131.

8. At age 65, General Edwin V. Sumner was the oldest general in the Army of the Potomac. Appointed a lieutenant in the Regular Army during 1819, he fought Indians on the frontier and served in the Mexican War. He was known as "Bull" because of his great booming voice. Behind his back, Sumner was also called "Bull Head," allegedly because musket-balls bounced harmlessly off his thick skull. He rose from a command of a division to a corps under McClellan. Sumner led the Right Grand Division under Burnside at Fredericksburg. Sifkakis, *Who Was Who In the Civil War*, pp. 634, 635. McCarter was obviously impressed by Sumner's military bearing.

9. McCarter paints an interesting portrait of "Hancock the Superb," one of the best generals of the Army of the Potomac. The general's biographers concur with McCarter's assessment of Hancock as a striking military figure and harsh disciplinarian. See, e.g., Glenn Tucker, *Hancock the Superb* (Indianapolis: Bobbs-Merrill, 1960). Hancock's profanity was also legendary. Father Corby remembered how Hancock stopped the whole Irish Brigade in its tracks with the bluest of oaths on the march to Gettysburg. The general believed that some of the men, in violation of orders, had killed a sheep belonging to civilians. When the sheep jumped out of the brush and ran off, Hancock took back his accusations and rode off. The Irish Brigade's chaplain wrote: "Addicted merely through force of habit to the use of profane language when excited, he [Hancock] would invariably stop short when he discovered the presence of a clergyman." Corby, *Memoirs of Chaplain Life*, pp. 173-174.

10. This comical incident shows Hancock's fiery temper in action. Did he actually frighten an Irish Brigade soldier so badly that the man deserted to the Confederates? We shall never know, but two "Richards" who enlisted as privates in the 116th, Company D, during the summer of 1862, were unaccounted for when the regiment mustered out. Mulholland, *116th Pennsylvania*, "Muster Roll."

11. As McCarter reports, Federal and Confederate pickets on the Rappahannock were within calling distance of each other, divided only by the narrow band of water. D. P. Conyngham recorded an interesting dialogue between an Irish Brigade soldier and a Confederate on the other side. "How are you today, Yank?" asked the Confederate. "I reckon I feel rather cold, Johnny," replied the Irishman. "Any coffee, Yank?" queried the Reb, holding up a canteen of moonshine whiskey. "Plenty, and tobacco, too," answered the Federal. Thus a trade was established and parties from both armies crossed the river to trade, exchange newspapers, and gossip. Conyngham, *The Irish Brigade*, p. 328.

12. The Army of the Potomac moved 147 pieces of artillery into these prepared positions. St. Clair A. Mulholland, "Annals of the War—Battle of Fredericksburg," *Philadelphia Weekly Times*, April 23, 1881.

13. McCarter notes that the enemy on the other side of the Rappahannock moved about without any interference from the Union troops. Stackpole reports that young Confederates pelted each other with snowballs as the Federals watched. Both sides waited impatiently for Burnside to attack. Stackpole, *The Fredericksburg Campaign*, p. 101.

Chapter 6

1. The prayer is based on Proverbs.
2. This is probably Capt. Patrick Carrigan of Company A. Mulholland, *116th Pennsylvania*, "Muster Roll," p. 422.
3. Few surviving tales about foraging by the Army of the Potomac have either the zest or humor of McCarter's account. See John D. Billings, *Hard Tack and Coffee: The Unwritten Story of Army Life* (Williamstown: Corner House Pubishers, 1887), pp. 231-249 for a detailed account of the science of foraging by hungry Union troops.
4. General Robert E. Lee concentrated his forces at Fredericksburg while Burnside marked time.
5. There is no basis for this rumor. Sigel's XI Corps did not fight a major engagement with the Confederates during late November 1862. Light skirmishing took place at Newtown, Virginia, on November 24. Long, *The Civil War Day by Day*, p. 289.
6. McCarter was not alone in his premonition that a Union attack on the entrenched Confederate lines at Fredericksburg would be a disaster. Father Corby, chaplain of the 88th New York, wrote that the Confederates "massed on the hills behind the city, on the south of the Rappahannock, built breastworks, and got all their artillery in the best possible positions." Corby, *Memoirs of Chaplain Life*, pp. 130, 131. Mulholland, McCarter's superior officer, described any effort to carry the place, "insanity." Mulholland, *116th Pennsylvania*, p. 29.
7. Irish immigrant soldiers who served in the Union Army have been accused by several historians of outright prejudice against the black slaves whom they were liberating. The typical argument advanced to support this theory suggests that the Irish feared displacement from their low-paying jobs by even poorer freed slaves. See, e.g., William L. Burton, *Melting Pot Soldiers: The Union's Ethnic Regiments* (Ames: Iowa University Press, 1988), pp. 112-154. McCarter's empathy towards the slave women who fed and solaced him dispels some of this stereotype.
8. While Lee had much of James Longstreet's artillery dug in at Fredericksburg, many of Jackson's cannons were still en route. There was nowhere near 400 guns waiting for the Federals. McCarter, being an Irishman, should be allowed a wee bit of leeway when exaggerating.

Chapter 7

1. McCarter does not consider the obvious. The three black slave women chose to stay with their owner despite the nearby presence of the Army of the Potomac. Those slaves who had been ill-treated or beaten already had fled their owners. Only the most loyal and comfortable slaves remained in bondage while Union troopers held sway in the Fredericksburg vicinity.

2. The young Irish private aptly describes the critical role which adjutants played at every level of command during the Civil War. Military secretaries recorded in writing essential orders and reports. McCarter's penmanship had marked him for headquarters duty when Meagher learned of his skill.

3. There is no record of a meeting between Meagher, Hancock and Burnside on November 28, 1862. But since McCarter was familiar with both Burnside and Hancock, it is possible that the rendevous occurred. Unfortunately, McCarter stepped outside the headquarters tent on the Irish Brigade and did not hear the conversation. It would be interesting to know the generals' thoughts on the eve of the Battle of Fredericksburg.

4. Irish slang for liquor. Also known in the Union army as "busthead," "dead shot," "how come you so," "knock-`em stiff," "rifle knock-knee," "rotgut" and "tarantula juice." Darryl Lyman, *Civil War Wordbook* (Conshohocken: Combined Books, 1994), p. 7.

5. McCarter's extremely favorable impression of Meagher was echoed in postwar biographies of the general. See, e.g., Michael Cavanagh, *Memoirs of Gen. Thomas Francis Meagher* (Worcester: Messenger Press, 1892), and W. F. Lyons, *Brigadier General Thomas Francis Meagher: His Political and Military Career* (New York: D & J Sadlier Co., 1870).

6. Brigaider General Henry J. Hunt reported that he had 147 pieces of artillery under his command overlooking the city of Fredericksburg when the hostilities commenced. His cannons were organized into four large divisions. *OR* 21, p. 181.

7. For a similar description of how winter quarters were built by Union troops, see Billings, *Hard Tack and Coffee*, pp. 541-57. According to Billings, no hut was complete until a sign appeared above the door, marked with charcoal. "Hole in the Wall," "Willard's Hotel" and "Astor House" were popular names.

8. Major General William B. Franklin, who commanded Burnside's Left Grand Division, wrote to St. Clair Mulholland about a council of war held by the high command of the Army of the Potomac during this first week of December. In Franklin's words, Burnside's division commanders talked to the commanding general "at arm's length." There was a total lack of harmony and

unity between Burnside and his subordinate generals, which boded poorly for the Union soldiers about to assault the Confederate troops. Letter from William B. Franklin to St. Clair Mulholland, January 6, 1881, Mulholland Papers, Box 1, Civil War Library and Museum, Philadelphia, Pennsylvania.

9. The pontoons had finally arrived. Burnside had the Army of the Potomac on the move to concentrate near the places where the bridges would be built. *OR* 21, pp. 87, 88.

Chapter 8

1. Federal soldiers on the march normally carried 40 rounds. Billings, *Hard Tack and Coffee*, p. 317.

2. The Army of the Potomac was finally ready to move on Fredericksburg. General Burnside abandoned a plan to flank Lee's Army of Northern Virginia at Skinker's Neck because Stonewall Jackson had moved in that direction. *OR* 21, pp. 87, 88. See also Marvel, *Burnside*, pp. 169, 170. Burnside believed that an attack into the city itself over pontoons would surprise the enemy and lead to victory. Ibid., p. 87. Burnside reasoned that the Army of the Potomac would catch the Confederates napping, swiftly capture Marye's Heights, and cut the Confederate forces into two halves which could be then defeated in detail.

3. Two designated Confederate guns replied to this barrage at 4:30 a.m. It was a signal to Longstreet's corps that the long-awaited crossing was about to start. Stackpole, *The Fredericksburg Campaign*, p. 133.

4. The 50th New York Engineers labored throughout the night constructing a span across the Rappahannock. By 6:00 a.m., growing daylight thinned the fog concealing the New Yorkers. Brigadier General William Barksdale's Mississippi brigade and the 8th Florida Infantry, hidden among buildings and cellars near the river, opened fire on the men working on the bridge. Major Ira Spaulding, who commanded the engineers, reported that the Rebs killed a captain and two enlisted men. *OR* 21, p. 175. Construction activity temporarily ceased.

5. Lieutenant Colonel Mulholland of the 116th Pennsylvania also witnessed the destructive effects of the Federal artillery barrage. "Tons of iron were hurled into the town; shells, solid shot, shrapnel and canister raked and swept the streets. We could not see yet; we could hear the walls crumbling and the timbers crashing; then a pillar of smoke rose above the fog; another, and another, increasing in density and volume, rose skyward and canopied the doomed city like a pall. Flames leaped high out of the mist—the city was on fire." Mulholland, "Annals of the War—The Battle of Fredericksburg," *Philadelphia Weekly Times*, April 23, 1881.

6. The Union cannons could not depress their barrels far enough down to hit the Confederates on the riverside. Further, the Southerners were hidden in cellars, ditches and behind stone walls. It would take infantry to dig the Confederates out. Richard F. Miller and Robert F. Mooney, "Across the River and into the Streets: The 20th Massachusetts Infantry and the Fight for the Streets of Fredericksburg," *Civil War Regiments: A Journal of the American Civil War*, Vol. 4, No. 4 (1996), pp. 101, 109-110.

7. Would Meagher have ordered McCarter back to the command tent if he found him in the ranks? The answer is most likely yes, since Meagher put McCarter in charge of his own personal possessions in the case of death or a wound. As McCarter's memoirs eventually reveal, the general forgave him for disobedience and tried to help him when he was in the Union Army hospital system.

8. Henry J. Hunt, chief of artillery, proposed at about 2:30 p.m. that Federal infantry fill pontoon boats and dash to the other side of the river. The foot soldiers would dislodge the stubborn enemy and allow the bridges to be completed. The plan was approved. *OR* 21, p. 183. At the Upper Bridge site (observed by McCarter), the 7th Michigan and the 19th Massachusetts volunteered to crew the boats. The 20th Massachusetts enthusiastically followed these two regiments across the water, with all three units under a heavy fire from Confederate sharpshooters. Ibid., p. 189.

9. McCarter offers one of the best written and dramatic accounts of the river crossing by Federal volunteers in pontoon boats. He rightly compliments the brave soldiers who accomplished the deed. George Henry Boker, poet, dramatist, and U.S. Minister to Turkey and Russia, wrote a poem titled, "The Crossing at Fredericksburg," to honor the brave young men from Massachusetts and Michigan. Miller and Mooney, "The 20th Massachusetts Infantry and the Fight for the Streets of Fredericksburg," p. 123.

10. McCarter is right in noting that three pontoon bridges were constructed. But he incorrectly described the planned deployment of the Union troops. General Sumner was to cross over the Upper Bridge with his Right Grand Division, supported by Hooker. General Franklin was to use the Lower Bridge and attack Lee's right flank. Marvel, *Burnside*, pp. 176-184.

11. See the Report of Brig. Gen. Winfield S. Hancock, First Division, Second Corps, for further information on the procession of Union troops across the pontoon bridges. *OR* 21, p. 226.

12. Unfortunately, the identity of Colonel "Whiskey Head" cannot be determined from available reports on the crossing into Fredericksburg.

13. St. Clair Mulholland also remembered this salvage operation in his regimental history. "Some barges laden with tobacco had been sunk. The boys

succeeded in fishing up great quantities of the weed and lined their blouses with it. After the fight, one heard of many of the men whose lives had been saved by the solid plugs of tobacco stopping the ball intended for their heart, still there was no tangible evidence of the fact." Mulholland, *116th Pennsylvania*, p. 37.

14. Union troops looted the city of Fredericksburg like an invading foreign army. Little or no restraint was exercised. Theft of clothing, blankets, household furnishings, and family treasures escalated into wanton destruction. It was like the sack of a medieval city. Marvel, *Burnside*, p. 179.

Chapter 9

1. McCarter was not alone in finding uncomfortable sleeping accommodations. Sergeant Peter Welsh, 28th Massachusetts of the Irish Brigade, wrote his wife that the men searched for a place to rest in ankle-deep mud. "We hunted up pieces of boards," he wrote, "and lay them down on the mud and covered ourselves up in blankets." Lawrence Kohl and Margaret Richard, ed., *Irish Green and Union Blue: The Civil War Letters of Peter Welsh, Color Sergeant, 28th Massachusetts Volunteers* (New York: Fordham University, 1986), p. 42.

2. Winfield Hancock's division numbered about 5,000 soldiers on the morning of December 13, 1862. It lost 2,013 killed, wounded, missing or captured during the assault of Marye's Heights. *OR* 21, p. 228.

3. Major General William Henry French's division led the Federal assault on Marye's Heights. Ibid., p. 94.

4. General Meagher ordered sprigs of evergreen placed in each man's hat to make sure that the Confederates knew they were facing the Irish Brigade. The green flags of the three New York regiments—the 63rd, 69th and 88th—had been so riddled by shot and shell that they had been returned to New York City for replacement. Only the 28th Massachusetts, which had recently received a green silk banner decorated with a golden harp, a sunburst and a wreath of shamrocks, carried the Irish emblem into battle. The replacement symbol of green boxwood stirred the hearts of the Irish Brigade. "We all looked gay and felt in high spirits," wrote Pvt. William McCleland of the 88th New York after he fixed his green sprig in his cap. Letter from William McCleland to Irish-American, January 10, 1863, Irish Brigade file, Fredericksburg and Spotsylvania National Military Park. Hereinafter cited as FSNMP. Lieutenant Colonel Mulholland of the 116th Pennsylvania wrote: "Wreaths were made and hung upon the tattered [U.S.] flags, and the national color of the Emerald Isle blended in fair harmony with the red, white, and blue of the Republic." Mulholland,

116th Pennsylvania, p. 44. According to another historian of the brigade, the ceremony with the green boxwood fired up the troops with unusual zeal and determination. Conyngham, *The Irish Brigade*, pp. 330-337, 341.

5. Another soldier of the 116th, Pvt. Samuel D. Hunter, remembered that the whole regiment, inspired by Meagher's ceremony with the sprigs of boxwood, left its position "cheering." Hunter penned that Meagher's own hat "was ornamented with three sprigs." Samuel D. Hunter, "Charge of the Irish Brigade on Marye's Heights," Grand Army Scout and Soldier's Mail, October 6, 1883, Irish Brigade file, FSNMP.

6. The Irish Brigade actually numbered about 1,200 men as the advance began. *OR* 21, p. 241.

7. McCarter is incorrect regarding the deployment of the brigade. The 69th New York was placed at the head of the column so that it would form the right flank, followed by the 88th New York, 28th Massachusetts, 63rd New York, and 116th Pennsylvania. Ibid., pp. 241, 242.

8. St. Clair Mulholland remembered, like McCarter, that "the wounded went past in great numbers and the appearance of the dripping blood was not calculated to enthuse the men or cheer them for the first important battle." Mulholland, *116th Pennsylvania*, p. 43.

9. Sergeant Marley was beheaded by the shell which wounded McCarter and killed three other men. Mulholland, ibid., p. 45.

10. McCarter's assessment of Burnside's downward spiral as a military commander hits the mark. After being relieved as commander of the Army of the Potomac, Burnside was transferred to the western theater of operations. His star shone slightly brighter when he captured Knoxville, Tennessee. Reassigned to the Army of the Potomac, Burnside led the IX Corps during Grant's Overland Campaign in 1864, and badly bungled the followup attack after the explosion of a mine under the Southern lines at Petersburg at the end of July. Following the Battle of the Crater, Burnside was sent on leave and was never recalled. After the war, he served as governor of Rhode Island and U.S. Senator. Sifkakis, *Who Was Who in the Civil War*, p. 94.

11. McCarter is incorrect. Major John Pelham's lone Napoleon cannon was located on the Confederate right at Fredericksburg, where it harassed advancing Union troops. Gregory A. Mertz, "`A Severe Day for the Artillery': Stonewall Jackson's Artillerists and the Defense of the Confederate Right," *Civil War Regiments: A Journal of the American Civil War*, Vol. 4, No. 4 (1996), pp. 70, 73, 74, 81. Lee's New Orleans Washington artillery, under Colonel Walton, did much of the damage to the Federal attackers at Marye's Heights. Edward P. Alexander, *Military Memoirs of a Confederate* (New York: Charles Scribner's Sons, 1907; reprint, Dayton: Morningside House, 1990), p. 303.

12. Hancock's brigades went in as follows: Zook first, followed by Meagher and Caldwell. *OR* 21, p. 227.

13. A fellow Irishman in the 8th Ohio, part of French's division, attempted to shelter himself by taking cover on the ground, from which point he observed the soldiers of the Irish Brigade as they charged the heights. "Every man has a sprig of green in his cap and a half-laughing, half-murderous look in his eye," he wrote. Captain Thomas F. Galwey, *The Valiant Hours* (Harrisburg, 1961), p. 62.

14. While the Irish Brigade took severe casualties from Confederate shells and canister, it was the heavy rifle fire from Thomas Cobb's Georgians that stalled the movement against Marye's Heights. "Round shot, grape and canister swept through the rank of five regiments, but not for a moment did they halt until fire from the `stone wall' became deadly—a steady, withering sheet of flame," remembered Maj. John Dwyer of the 63rd New York. "Address of John Dwyer," December 12, 1914, New York City, N.Y., Irish Brigade file, FSNMP. "None of our company fell until we were within 30 or 40 yards of the rifle pits, where we met dreadful showers of bullets from three lines of the enemy, besides their enfilading fire," wrote Pvt. William McCleland, a New Yorker from the 88th regiment. "Our men were mowed down like grass before the scythe of the reaper." Letter of William McCleland to Irish-American, January 10, 1863, Irish Brigade file, FSNMP.

15. The Confederate defensive fire was so intense that it literally tore clothing and equipment off the soldiers of the Irish Brigade. Captain W. J. Nagle of the 88th New York wrote: "Lt. Granger was struck by a piece of shell, tearing through all his clothes and the flesh over his bowels—one inch closer and he would have been killed. A piece of shell struck my haversack, tearing it off me, and throwing me over." Letter from W.G. Nagle to father, Irish-American, December 27, 1862, Irish Brigade file, FSNMP.

16. Many of Cobb's Georgians were Irish immigrants themselves. Lieutenant Colonel Mulholland alleged that these Southerners recognized the green flag of the 28th Massachusetts and the symbolic sprigs of green in their opponents' caps. "`Oh, God, what a pity! Here comes Meagher's fellows!' was the cry in the Confederate ranks," penned Mulholland. The likelihood of his having heard such a shout about the tumult of battle is, of course, virtually nil. Nevertheless, Cobb's Georgians decimated the ranks of the Irish Brigade with accurate rifle fire. Mulholland, *116th Pennsylvania*, p. 57.

17. McCarter must have confused General Meagher with another senior Irish Brigade officer, an easy thing to do with all of the smoke and noise on Marye's Heights. Meagher was unable to participate in the charge because of an ulcerated knee joint. He got as far as the low ground beyond the canal and

ordered the advance before returning to the town in search of his horse and staff officers. *OR* 21, pp. 241, 242.

18. Like McCarter, Col. Robert Nugent, commanding the 69th New York, was overwhelmed by the casualties and brutal Rebel musketry. "The fire was terrific," he wrote, "no pen can describe the horrors of this battle. The casualties were enormous. It was a living hell from which escape seemed scarcely possible. I was myself carried off the field, having been shot through the right side." Robert Nugent, "The Sixty-ninth Regiment at Fredericksburg," Third Annual Report of the Historian of the State of New York, 1897 (Albany, 1898), p. 42.

19. Colonel Brynes, of the 28th Massachusetts, and Col. Patrick Kelly, of the 88th New York, met a fenceline not far below the stone wall and agreed to retreat, collecting what remained of the Irish Brigade. *OR* 21, p. 252. General Meagher met groups of survivors as they stumbled back down the slope, directing them toward a relatively safe location in town. By late afternoon, he had collected only 250 of the 1,200 men in the brigade who had made the assault. Ibid, p. 243.

20. Lieutenant Christian Foltz was the only officer in the 116th Pennsylvania to be killed outright at Marye's Heights. Lieutenant Robert Montgomery was mortally wounded, dying later that day, while Lt. Robert T. McGuire died of his wounds received at Fredericksburg during the spring of 1865. Mulholland, *116th Pennsylvania*, "Roll of Honor—The Dead of the 116th Pennsylvania."

21. An endless debate has raged since the battle about how close the Federal troops got to the stone wall on Marye's Heights. Captain Galwey of French's division wrote that the Irish Brigade charged "within a stone's throw" of the wall and sunken road. Galwey, *The Valiant Hours*, p. 62. A Confederate observer suggested that the forward element of the Irish Brigade actually reached a point 25 paces from the wall. William Miller Owen, "A Hot Day on Marye's Heights," reprinted in William Marvel, *The Battle of Fredericksburg* (Fredericksburg: Eastern National Park and Monument Association, 1993), p. 36. It will never be possible to resolve the varying claims with the truth. Good evidence exists, however, that the soldiers of the Irish Brigade got closer than any other Union troops to the enemy. Colonel William R. Brooke, who commanded the 53rd Pennsylvania in Zook's brigade, wrote to St. Clair Mulholland after the war: "The dead found nearest the enemy on that field belonged to the 1st Division, 2nd Corps, 69th New York. The color sergeant of the 69th New York moved forward about 20 feet beyond the point of our advance to a low place in the ground for better protection. There I found him and all who went with him dead. These few men, as nearly as I can remember, were about 20 feet in advance of the point which the three regiments, 53rd Pennsylvania, 5th New Hampshire, and 69th New York marched." Letter from Wm. R. Brooke to St.

Clair A. Mulholland, January 8, 1881, Mulholland Collection, Box 2, Civil War Library and Museum, Philadelphia, Pennsylvania. See Appendix A for the full text of Brooke's letter.

22. From McCarter's description, it appears that he observed the deployment of Captain Hazard's Battery B, 1st Rhode Island Artillery, at 3:30 p.m. The Confederate cannoneers immediately focused their attention on Hazard's six twelve-pounder Napoleons. Within 15 minutes, Southern counter-battery fire had dropped 16 men and 15 horses. Hazard's battery was withdrawn, with one gun so disabled that it had to be drawn off by hand. *OR* 21, p. 185.

23. Major General Oliver O. Howard's attack failed as miserably as the ones that preceded it.

24. Numerous Federal troops took shelter in and behind a brick farmhouse on the slope of Marye's Heights. The wounded in particular sought shelter there. Galwey, *The Valiant Hours,* pp. 60, 61.

Chapter 10

1. McCarter probably observed the attack of General Humphrey's division from the V Corps. *OR* 21, p. 95, and Marvel, *Burnside,* pp. 192-195. Getty's division also assailed Marye's Heights after dark immediately after Humphrey's men fell back. Both charges were signal failures.

2. Union casualties were 1,180 killed, 9,028 wounded and 2,145 missing. *OR* 21, p. 97. Lee lost about 5,588 men killed, wounded and missing. Ibid., p. 562.

3. The 116th Pennsylvania reported 88 men killed, wounded or missing at Fredericksburg. Ibid., p. 128.

4. Several other Irish Brigade soldiers escaped from Marye's Heights after darkness fell. Captain Jack Donovan of the 69th New York was struck down by a piece of shell during the Irish Brigade's attack. When he regained consciousness after the sun set, Donovan viewed the dismal scene that surrounded him. "Who are these lines of men that lie stretched along to my right and left, as if asleep on their arms?" he asked. A sergeant from the 69th New York replied, "They are the dead and wounded of the 69th and 88th New York, as well as the 5th New Hampshire." Donovan then gave the order to the sergeant and all others that could hear it to fall back. About a dozen men rose from among the dead and followed Donovan. On his way down the slope of Marye's Heights, Donovan had his hat shot off his head. Letter from Cpt. John Donovan to friend, Irish American, January 3, 1863, Irish Brigade file, FSNMP.

5. Rescue parties from the Irish Brigade searched all over on the night of December 13, 1862. Some were not as lucky as Sergeant Stretchabok and his comrade who found McCarter. "The Confederates savagely fire at any of our men who go out, even to give the wounded a drink," wrote an officer of the Irish Brigade. "Cpt. Hart went out with a party to try and bring in some. One man and two horses were shot. Lt. McCormack, of Co. F [88th New York], got shot in a like laudable effort." Letter from Irish Brigade officer, *Irish American*, December 27, 1862, Irish Brigade file, FSNMP.

6. St. Clair Mulholland paints a picture of the Union defeat very similar to that written by McCarter. "The immense crowd of wounded began crawling, struggling, dragging themselves towards the city, those who were slightly hurt assisting the others who were more seriously injured. Those with shattered limbs using muskets for crutches, many fainting and falling by the way. And when in the town, how hard to find a spot to rest or a surgeon to bind up the wounds. More wounded than the city had inhabitants, every public hall and house filled to overflow, the porches of the residences covered with bleeding men, the surgeons busy everywhere." Mulholland, *116th Pennsylvania*, p. 52.

7. McCarter offers an interesting scenario. Could General Robert E. Lee have descended from the heights of Fredericksburg and rolled up the Union forces? It is an interesting question that can never be answered. Perhaps Lee did not realize the full extent of the demoralization and chaos in the Army of the Potomac. As bad as the Union casualties had been, however, Burnside's army still greatly outnumbered Lee's. Marvel, *Burnside*, pp. 197-199.

8. Mulholland, himself wounded, wrote a somewhat rosier (and less believable) account than McCarter's about the morale of the wounded: "Lying there in deep pools of blood they waited, very patiently, almost cheerfully, their turn to be treated; there was no grumbling, no screaming, hardly a moan; many of the badly wounded were smiling and chatting, and one—who had both legs shot off—was cracking jokes with an officer who could not laugh at the humorous sallies, for his lower jaw was shot away." Mulholland, *116th Pennsylvania*, p. 53.

9. The ball caused such a serious wound to his arm that McCarter received a pension for "atrophy and paralysis" after the war ended. "Surgeon's Certificate," September 24, 1873, William McCarter Pension Records, National Archives and Records Administration, Washington, D.C.

10. *OR* 21, p. 95. Burnside originally had planned another Union assault on Marye's Heights on the morning of December 14. His corps commanders talked him out of the idea. Marvel, *Burnside*, pp. 196-198.

11. Burnside conducted a skillful withdrawal at night in a pouring rainstorm, and the Army of the Potomac silently stole away from Lee's army.

12. The United States Christian Commission was an outgrowth of the Y.M.C.A. It was formed in New York City during the autumn of 1861 at the suggestion of Vincent Colyer, a pious artist, who had gone to Washington after First Bull Run to distribute bibles, tracts and hymnbooks to soldiers. The society worked in conjunction with army and navy chaplains. The Christian delegates held services in camps and knelt in prayer beside the dying in the hospitals. The U.S. Christian Commission ministered to the body as well. While the Army Medical Bureau was slow to supply the wounded after Fredericksburg, the U.S. Sanitary Commission and U.S. Christian Commission, civilian volunteers, sent enormous shipments of food and medical supplies. Leech, *Reveille in Washington*, pp. 269, 270, 399, 400.

Chapter 11

1. McCarter was lucky to be assigned to an army hospital. After Fredericksburg, Washington, D.C., was flooded with wounded Union soldiers. Hotels were taken over by the U.S. Army to be used as hospitals. Louisa May Alcott, author of Little Women, ministered to the wounded at the Union Hotel in Georgetown. Leech, *Reveille in Washington*, pp. 275-278.

2. General Meagher's concern for his aide, William McCarter, is touching. Shortly after Fredericksburg, Meagher visited President Lincoln and asked that the Irish Brigade be relieved from duty to recruit replacements for its depleted ranks. Permission was denied. Conyngham, *The Irish Brigade*, pp. 365-372.

3. The Cooper Shop Volunteer Refreshment Saloon provided food to Union soldiers who passed through Philadelphia on the way to the front throughout the entire war. The Cooper Shop Hospital ministered to the sick and wounded like McCarter. The volunteers who staffed the facility were proud to note that they even fed large numbers of Confederate prisoners on their way to prisons in the North. Taylor, *Philadelphia in the Civil War*, pp. 210-214.

4. Philadelphia hospitals cared for some 157,000 wounded Federal soldiers during the war. Ibid., p. 226.

5. McCarter filed for a pension because of the severity of his wound. He was initially awarded $6.00 per month, but the pension was reduced by $2.00 when McCarter regained partial use of his arm and hand. "Surgeon's Certificate," September 25, 1875, William McCarter Pension Records, National Archives and Records Administration, Washington, D.C.

Bibliography

Manuscripts

Dwyer, John. Address of, December 12, 1914, New York City, N.Y., Irish Brigade File, Fredericksburg/Spotsylvania National Military Park, Fredericksburg, Virginia.

McCarter, William. Military Records and Pension Records, National Archives and Records Administration, Washington, D.C.

— My Life in the Irish Brigade, Historical Society of Pennsylvania, Philadelphia, Pennsylvania.

Mulholland, St, Clair, Papers, Civil War Library and Museum, Philadelphia, PA.

Smith, William A. Letters, Lewis Leigh Collection, U.S. Army Military History Institute, Carlisle Barracks, Pennsylvania.

Books and Articles

Alexander, E. P. *Military Memoirs of a Confederate* (New York: Charles Scribner's Sons, 1907; reprint, Dayton: Morningside House, (1990).

Athearn, Robert G. *Thomas Francis Meagher: An Irish Revolutionary in America* (Boulder: University of Colorado Press, 1949).

Billings, John D. *Hard Tack and Coffee: The Unwritten Story of Army Life* (Williamstown: Corner House Publishers, 1887).

Burton, William L. *Melting Pot Soldiers: The Union's Ethnic Regiments* (Ames: Iowa University Press, 1988).

Catton, Bruce. *The Army of the Potomac: Mr. Lincoln's Army* (New York, 1951)

Cavanagh, Michael. *Memoirs of Gen. Thomas Francis Meagher* (Worcester: Messenger Press, 1892).

Conyngham, D. P. *The Irish Brigade and Its Campaigns* (New York,1867; reprint, ed. Lawrence P. Kohl, New York: Fordham University Press, 1994).

Corby, William. *Memoirs of Chaplain Life* (Chicago: La Monte, O'Donnell, and Co., 1893; reprint edition, ed. Lawrence P. Kohl, New York: Fordham University Press, 1992).

Engle, D. *Yankee Dutchman: The Life of Franz Sigel* (Fayetteville, 1993).

Galwey, Thomas F. *The Valiant Hours* (Harrisburg, 1961).

Hill, Lois, ed. *Poems and Songs of the Civil War* (New York, 1990).

Hunter, Samuel D. "Charge of the Irish Brigade on Marye's Heights," *Grand Army Scout and Soldier's Mail*, October 6, 1883.

Kohl, Lawrence and Margaret Richard, ed., *Irish Green and Union Blue: The Civil War Letters of Peter Welsh, Color Sergeant, 28th Massachusetts Volunteers* (New York: Fordham University, 1986).

Leech, Margaret. *Reveille in Washington: 1861-1865* (New York: Harper and Row, 1941; reprint, New York: Time-Life, 1962).

Long, E. B. *The Civil War Day by Day: An Almanac* (Garden City: Doubleday, 1971; reprint, New York: Da Capo Press, 1985).

Lyman, Darryl. *Civil War Wordbook* (Conshohocken: Combined Books, 1994).

Lyons, W. F. *Brigadier General Thomas Francis Meagher: His Political and Military Career* (New York: D & J Sadlier Co., 1870).

Marvel, William. *Burnside* (Chapel Hill: University of North Carolina Press, 1991).

McCarter, William. "Fredericksburg's Battle," *Philadelphia Weekly Times*, September 8, 1883.

Menge, W. Springer and J. August Shimrak, ed., *The Civil War Notebook of Daniel Chisholm: A Chronicle of Daily Life in the Union Army, 1864-1865* (New York: Orion Books, 1989).

Mertz, Gregory A. "'A Severe Day for the Artillery': Stonewall Jackson's Artillerists and the Defense of the Confederate Right," *Civil War Regiments: A Journal of the American Civil War*, Vol. 4, No. 4 (1996), pp. 70-99.

Miller, Richard F. and Robert F. Mooney, "Across the River and into the Streets: The 20th Massachusetts Infantry and the Fight for the Streets of Fredericksburg," *Civil War Regiments: A Journal of the American Civil War*, Vol. 4, No. 4 (1996), pp. 101-126.

Mulholland, St. Clair A. "Annals of the War—Battle of Fredericksburg," *Philadelphia Weekly Times*, April 23, 1881.

— *The Story of the 116th Regiment, Pennsylvania Volunteers* (Philadelphia: F. McManus & Jr., Company Printers, 1903); reprint, ed. Lawrence P. Kohl, New York: Fordham University Press, 1996).

Nevins, Allen. *The War for the Union* (New York: Charles Scribner's Sons, 1960).

Nugent, Robert. "The Sixty-ninth Regiment at Fredericksburg," Third Annual Report of the Historian of the State of New York, 1897 (Albany, 1898).

O'Brien, Kevin E. "'The Breath of Hell's Door': Private William McCarter and the Attack of the Irish Brigade on Marye's Heights—An Unpublished Memoir," *Civil War Regiments: A Journal of the American Civil War*, Vol. 4, No. 4 (1996), pp. 47, 48.

— "Sprig of Green: the Union Army's Irish Brigade," *The Recorder: Journal of the American Irish Historical Society*, vol. 6, no. 2 (Fall 1993), pp. 45-53.

O'Flaherty, Rev. Patrick D. *The History of the Sixty-Ninth Regiment in the Irish Brigade* (New York: privately printed, 1986).

Owen, William Miller. "A Hot Day on Marye's Heights," reprinted in William Marvel, *The Battle of Fredericksburg* (Fredericksburg: Eastern National Park and Monument Association, 1993).

Pakenham, Thomas. *The Year of Liberty: The Great Irish Rebellion of 1798* (London: Granada Publishing, 1969).

Sears, Stephen W. *Landscape Turned Red: The Battle of Antietam* (New York: Ticknor and Fields, 1983).

Sifkasis, Stewart. *Who Was Who In the Civil War* (New York: Facts on File, 1988).

Stackpole, Edward J. *The Fredericksburg Campaign: Drama on the Rappahannock* (2nd ed.; Harrisburg: Stackpole Books, 1991).

Taylor, Frank H. *Philadelphia in The Civil War: 1861-1865* (Philadelphia: By the City, 1913).

Tucker, Glenn. *Hancock the Superb* (Indianapolis: Bobbs-Merrill, 1960).

United States War Department. *The War of the Rebellion: A Compilation of the Official Records of the Union and Confederate Armies*, 128 vols. (Washington, D.C.: Government Printing Office, 1880-1901).

Wycoff, Mac. *A History of the 2nd South Carolina Infantry: 1861-1865* (Fredericksburg: Sergeant Kirkland's Museum, 1994).

Newspapers

Grand Army Scout and Soldier's Mail
Irish-American, New York City
Philadelphia Weekly Times
Boston Pilot

INDEX